A curriculum for the pre-school child

First published in 1986, this book has been enormously influential in the training and professional development of early years workers. This new edition has been fully revised to take into account changes in the National Curriculum, the introduction of *Desirable Outcomes for Children's Learning* and the introduction of baseline assessment.

The new edition also includes sections on: the effects of developmental psychology on the early years curriculum; working with young children on self-awareness and social skills; developing communication, motor, analytical and problem-solving skills; fostering aesthetic and creative awareness; play and the learning environment; record keeping and assessment; the involvement of parents; and continuity from pre-schooling to statutory schooling.

Audrey Curtis is an education consultant and former senior lecturer at the Institute of Education, London University.

A curriculum for the pre-school child

Learning to learn

Second edition

Audrey Curtis

London and New York

First published in 1986 by NFER-Nelson Publishing
This edition first published 1998
by Routledge
11 New Fetter Lane, London EC4P 4EE

Simultaneously published in the USA and Canada
by Routledge
29 West 35th Street, New York, NY 10001

Reprinted 2000 by RoutledgeFalmer

RoutledgeFalmer is an imprint of the Taylor & Francis Group

© 1986, 1998 Audrey Curtis

Typeset in Times by LaserScript, Mitcham, Surrey
Printed and bound in Great Britain by
TJ International Ltd, Padstow, Cornwall

British Library Cataloguing in Publication Data
A catalogue record for this book is available from the British Library

Library of Congress Cataloguing in Publication Data
Curtis, Audrey.
    A curriculum for the pre-school child: learning to learn/Audrey Curtis – 2nd ed.
p. cm.
    Includes bibliographical references and index.
    1. Education, Preschool – Great Britain – Curricula. 2. Education, Preschool – United States – Curricula. 3. Child development. 4. Education, Preschool – Activity programs. I. Title. LB1140.4.C89 1998
372. 19–dc21
97–14150
CIP
ISBN 0–415–13976–7

Contents

Introduction

In the years since the first edition of this book appeared there have been many changes within the education system. The introduction of the National Curriculum and the move towards a centralised system of teacher education have been responsible for a more subject-based approach to primary education and this in turn has had an effect upon the programmes offered to children under statutory school age. Unlike many of our European counterparts, we do not offer state nursery education for the majority of our three- and four-year-olds, but prefer to rely upon a mixture of state, private and voluntary provision, or a policy of admitting children into primary classes at the beginning of the year in which they will be five; for some children this is when they are barely four years of age. This is not seen as a desirable situation by most early years professionals, particularly as our children already commence full-time schooling earlier than in most countries.

As it was not deemed possible to provide all children with free nursery education, it was decided to introduce a nursery voucher scheme for all parents of four-year-old children to be used in the institution of their choice (state nurseries or nursery classes, private nurseries, play groups or primary schools). However, if state money is to be used to support children in private and voluntary institutions then there must be some control over the education offered and to this end two major changes have been introduced. First, the Schools Curriculum and Assessment Authority issued guidelines for *Desirable Outcomes for Children's Learning* (SCAA 1996b) on entering compulsory schooling; and, second, a system of inspection has been introduced to safeguard the quality of provision offered in the institutions receiving the vouchers. Both these changes continue even though the nursery voucher scheme has been abolished.

These inspections, more rigorous than those required under the Children Act, are to be carried out in all the institutions which intend to accept the nursery vouchers. This is a very positive move as it should help to overcome the disparity in quality of provision which exists throughout the country, and hopefully inspections will be extended eventually to all institutions, whether or not they accept vouchers. Although the *Desirable Outcomes for Children's Learning* are meant to be goals for learning for children by the time they reach statutory school age (the term after the child's fifth birthday), many early childhood educators, including myself, are concerned that they provide a narrow approach to learning in the early years of schooling. Furthermore, as they are designed to link closely with the National Curriculum, which is defined in terms of subjects, and favours summative assessment, there is a danger that some children will be placed in a 'subject-based' learning mould before they are five, as early childhood institutions are pressurised by parents and others into offering children too many 'desk-top' activities, particularly in relation to reading and writing.

There is no doubt that the National Curriculum, with its subject-based approach and its emphasis upon assessment and evaluation, has put pressure upon early childhood educators. This, combined with the introduction of Baseline Assessment for children shortly after their entry into primary school, has made many early years workers feel that they need to be assessing children from the time they begin in the nursery in a formal way, not the informal approach which is part of good practice. If early years educators look closely at the *Desirable Outcomes for Children's Learning* and some of the attainment targets at Key Stage 1, particularly with regard to language and literacy, it is possible to show that some children are able to carry out some of these tasks at level 1, for example, 'listen to others and usually respond appropriately' in an informal setting, by the time they leave the nursery, although they could not meet the requirements of a Standard Assessment Test (SAT). Early childhood educators should not feel pressurised into taking a subject approach to the early years curriculum even though the government guidelines for children below statutory age are subject-based.

This book aims to provide educators, in whatever setting, with the knowledge and understanding to stimulate and encourage children aged between two-and-a-half years and five: boys and girls whose lively personalities, enthusiasm and energy present a challenge to all those adults with whom they come into daily contact. The age range has been lowered slightly since the first edition as so many of the nurseries and play groups in the private and independent sector are now enrolling younger children as the four-year-olds leave for primary school, leaving nurseries and play-groups with the two-and-a-half- and three-year-olds only.

The *Desirable Outcomes for Children's Learning* have provided early childhood educators with a content framework but there is still a need to ask a number of basic questions about 'good practice' and the role of the educator in helping to provide children with the skills and competencies they will need as they progress through school and later life.

In attempting to outline a curriculum for children within this age range I am very conscious that each child is unique, with different aptitudes and interests, and will bring into the early childhood institution a variety of experiences upon which the adult must build. Nevertheless, I hope that this book will provide a useful framework for adults working with children in the two-and-a-half- to five-year age range whether they are in playgroups, day nurseries, nursery schools or classes in the primary school.

There now appears to be general acceptance that quality nursery education is beneficial to young children and has positive later benefits. The longitudinal findings of the High Scope Perry Preschool Study through to age twenty-seven (Schweinhart and Weikart 1993) have shown that disadvantaged children who participated in this pre-school programme have become economically self-sufficient, socially responsible adults.

However, quality nursery education is now no longer seen as a programme for the disadvantaged but for all children. Research from Sweden has found that day-care experience gave children a better chance in school (Andersson 1992), while in this country Jowett and Sylva (1986) compared two groups of children entering reception classes, one group coming from state nursery provision and the other from voluntary playgroups and found that those coming from nursery classes engaged in more purposeful play and complex activity and chose more demanding educational activities than children coming from playgroups.

There is also evidence that attendance at pre-school institutions had a positive effect upon performance in Standard Assessment Tests at Key Stage 1. Shorrocks *et al.* (1992) carried out a rigorous study of the 1992 SATs results and found that children who had attended 'nursery' performed better in English, Science and Mathematics. Quality nursery education is beneficial for all children.

Analysis of programmes which have been successful in several countries throughout the world suggests that they contain the following features, although their emphasis may be different:

1 Parents were included in their children's education.
2 Emphasis was placed on developing an atmosphere based on sound human relationships.
3 A balance was maintained between child-directed and teacher-directed activities.
4 The curriculum was planned with specific objectives in mind.
5 The curriculum was geared to the needs of individual children.
6 The programme emphasised that nursery school was fun.

When the first edition of this book was written there were no *Desirable Outcomes for Children's Learning* to act as guidelines for early childhood workers and although these are helpful, they are indicative of content rather than an analysis of the skills and competencies which children will need to develop in a flexible and child-centred environment. We must be certain that there is ample material with which to challenge and extend children without offering them a 'watered-down' National Curriculum. There should be continuity and progression but it should be a 'bottom-up', not a 'top-down', approach.

Nursery education is about challenging children and encouraging them to develop into motivated learners and thinkers, full of curiosity about the world around them, and helping them to 'learn how to learn'.

The book is divided into two sections. The first main section deals with important aspects concerning the education of young children. The first chapter looks at the contribution of five eminent early childhood pioneers – Friedrich Froebel, Maria Montessori, Margaret McMillan, Rudolph Steiner and Susan Isaacs – to our current thinking and discusses their relevance to modern pre-school education, followed by a chapter which discusses briefly several modern approaches to the curriculum.

Chapters Two to Seven identify the skills and competencies which it is felt should be developed with two-and-a-half- to five-year old children; these relate to personal and social development, communication skills, physical skills, analytical and problem-solving skills, and creative and aesthetic awareness. Each area is discussed briefly in the light of current research and is related to both *Desirable Outcomes for Children's Learning* and the National Curriculum.

Chapter Eight takes a critical look at the learning environment, the ethos of the classroom, as well as the apparatus and materials required for both indoor and outdoor activities. Discussion centres on how this environment meets the needs of the young child and stresses the importance of play as a means of learning, and the role of the adult as facilitator and enabler. Chapter Nine is a discussion on assessment and record keeping since implementing a curriculum and providing a suitable learning environment must be accompanied by some form of planning and assessment to ensure that each child is receiving the appropriate experiences.

A new chapter for this edition, Chapter Ten, considers the role of parents in their children's learning, as educators are well aware that home influences are important in children's overall development. The issues arising when the children transfer from pre-school to statutory schooling are tackled in Chapter Eleven, and suggestions made as to how educators and parents can help overcome the problems inherent in this move.

In the second section of the book there is a collection of activities appropriate for children aged between two-and-a-half and five years which educators may find useful to help develop the various skills and competencies discussed earlier.

All children must be offered a curriculum which provides equal opportunities and which is based upon an anti-bias approach. It is for this reason that I have not identified any particular groups of children who may have special educational needs as I believe that the skills and competencies which we are trying to foster are appropriate for all children, as are the activities in the last section. It may well be that some adaptation will be necessary but the majority of children with special educational needs will be able to achieve the desired levels of skill and awareness, although they may take longer to reach their goals.

Unlike those in other countries, our young children are provided for in a wide range of institutions and are the responsibility of people from a wide range of training backgrounds. There will be some readers who are trained nursery teachers, others may be teachers who are trained to work with an older age range and there will be others, such as nursery nurses and play-group leaders whose training will have been shorter and less education biased. As I hope this book should be helpful to educators in all these groups, I have interchanged the terms educator, early years worker and teacher throughout.

Finally, some explanations. As it is cumbersome to refer to a child as s/he and write the possessive pronouns as his/her in the text, I have adopted a sexist approach and referred to every child in the feminine gender. Again for the sake of style and clarity I have adopted the term 'black' for all the non-whites in our community. May I offer my sincerest and humble apologies for any aggravation or offence this terminology may give to any readers.

Part I

1 Early educators and their influences on the curriculum

No book concerned with the curriculum for children between the ages of two and five can afford to ignore the effect which the early childhood educators have had on our current thinking. In this chapter, the names of five educationalists have been singled out: Friedrich Froebel, Rudolph Steiner, Maria Montessori, Margaret McMillan and Susan Isaacs, each of whom is still exerting an influence on early childhood education today, either directly or indirectly. These five all held the view that the young child is first and foremost a whole person, with thoughts, feelings and imagination that need to be cared for and cherished. That young children no longer sit in rows of desks all day and are free to carry out various activities inside and outside the classroom is due in the main to these early thinkers who had a child-centred approach to education and who believed that young children are intrinsically motivated and wish to learn.

FRIEDRICH FROEBEL

The earliest of the five educationalists I am going to consider is Friedrich Froebel, who died more than a century ago yet still exerts an important influence upon early childhood education in this country. Although his pedagogy has long been considered sterile there is no doubt that Froebel pioneered a new approach to our understanding of children's activities and ways of learning, demonstrating that children need a vast number of experiences before they can arrive at an awareness of themselves and the world.

Froebel, influenced by both Rousseau and Pestalozzi, argued that play was a serious and deeply significant activity for the young child. He wrote (1896, para. 30): 'at this age play is never trivial; it is serious and deeply significant. ... The focus of play at this age is the core of the whole future, since in them the entire person is developed and revealed in the most sensitive qualities of his mind.'

The kindergartens, for him, were institutions where children instruct and educate themselves and where they develop and integrate all their abilities through play, which is creative activity and spontaneous instruction. That children learn through play is indeed a basic tenet of Froebelian philosophy and one which has been embraced by many early childhood educators. However, Froebel did not believe that the play of young children should be unstructured, as was the approach of many of his later followers. For him play was too important to be left to chance and in discussing the pedagogies of the kindergarten he wrote:

> just because he learns through play, a child learns willingly and learns much. So play, like learning and activity has its own definite period of time and it must not be left out of the elementary curriculum. The educator must not only guide the play, since it is so very important, but he must also often teach this sort of play in the first instance.
>
> (Lilley 1967, p. 167)

In order to help children learn through play Froebel devised a series of playthings and games. The six sets of playthings or 'gifts' which Froebel designed formed a sequence beginning with a number of soft balls leading on to wooden spheres, cubes and cylinders. There were also 'occupations' which trained children in activities such as drawing or modelling.

The 'gifts' and 'occupations' were a fundamental part of Froebel's doctrine of innate ideas but stripped of their symbolism they are the timeless playthings of childhood. Balls, boards, sand, clay, for example, have made up children's play activities throughout the ages. The role of the adult was to plan and supervise these activities. In the Froebelian kindergarten the gifts, occupations, singing games, stories and talk made up the curriculum in contrast to the stark infant schools of the time where the 3Rs occupied most of the daily routine.

Our modern infant schools owe much to the influence of Froebel and most of the experiences which we offer children in present-day nurseries and reception classes have their roots in the 'occupations' of the Froebelian kindergarten, although these have been extended and amended to meet the needs of children in the late 1990s.

The idea of treating the school day as a complete unit in which activities continue for varying lengths of time to enable children to pursue their own interests is but another of the legacies which the modern primary schools have inherited from the Froebelian tradition. Friedrich Froebel was one of the great pioneers of early childhood education and although his influence can still be seen throughout our primary schools, his writings are little read today by students, since his main work, *The Education of Man* (1896), is not the lightest of reading.

RUDOLPH STEINER

Rudolph Steiner, an Austrian philosopher and theosophist, opened the first Waldorf School in Stuttgart for the children of cigarette factory workers. Although designed for children of all ages, there is currently an increase in the number of Rudolph Steiner nursery schools in this country and in many other parts of the world. Steiner was concerned primarily with the whole child and his principles are based upon a specific view of child development. The philosophy behind the curriculum is that through understanding the nature of children it is possible to develop their individuality. If children are presented with a creative curriculum which offers them balanced experiences of both the arts and sciences, and opportunities to develop processes of thinking, feeling and willing then they will grow into flexible and creative adults. For him the best nursery teacher is one who can create the atmosphere of a home in the school setting.

There is a strong emphasis upon free play and the use of toys that are multipurpose so that they encourage children's play and imagination. In Steiner nursery schools there are such natural materials as pine cones, shells, pieces of wood and textiles always available and children are encouraged to sew, draw and engage in woodwork. In the woodwork area children have access to miniature, but real, tools so that they can make their own toys to use in their imaginative play. Outdoor play is encouraged, but the amount of commercial equipment is minimal, although there are plenty of natural playthings (e.g. trunks and logs for children to climb over). This lack of commercial materials is intentional so that children become more creative and imaginative in their play. While visiting a Steiner school in Hungary recently I was able to see this philosophy in practice as children between the ages of three and six demonstrated high levels of concentrated imaginative play using the few natural 'props' that were available.

Children are also encouraged to use colour in a variety of ways, as Steiner believed that children should think of colours as living and active entities, but the children do not necessarily need to be painting something. Singing and singing games are seen as important, as is eurhythmy, a new art of movement developed by Steiner which involves movement to both music and speech. Storytelling is also important in the Steiner curriculum as he argued that if a story is read the book comes between the storyteller and the children. The children will be better able to imagine the situation if they do not have pictures in a book to destroy their own images.

Children are not offered any instructional materials nor is any attempt made to force children to read and write. Maybe this is one of the reasons for the increase in interest in Steiner nursery schools by parents who are becoming concerned about the 'academic' pressure which is being placed upon children in many nurseries today.

MARIA MONTESSORI

The ideas of Maria Montessori, the doctor who worked among the socially and mentally handicapped children of Rome in the early years of the twentieth century, have been more widely adopted in the USA than in Britain, although there is currently a revival of interest in her methods.

Maria Montessori, in the same way as Froebel and Pestalozzi, saw development as the inevitable unfolding of a biological programme. From her observations in her Children's House (the name she gave to her nursery schools), she concluded that each child passes through sensitive periods of development when it appears that certain skills and concepts are learned more readily. Her stages covered the periods 0–6, 6–12 and 12–18 years. She believed that children learn from their own spontaneous activities and therefore a prepared environment was all important. She argued that the child under six cannot reason or use language in the same way as the older child and therefore adults need to be aware that they do not use language which cannot be understood by small children.

She considered that every child is unique and is profoundly affected by society and the environment, and in the quiet surroundings of the Children's House the child is able to develop her natural potential. She also believed that children have an intrinsic love of order and expected each one to take responsibility for taking and replacing materials and equipment in good order.

The Montessori method rests on a sequence of activities which must be followed exactly with every child. In *The Absorbent Mind* (1964, p. 205) she wrote, 'We take certain objects and present them in a certain fashion to a child and then leave the child alone with them and do not interfere.' Within these restrictions the child has the freedom to explore and interact with the prepared environment, choosing from a variety of materials appropriate to her stage of development, but that does not mean a licence for children to do as they please. Montessori argues that we cannot be absolutely free if we wish to live in society.

The role of the directress in the Montessori schools is to prepare the environment and act as a link between the child and the materials. This is achieved through close observation so that the directress is able to help out at appropriate moments but overall her approach is to emphasise independence in children's development. By using the prepared environment, Maria Montessori argued that it would be possible for children to learn even if the directress was not of a very high calibre, the skill of the teachers being of less importance than the method. This is a view which may seem alien to current readers but which was a very important issue at the beginning of the twentieth century when many early years teachers were untrained, particularly in Italy.

Another of Maria Montessori's viewpoints which has been widely criticised concerns her attitude to play, and to imaginative play in particular. Montessori argued that 'play is the child's work', but the only form of play that was acceptable was that which had a preparatory function for adult forms of interaction. Thus the concept of imaginative play is not admissible because it takes children away from adaptive learning and therefore was of very little value. It is interesting to note that many years later Corinne Hutt adopted this view when she argued that during 'ludic' play activities there was little or no learning taking place, whereas during exploratory play, adaptation and learning occurs. Montessori and her followers considered fantasy play to be essentially dishonest, because in talking about stories involving witches and ogres or talking animals, children were being presented with a false picture of reality; an approach which is opposed to that of many pre-school educators in Britain today.

Few modern educators would disagree with the need for a planned environment, but the rigidity of the Montessori method, with its sequential stages, has been criticised as it is argued that there is no place for spontaneous, incidental learning, and no opportunity for teachers to build on experiences which the children may bring from outside the school environment. Modern critics point out not only that Maria Montessori's methods do little to encourage language development or symbolic thought but also that her approach fails to take into account the possibility that a child's development might deviate in any way, thus necessitating the modification of the method. This is a strange criticism when one considers that her original method was devised for children with learning difficulties.

In spite of these criticisms, few would disagree that Maria Montessori has made a number of contributions to early childhood education which have become basic to our thinking about small children. At a practical level it was Maria Montessori who was responsible for introducing child-sized furniture into our nursery schools and classes, a regular feature nowadays in all classrooms for young children. Likewise, much of the mathematical and sensorial equipment which is used with young children stems from the principles of Montessori education. Above all, Maria Montessori brought to early childhood education a respect for young children as individuals. At a time when most young children throughout the world were being instructed in large groups she was advocating the need for them to engage in modes of learning which would lead them to become independent, spontaneous thinkers. Her attitude towards children was that they were active, intrinsically motivated beings, not passive learners who had to be 'force fed' with information.

The prepared environment in which each child could work to achieve autonomy has been adopted with modifications by several generations of nursery educators who may not appreciate the contribution which Maria Montessori has made to their thinking. Her influence pervades much of the work carried out in early childhood education today and although her method is seen by many as static and inappropriate in the 1990s, we nevertheless owe much to this forward-thinking doctor. Many of her most deep-thinking followers, particularly in the USA, although they do not challenge her philosophy, are reconsidering some of the approaches to teaching in the light of modern educational thought, as they appreciate that however useful the method, changes must be made to meet the needs of present-day society if the movement is to survive.

MARGARET McMILLAN

Margaret McMillan was one of the most practical educational innovators of her time, once termed by J.B. Priestley as 'the nuisance who worked miracles'. P. Ballard, a nursery inspector, wrote in 1937 that 'the modern nursery school is the product of Miss McMillan's genius'. A brief look at her ideas and career will give some idea of the truth of this statement and show how in the late 1990s her views have relevance, and that much of what she strived for is pertinent today.

Margaret McMillan and her sister Rachel were both concerned with the health and home conditions of the poor children and their families among whom they lived. Starting with medical treatment centres, Margaret McMillan attempted to improve the health of children first in Bradford and later Deptford, arguing that 'health was the working-man's capital', since in those days when there was no National Health Service, ill health for an average worker was synonymous with poverty.

Margaret McMillan was one of the first to appreciate the educational value of the home. In acknowledging the importance of the home she also fully realised, as a former governess, the great gulf between the experiences of the middle-class child and those of the working-class child where either the mother was working or else was tied down to coping with a large number of children all living in one room. It was this deep concern for the community and family life in which the children were brought up that led Margaret McMillan to consider the value of crèches. Some writers have suggested that the concern for the neighbourhood as a whole was, at least in part, the result of her Fabian training since education of the community as a whole was a Fabian objective.

Margaret McMillan saw both the home and the community as contributors to the education of young children. In this, and in her appreciation of the supreme importance of the first few years of life in children's development, she was well in advance of her time, arguing that love and security were as vital to the child's overall progress as material well-being. Her views on this are clearly expressed in *The Nursery School* (1919), a small book full of sound ideas and written in a clear style. She realised very early on that if any progress was to be made, parents must be involved in their children's education. Nursery schools alone could not overcome the ills of society, but rather parents must be helped to improve their own child-rearing practices and to develop their own potentialities.

In the early decades of this century, Margaret McMillan was advocating to her helpers and trainee teachers the need for close links and cooperation between home and school, in the way that official government reports are suggesting to us today. It is no wonder that many nursery teachers trained under the influence of her thinking are surprised when these ideas come forth as new edicts, when in many nursery schools throughout the country close links have been maintained between home and school for decades. The concept of the nursery school as an extension of and not a substitute for the home has long been an accepted principle of Margaret McMillan and her successors. Likewise, her ideas on helping parents grow as people have been translated into practice by many nursery schools and centres today where parents are involved in hobbies, language classes, and so on, as well as in activities related to child rearing. In reading her writings one is struck by the similarities that exist between the ideas of this early educator and the views of the Head Start planners in the 1960s, in that she was convinced that specially devised pre-school education would counteract the effects of a poor material environment. She, like them, felt that educational attainment and a better start in life were linked to nursery education, and argued for this nurture to be available to all children whose parents wished them to have it. This must seem to many readers to be a reminder of the recommendations made in the Plowden Report (1967) and the views expressed in *Education: A Framework for Expansion* (DES 1972a).

It is interesting to note that in 'rediscovering' the potential of the nursery school for increasing educational attainment, the Head Start planners envisaged programmes emphasising the intellectual development of the child within the school. Not until most of the early programmes had failed did the administrators involve parents in their children's education with apparently successful outcomes. Margaret McMillan was indeed ahead of her time!

Her views on home–school relationships and her approach to classroom organisation set her apart from most of her contemporaries in early childhood education. Although changes in living standards and improved health care have done away with the need for the open-air schools designed in the ways she suggested, children of nursery-school age are still encouraged to run freely between the indoor and outdoor environment and fresh air is still seen as a vital ingredient in early education.

Margaret McMillan appreciated the need to foster development and adapt one's method of teaching to keep pace with the child's overall progress. She encouraged her teachers to experiment with the nursery curriculum and place increasing demands upon the child, not wait for the child to learn. Their role was to recognise the teachable moments and intervene at the appropriate time. Her views on the need to develop children's imagination and language through story and rhyme and her encouragement of imaginative play wherever possible were totally opposed to those of Maria Montessori. However, in other respects these two early educators had much in common, certainly more than Margaret McMillan would have cared to admit. Both believed in the need to provide an environment for young children in which learning would be almost inevitable and where children were free to choose the apparatus, thus helping them to learn to exercise responsible choice and to find out for themselves what they were or were not interested in. It was in the actual preparation of the environment that they differed. Montessori provided children with specific sense-training apparatus which she expected them to use in an exact manner within the classroom, whereas Margaret McMillan believed children gained better sensory experience by playing in the garden.

She was an imaginative and inventive teacher who expected her teachers to be the same; in their training she ensured that they learned to use the environment effectively and were fully aware of the importance of language in a child's overall development. The teachers thus had an important role to play in the education of young children, whereas for Montessori, as we have seen, it was the method, not a directress, which counted.

Because Margaret McMillan appreciated that little children cannot learn if they are unhealthy, all her efforts were specifically designed to improve their health. This emphasis upon nurture was interpreted by some of her later followers to imply that she believed in fostering physical development at the expense of cognitive and intellectual development and that she advocated leaving children to play freely on their own without any form of intervention. A close look at the writings of Margaret McMillan, for example *The Nursery School* (1919) and *Education through Imagination* (1904), as well as her numerous articles, shows quite clearly that her own views were that once the children were restored to health they were to be encouraged to respond to the instructive environment and the stimulating enrichment programme laid down for them. Like Froebel, she saw play as a vehicle for education and, for her, the objective of the nursery-school curriculum was to provide 'the organic and natural education which should precede all primary teaching and without which the work of the schools is largely lost' (Lowndes 1960, p. 107). When in the garden children would be learning the rudiments of science and geography and in talking and singing the beginnings of literacy and musical appreciation.

The records and observations kept by Margaret McMillan and her teachers on the many children who passed through the nursery school, and the contact she maintained with them when they later moved on to infant schooling, led this educational visionary to advocate that children should remain in nursery education until they were seven years of age, as occurs in some other countries of the world. She argued for progression and continuity in the curriculum as she found that many of her children regressed when they left the nursery to proceed to infant school. Her views, put forward in the 1920s, foreshadowed those recommended by the HMI report *Primary Education in England* (DES 1978), the research into continuity of children's educational experience (Cleave, Jowett and Bate 1982) and, more recently, the SCAA document *Desirable Outcomes for Children's Learning* (1996b).

Readers who take the trouble to look at some of the original writings will discover that many of her ideas on curriculum and teacher training have much in common with current philosophy. The concept of school-based teacher training, with the staff in the nursery acting as professional tutors, was one which was incorporated into the college at Deptford and which is now part of the education of teachers. Likewise, her views on in-service training and the need for a workshop approach could be recommendations from the current government committees.

Not all of the views she held are appropriate today. For example, Margaret McMillan wanted nursery schools for up to 200–300 children divided into groups, a view which would not be acceptable today in the light of our current knowledge of children's development. She was also an advocate of nursery schools as opposed to nursery classes attached to infant schools, a view contrary to prevailing opinion. However, it is interesting to note that there are still members of the teaching profession who are against nursery education taking place in infant schools. Whatever the current arguments for and against nursery education being continued in separate schools, there is no doubt that Margaret McMillan based her views on the knowledge that in her time infant-school practice was very different from that occurring in the nursery school.

The 'nuisance who worked miracles' has left her mark on current early childhood practice and many of her ideas on parental involvement, teacher education and continuity and progression are as relevant today as they were more than half a century ago.

SUSAN ISAACS

The final early childhood educator whose work will be discussed in this brief overview of eminent educationalists is Susan Isaacs, the centenary of whose birth was celebrated in 1985. Intellectually an outstandingly able woman, her detailed observations of the children who participated in the pioneer experiment at Malting House School, Cambridge, have contributed a great deal to our understanding of the social and intellectual development of young children.

At a time when little was understood about the inner feelings of young children, Susan Isaacs, influenced by the views of Freud and later Melanie Klein, made every effort to ensure that children had freedom of action and emotional expression. At Malting House School, emotions such as hostility, anger, fear and aggression were openly encouraged as she rightly believed that their suppression would harm the unconscious mind of the children. Susan Isaacs' insightful comments on the behaviour of young children were later recorded in *Social Development in Young Children* (1933) and have helped many teachers towards an understanding of the inner conflicts and fears experienced by three- to five-year-old children.

Susan Isaacs encouraged teachers to record accurately the behaviour of children, but as a psychoanalyst she warned against amateur interpretation of events since she was well aware of the dangers inherent in such a course. Non-analysts should observe and record, only the trained analyst should interpret.

As with Froebel, Susan Isaacs emphasised the importance of play in children's learning, particularly play with other children. In her pamphlet *The Educational Value of the Nursery School*, whose message is as pertinent today as it was forty years ago, she wrote:

> play with other children gives the child confidence in himself, no less than in his little friends, and not only helps him to feel less suspicious and aggressive to others but by giving him the delight of action and sharing and helping him to discover the way in which he can carry out his own practical and imaginative pursuits with others lays down the foundation for a co-operative social life in the later school years.

(1954, p. 16)

Make-believe play received special emphasis from Susan Isaacs as she believed that it not only helped children to solve intellectual problems but helped them to 'achieve inner balance and harmony through active expression of [their] inner world of feelings and impulses'. Her emphasis upon the importance of imaginative play for young children has much in common with the philosophical approach of Rudolph Steiner.

Although a strong advocate for children's freedom of action, Susan Isaacs was also aware of the young child's need for order and stability. The approach to the curriculum in Malting House School stressed individual development and to this end the Montessori apparatus was available and the Montessori method used for reading and writing. However, in her approach to children's intellectual development Susan Isaacs reflected the thinking of Dewey, believing that the central task of teaching was to train children to think in a logical, reasoned way. In *Intellectual Growth in Young Children* (1930) she pointed out that one of the chief educational aims for children was to give them the best possible start with regard to clear thinking and independent judgement. She recognised the ability of young children to solve problems and queried Piaget's view that they were egocentric and unable to reason. It is interesting to note that a half-century later many modern psychologists agree that young children can understand and express ideas at a complex level if they are motivated, if they fully appreciate the language used and if they are working with an adult who poses challenging, meaningful questions which are of interest to them.

Scientific experiments and the testing of hypotheses were all part of the broad curriculum offered to the children at Malting House School. During her years at the school, Susan Isaacs kept meticulous, detailed records of the children and it was these observations which formed the basis of much of the teaching she gave to higher degree students and to teachers on in-service courses at the University of London Institute of Education.

Through her in-service education courses Susan Isaacs was to become a major influence on nursery and primary education in the post-war years. She helped teachers who still relied heavily on didactic teaching material to appreciate that the young child had a scientific interest in problem solving and that in play she can test out her hypotheses against real facts and even at such a young age can be, and is, a thinker. Above all, Susan Isaacs' major contribution to early childhood education is that through her clear and cogent writings, both to teachers and to parents, under the pseudonym of Ursula Wyse, she was able to bring about an understanding of the intensity of young children's emotional feelings.

As with Margaret McMillan, Susan Isaacs saw the nursery school as an extension of the function of the home, not a substitute for it. Both these early educators were concerned that parents be involved with the nursery school, although possibly for different reasons, and both, I believe, would have concurred with the statement written by Dorothy Gardner, Susan Isaacs' most ardent disciple that: 'a great value of the nursery school is that it provides a common meeting ground for parents and young children, since they can often learn that children have common problems, fears and anxieties' (1956, p. 79).

2 Curriculum in the early years

In the last chapter we looked at the work and ideas of some of the great early childhood educators of the past and considered their contribution to present practice. Although many of their ideas have become distorted and misunderstood, we can still see clearly their influence upon the current scene. For example, the stress on the prepared environment with a minimum of adult intervention owes much to the thinking of Maria Montessori, but learning through interaction with materials needs very careful monitoring of the equipment and apparatus, since a poorly prepared environment with little or no adult intervention provides ammunition for the critics of nursery education. Likewise, Margaret McMillan's stress on the relationship between care and education, with its emphasis on eating, sleeping and outdoor activities, so essential for the children for whom she was catering, has been seen as fundamental to her nursery-school programme, but we must not forget that she also provided academic instruction and specific learning activities.

In the first section of this chapter we shall be considering the underlying principles of early childhood education and discussing some of the approaches to curriculum which can be found in our nurseries. In the second section attention will be drawn to the influence of developmental psychology on current practice and on the model which is being offered here.

WHAT ARE THE AIMS OF THE NURSERY CURRICULUM?

Due to a misinterpretation of the principles underlying early childhood education there grew up during the 1950s and 1960s an image of the nursery school as a 'cosy' place in which children are able to play freely, follow their own interests with little or no guidance of their activities, a place which Blank (1974) termed 'a secure, benign environment', a criticism which was seriously challenged by practitioners at the time. This attack prompted early childhood educators to think about and overtly declare their policies, aims and objectives and the curriculum they offer young children.

The first large-scale attempt to research into the aims of nursery education was carried out in 1972 by Taylor, Exon and Holley who asked 578 teachers to complete a questionnaire on the main purpose of nursery education. The aims of the study focused on the following major areas:

1 The intellectual development of the child, i.e. encouraging her use of language, helping her to learn how to learn, stimulating her curiosity and encouraging the development of her ability to use concepts.
2 The social and emotional development of the child, i.e. helping her to form stable relationships, encouraging her sense of s responsibility, her consideration for others, her self-confidence, independence and self-control.
3 The aesthetic development of the child, i.e. giving her opportunities to experiment with a variety of materials in art and music, encouraging her to be creative and expressive and awakening in her a growing awareness and appreciation of beauty.
4 The physical development of the child, i.e. helping the child to use her body effectively by providing fresh air, space to play and sleep, good food, training in personal hygiene and regular medical attention.
5 The creation of an effective transition from home to school, i.e. providing mutually supportive conditions for the child's development in both the home and the school.

Another section of the questionnaire related to objectives with goals specifically linked to the aims. The authors of the questionnaire derived thirty objectives representing a range of capabilities, skills, attitudes, values and dispositions which were related to the four major developmental areas. The teachers were asked to rank the aims in order of priority relative to the other aims; each objective had to be rated on a five-point scale. The findings from the research indicated that nursery teachers placed greater emphasis on the social and emotional development of children than on intellectual development which led Van der Eyken (1977) to report that the nursery school fails to 'place emphasis where it belongs – on educational needs'. Before we conclude that nursery teachers place low priority on intellectual development, thereby laying themselves open to the criticism that nursery school is a place solely for socialising and play, we should look again carefully at this questionnaire and its methodology. If you are asked to place five aims in rank order, even if you think some may be of equal importance, and are not permitted to stipulate any reasons for your decisions, then you have the choice of either complying with the request or refusing to answer the questionnaire. Either way, you are unable to reflect your true feelings. Taylor, Exon and Holley also commented that no great gulf separated any one of the objectives from another. All are considered of importance though it is reasonable to infer that some will be given priority depending on the child and the circumstances.

Awareness of the difficulties involved in attempting to differentiate between aims of nursery education and the rest of education may have been one of the reasons why Webb came to the conclusion that the aims of education are the same at all levels. She states that:

> education is . . . that process by which an individual is aided by informed instruction, guidance, demonstration, provision, and opportunity to pursue worthwhile activities to as high a degree of critical awareness and retains personal autonomy as possible to him.
>
> (1974, p. 58)

Her view was reiterated in the HMI report (1989, p. 19) when they stated:

> Certain general principles that inform the planning and evaluation of the curriculum for children of non-compulsory school age hold true for the under fives. As for older pupils, the curriculum for young children needs to be broad, balanced, differentiated and relevant: to take into account the assessment of children's progress; to promote equal opportunities irrespective of gender, ethnic grouping or socio-economic background; and to respond effectively to children's special educational needs. The Educational Reform Act calls for a balanced and broadly based curriculum which:
>
> 1 promotes the spiritual, moral, cultural, mental and physical development of pupils at the school; and
> 2 prepares such pupils for the opportunities, responsibilities and experiences of adult life.

Although early childhood educators did not disagree with this broad general statement there was some concern that there might also be a subject-based curriculum with its set programmes of study for children under statutory school age. The National Curriculum is based upon an approach that assumes that every child should acquire certain knowledge and information, and concentrates upon what children are to become rather than upon what they are now. This model is very similar to what is associated with secondary schooling and fails to take into account what we know about the ways in which young children structure their learning. As far as early childhood education is concerned, the National Curriculum has placed a 'downward pressure' upon children under statutory school age, even though the curriculum framework which emerged from the Rumbold Committee (Department of Education and Science 1990) was not subject based. This committee advocated that:

> It is the educator's task to provide experiences which support, stimulate and structure children's learning to bring about a progression of understanding appropriate to the child's needs and abilities. Careful planning and development of the child's experiences, with sensitive and appropriate intervention by the educator, will help nurture an eagerness to learn as well as enabling the child to learn effectively.
>
> We believe that, in fulfilling this task for the under fives, educators should guard against pressures which might lead them to over-concentration on formal teaching and upon the attainment of a specific set of targets. Research points to the importance of a broad range of experiences in developing young children's basic abilities.
>
> The educator working with under fives must pay careful attention not just to the content of the child's learning, but also to the way in which that learning is offered to and experienced by the child, and the role of all those involved in the process. Children are affected by the *context* in which learning takes place, the *people* involved in it and the *values and beliefs* which are embedded in it.
>
> (1990, p. 9)

The content of the curriculum was to be based on areas of learning experience: aesthetic and creative; human and social; language and literacy; mathematics; physical; science; moral and spiritual; and technological.

In spite of this reassurance from a government committee the feeling of a 'top-down' pressure increased and was reinforced by the publication of *Desirable Learning Outcomes for Children's Learning* (1996) which looked at five areas of learning: personal and social development; language and literacy; mathematics; knowledge and understanding of the world; physical development and creative development. This, too, is subject based and in many ways inappropriate to young children's learning; although they are guidelines, not programmes of study.

A genuine concern for the principles of early childhood education by everyone working in the field of early childhood education prompted the setting up of the Early Years Forum – a group of early childhood educators from all sectors of the field (public, voluntary and private, including the Montessorian educators) whose aim was to produce a set of underpinning principles with regard to children's learning. One of the very positive things to come out of this venture was the awareness that whatever the methodological approach of the members of the group they all shared common principles (Early Childhood Education Forum 1997, np):

- learning begins at birth
- care and education are inseparable – quality care is educational and quality education is caring
- every child develops at his or her own pace, but adults can stimulate and encourage learning
- all children benefit from developmentally appropriate practice and education
- skilled and careful observations are the keys to helping children learn
- cultural and physical diversity should be respected and valued: a proactive anti-bias approach should be adopted and stereotypes challenged
- learning is holistic and cannot be compartmentalised: trust, motivation, interest, enjoyment and physical and social skills are as important as purely cognitive gains
- young children learn best through play, first-hand experience and talk
- carers and educators should work in partnership with parents, who are their children's first educators
- quality care and education require well-trained educators/carers and on-going training and support.

These principles support a process model of curriculum rather than the traditional model of education with its emphasis upon subject knowledge and the implication that we know what subject knowledge children need in order to live in the next century. The basis for a process model was laid down in the Hadow Report on the Primary School (Consultative Committee 1931) which suggested that: 'the curriculum be thought of in terms of activity and experience rather than knowledge to be acquired and facts to be stored. Its aim should be to develop in a child the fundamental human powers and to awaken him to the fundamental interests of civilized life so far as these powers and interests lie within the compass of childhood' (p. 93).

The educator is concerned with the process of education rather than with its possible products and is actively engaged in encouraging children's intellectual growth through discovery and inquiry. However, when designing curricula based on activities and experience the educationalist needs to consider which activities and fields of knowledge are 'worthwhile'. Peters (1966) queried what is meant by worthwhile, and asked how one can justify what is included in the curriculum for young children, and whether we are justified in teaching children to 'know how' rather than to 'know that'. Does it mean that to be termed 'worthwhile' every activity must have a cognitive content? If so, what about teaching some skills which are a necessary part of every curriculum? How much cognitive involvement is there in learning to get dressed and undressed?

Peters states that a worthwhile activity must have certain characteristics; it must engage the whole mind of the participant so that the child is totally absorbed. For him, 'worthwhile activities' are always 'infinitely extend-able', the main point being that the involvement is in the process, the activity itself, not the product. When we think about the activities offered to our young children, can we really justify adding the adjective 'worthwhile' to all of them? How meaningful are such activities as drawing round templates, or sticking pieces of screwed-up paper on to teacher-drawn shapes? Just as Peters has drawn our attention to the nature of the 'activities' which we present to the children, so Hirst (1969) has pointed out that 'experience in itself is quite inadequate for developing a body of concepts'. Therefore, in devising a curriculum around interests and activities we must ensure that children are able to learn from the experiences we offer.

Although the government has introduced the *Desirable Outcomes for Children's Learning* they are only guidelines and nurseries are free to organise their programmes of study in whatever way they choose and adopt a curriculum model to suit their own philosophy, provided the children have the appropriate experiences to enable them to attain the learning outcomes by the time they reach statutory school age. We have already looked at the curriculum framework offered by the Rumbold Report (1990) but it may be helpful to consider a few definitions of the term 'curriculum' before we look at some of the models currently in practice.

Drummond *et al.* (1989) state that the curriculum for young children includes:

- all the activities and experiences provided for them by adults
- all the activities they devise for themselves
- the language that adults use to them and that they use to each other
- all that they see and hear in the environment around them.

The Rumbold Report highlighted the concepts, knowledge, understanding, attitudes and skills that a child needs to develop, while Ball (1994) stressed that the curriculum includes all the activities and experiences (planned and unplanned, formal and informal, overt and hidden) from which a child learns. In its broadest form, the curriculum involves a consideration of the process of learning (how a child learns), the learning progression (when a child learns) and the learning context (where and why a child learns).

My own definition, which I use when I am working with early childhood educators, is slightly broader than those above. The curriculum is everything that affects the child in the learning environment, overt and covert. It covers not only the activities, both indoors and outdoors, offered to young children, but the attitudes of the staff not only towards the children but to each other, to parents and anyone who visits the setting.

What do these definitions have in common? Three of the definitions mention the importance of the learning environment. Three also consider the role of the adult. Overall these definitions adopt a broad perspective of curriculum, embracing a subject-based curriculum such as the National Curriculum with its programmes of study, specifying the knowledge and understanding which all children need to know and understand, as well as an informal curriculum, overt or hidden, which includes children learning about themselves and the social world in which they live.

To date there is no curricular entitlement for children under statutory school age in this country although the introduction of the Desirable Outcomes will go some way to ensuring that all early childhood institutions will offer certain programmes of learning.

SOME DIFFERENT APPROACHES TO CURRICULUM IN THE UK

Although the majority of early childhood settings in this country offer children a curriculum based upon their interests and activities, there is a relatively small number of nurseries which offer a very specific approach. Among the most popular and steadily increasing in number are the Montessori nurseries. Although some of these nurseries adhere strictly to her method, there is an increasing number which combine Montessori education with a more traditional approach, particularly in relation to play and creative activities.

We have already discussed the influence of Maria Montessori and Rudolph Steiner on early childhood education in Chapter One, but as there are still early childhood settings which adhere to their philosophies, it may be helpful to discuss in greater detail how they work in practice.

Montessori education

The Montessori classroom is designed to allow the children to develop their fullest potential through their own efforts, as, for her, the young child learns through observation, movement and exploration, and must not be educated in the same way as the older child. A key feature of Montessori education is the prepared environment, which includes both indoors and outdoors, as well as the organisation of space and resources. The

Montessori classroom is organised into areas of learning, and on the shelves, which are all low enough for children to collect easily whatever material they require, is specific equipment to help develop all the sensory abilities of the children. Everything the child requires for a particular activity is to be found in one particular area of the classroom and this is always in the same space, in order to provide security for the children.

The teacher, whom Montessori called a directress, is not there to direct the child, but, where possible, the direction and correction for the young child should be inherent in the structure of the environment, hence the self-correcting exercises and apparatus. A feature of Montessori education which is different from the other models to be discussed is that the child is not allowed to work with any of the structured materials until shown how to do so by the directress. The directress has four main tasks:

1 To prepare herself.
2 To prepare the environment and provide a stimulating and challenging environment which will help children by creating a spontaneous learning situation.
3 To act as a link between the child and the materials. Teachers do this by demonstration and example.
4 To observe each child and note her interests and the way she works. These observations are used to decide what next should be presented to the child, how it is presented and when. Once the child has been shown the materials she is free to use them in her own way.

The curriculum is governed by Montessori's belief that the child has two 'creative sensibilities'; an 'absorbent mind' and 'sensitive periods' which are aids to help the child adapt to the environment. Montessori refers to freedom within a structured environment, but that does not mean a licence to do what one wants. She argues that we cannot be absolutely free or we would not be able to live in society.

Another key feature of the approach involves the 'normalisation' of children. Montessori sets out the characteristics of the normalised child, which include: the ability to work at her own pace; the freedom to watch; and the possibility of choosing her own activities and following her own natural rhythm and work pattern. As far as Montessori is concerned, once the child has completed her work she will experience pleasure and success and will have learned the importance of the powers of concentration. Normalisation is most likely to work between the ages of three and six. In Montessorian terms the ideal environment does not happen by chance. For example, so that each child has to learn to take turns and wait there is only one set of didactic materials in the classroom. Montessori always placed children in a mixed-age-group class in order to give them the opportunity to be both an older and a younger member of a group. She believed that her environment provided infinite opportunities for role playing within a real setting with real activities.

Within this prepared environment the child follows a programme of learning which includes: exercises in practical and sensorial life that help children understand the world around them; a mathematical programme based on the highly structured apparatus devised by Montessori; a language programme which introduces quite young children to reading through the phonic approach; and activities around cultural and creative subjects.

Steiner education

The principles of a Steiner education are based upon a specific view of child development that children grow through different stages and the education offered must be appropriate to these stages. The philosophy behind the curriculum is that if the child is offered a creative and balanced curriculum then the child will grow into a flexible and creative adult.

Each morning there is a routine organised by the teacher. It may begin with circle time, with singing and circle games with plenty of opportunity for movement before the children are guided, sometimes through a story, into their play. The children may play alone or with others or they can draw or sew. The teacher is always ready to help them if required but there is no attempt to introduce them to number or reading skills or offer them any instructional materials.

The classroom is always painted in a warm colour with soft materials and few sharp corners. The materials in the room are natural and always at the child's own level and are stored in aesthetic containers, such as wooden baskets, which can be incorporated into the children's play. All the play materials are natural, and there are always wooden blocks of every shape and size. There is often a three-year age range in the nursery which enables children of different ages to work together. There are small felt dolls and puppets and a workbench available with miniature, but real tools where the children can make their own toys, such as wooden boats.

There is a mid-morning snack time, when the children all sit together around tables with tablecloths and flowers according to the season. Outside there is very little commercial play equipment but plenty of natural play things – trunks and logs for children to scramble over and so on: the philosophy being that the lack of equipment encourages children to become more creative and imaginative.

The role of the teacher is to help children learn to do things as well as possible: for example, the children are only given primary colours and have to experience the pleasure themselves of seeing colours change.

At the end of the morning the teacher gathers the children together in a special part of the nursery and a child is asked to light the 'story candle'. The story is always told, never read, as it is felt that the book comes between the children and the storyteller, and they will be better able to imagine the situation without pictures in a book to destroy their own images.

High Scope Curriculum

The High Scope Curriculum, which was derived from a programme for disadvantaged children in Ypsilanti in the 1960s, has been one of the most well publicised of recent programmes. It has been embraced by a number of local authorities in Britain for both nursery and young primary children and can be found in many parts of the world.

The programme

The programme encourages children to become problem solvers and decision makers and to develop their independence. It is a framework which places greater responsibility upon children for planning and executing their own activities than the traditional nursery programme. It works on a philosophy of *plan*, *do* and *review*, where the environment is arranged so that it optimises children's learning, using key experiences to observe and plan for the individual needs of children.

Implicit in the High Scope concept of children being active learners are the key experiences focused on five areas:

- using language, e.g. describing objects, events and relationships
- active learning, e.g. manipulating, transforming and combining materials
- representing ideas and experiences, e.g. role playing, pretending
- developing logical reasoning, e.g. learning to label, match and sort objects
- understanding time and space, e.g. recalling and anticipating events, learning to find things in the classroom.

These key experiences provide the framework for planning and evaluating activities and enable the staff to guide children from one learning experience to another. It is a child-centred approach that ensures that children are making choices and decisions about what they will do, while the adults play a guiding, supportive role.

The sessions are organised for both small- and large-group activities and include both snack time and tidy-up time, the latter being an important part of the child's learning process.

The High Scope Curriculum has two other characteristics: team teaching, that is, consultation between staff members regarding the needs of individual children; and parental involvement. It is the belief of the High Scope programmers that parents and staff need to work together in the best interests of the child.

Developmentally appropriate practice

This philosophical approach, based upon a child-centred philosophy, is, in Woodhead's (1996) view steeped in deep-rooted beliefs and ideals widely shared among Western-educated specialists, based entirely upon Western psychological theory. According to Kelly (1994), the term 'developmentally appropriate practice' indicates that the focus of the early childhood curriculum must be on the child and her development rather than on subjects and knowledge, the process being more important than the product. This approach, as has already been mentioned, was advocated by the Hadow Report (1933), which argued that the curriculum needs to be framed in terms of activity and experience rather than knowledge to be acquired and facts to be stored.

In practical terms developmentally appropriate practice is based on universal, predictable sequences of growth and change, and requires the educator to take account of the age of the child, and her individuality, in terms of growth pattern, personality, learning style and family background. It argues that children learn best through play which is self-initiated, self-directed and self-chosen.The role of the teacher is to provide a rich variety of activities and materials, and to support the children's play through talk and materials.

Recently this approach has been challenged as being insensitive to the cultural diversity in children's family experiences and parenting practices, and it risks, according to Mallory and New (1994), resurrecting discredited judgements about deprived environments and the need for compensation. The National Association for the Education of Young Children (NAEYC), although it supported the guidelines on developmentally appropriate practice (Bredekamp 1987), has issued a position statement of advocating responsiveness to linguistic and cultural diversity.

Foundations for early learning

These are curriculum guidelines developed from principles of observation and discussion of practice in action by the members of the Early

Childhood Education Forum who are participating in the Quality in Diversity Project based at Goldsmith's College. The guidelines work on the premise that children learn from all the experiences, planned and unplanned, that they encounter. The role of the adult is to plan appropriate learning experiences for them.

The framework which has been developed for goals for children's learning offers a different approach to thinking about curriculum in that it does not involve discrete areas of learning but places the observations of practitioners at the heart of curriculum planning.

The goals for learning are:

- belonging and connecting: involving relationships with children and adults in families, communities and group settings; learning to be a member of your own cultural group
- being and becoming: using the notion that effective learning builds upon self-respect, feelings of personal worth and identity, including care of self, health and safety of the individual
- doing and being active: effective learning builds upon what the children have already achieved and stresses the importance of the processes in learning as contributing to attitudes to learning and achievement
- contributing and participating: involving the need for learning to be responsible and to make appropriate choices in a group
- thinking, understanding and knowing: in order to learn effectively children build upon their own understanding through active processes such as play, discovery and encounters with world knowledge and culture.

Although the Montessori and Steiner methods of education relate very closely to their underlying principles and philosophy, the other approaches are more general and based on our understanding of developmental psychology.

INFLUENCE OF DEVELOPMENTAL PSYCHOLOGY

Psychology has long played an important part in the shaping of the school curriculum and the work of Piaget has probably been one of the most powerful influences on educational thinking in the nursery and primary school. Piaget argued that the individual is not a passive organism but an active participant in her own development, the source of knowledge is action and the child learns through interacting with the environment. From his observations of children covering several decades, Piaget postulated that cognitive development occurs through the processes of assimilation and accommodation. First the child uses existing mental schemas or structures to assimilate the new information, but if she finds that these are inadequate, then she will be in a state of disequilibrium. In order to restore the cognitive imbalance, that is, to take in the new information, it will be necessary to adapt or accommodate the existing schemas. Development occurs when the learner has resolved the conflict and restored equilibrium.

However, the process of equilibration is not a static one. It is what Inhelder (1962) referred to as 'an active system of compensation'. Changes will occur throughout life as new information is encountered which is at variance with existing mental structures. For example, the small child who first encounters a ball as a 'red woolly object' will need to alter her internal structures on many occasions before fully coming to understand the concept. It is the process of equilibration which produces the stages of intellectual development and which led to Piaget postulating that the child's thinking is qualitatively different from that of an intelligent adult. These two notions, that of the individual being an active participant in her own learning and the view that children's thinking is qualitatively different from that of the adult, are central to Piaget's theory and have had an important bearing upon the curriculum of the young child.

The period covering roughly the three years leading to formal schooling have been described by Piaget as the pre-operational stage of intelligence, when children's thinking is characterised by the development of language and the ability to represent the external world to themselves. It is a phase which has also been described as prelogical and magical because of the idiosyncratic remarks that children can make during conversation.

During the nursery years children frequently make bizarre statements, but these should not be viewed in a negative manner, rather we should consider that the mistakes are a valuable way of coping with reality and of reaching a more mature way of thinking which is characteristic of the next stage of development. Not only may children distort reality in their attempts to assimilate new schemas into their existing frameworks, but they may appear more egocentric in that they concentrate on their own points of view rather than seeing things from another perspective. Piaget based much of his thinking about childhood egocentricity on the experimental observations he made when working with Inhelder during the late 1940s and early 1950s. In his famous 'three mountains' experiment, he demonstrated that young children could not cope with the problems of spatial perspective. However, during the last few years, a number of researchers (Donaldson 1978, Chandler and Boyes 1982) have pointed out that if children are either given a more simple task or are able to identify very closely with some aspect of the problem, they can understand another perspective once they understand what is expected of them. Chandler and Boyes showed that in a simple task where children are shown a picture of a teddy and a duck on opposing sides of an otherwise blank block they realise that when they can see the teddy, the person on the other side of the table can see the duck, and vice versa. Once the children have come to understand that the object has two sides they are able to cope with the problem. The important things for the children to realise are the properties of objects, and only then will they realise that others have different perspectives and what those perspectives are.

All the researchers in this field have demonstrated that children can decentre if they are made aware of the difficulties and, what is more important, can understand what is required of them by the experimenters. Much of the criticism of Piaget's work has stemmed from the fact that the language used in the tests may produce negative results not because of the child's lack of ability, but because of her lack of understanding of the task.

Children's ability to 'role-take' or put themselves into 'other people's shoes' can be affected by other factors. Light (1979) studied differences in role-taking abilities in children aged four-and-a-half and found that they could be related to their mode of interaction with their mothers. In families where mothers appeared to take the child's viewpoint into consideration during discussion there was less evidence of egocentrism than in families where no deference was made to the child's wishes or opinions. This piece of research has important implications for the ways in which teachers behave towards their pupils.

Although the aspect of Piaget's work which is most widely known is related to his theory of stages, it is probably the notion of equilibration which is his greatest contribution to education. In adopting this model the educator facilitates development by providing opportunities for children to experience cognitive conflict, which throws them into a state of disequilibrium and necessitates the restructuring of their schemas if a state of equilibrium is to be restored.

In order to use this approach effectively it is vital that the educator has a sound knowledge of child development so that she can diagnose accurately the current level of the child's understanding and know which materials and activities will foster future development. Piaget's work, though, is descriptive, and as Bruner (1966) has pointed out, he is deeply concerned with the nature of knowledge *per se*, knowledge as it exists at different points in the development of the child. He is considerably less interested in the processes that make growth possible. It is this descriptive quality which has made critics such as Dearden (1976) point out that Piaget's theory offers no practical support to teachers as to how to promote intellectual development. On the other hand, Bruner has postulated a theory of instruction which interacts with his theory of cognitive development. For him learning is purposeful and he argues that the learner is constantly striving to understand the complexities of the world through the use of three modes or strategies.

Bruner terms his three modes enactive, iconic and symbolic. In the enactive mode the learner comes to represent the world through action. Bruner (1973, p. 328) terms this 'a mode of representing past events through appropriate motor-responses'. At the next stage, the iconic mode, children replace action with an image or a spatial scheme; images, therefore, stand for objects as does a picture on a map. The final, symbolic stage is a mode of representation emerging at about the age of six or seven years and is based on language and symbols. It is only at this stage that children are free to 'go beyond the information given'. Although these modes emerge sequentially and will be stronger at different ages, each will nevertheless continue to function and interact with the two others throughout life.

In his theory of instruction, Bruner advocates a prescriptive approach, arguing that the learning process can be accelerated by providing materials appropriate to a child's level of understanding. The role of the teacher is to provide what Bruner terms a 'scaffolding' to enable the child to acquire the skills, knowledge and concepts of a particular culture. Acquiring skills and competencies involves the solving of a series of problems; for example, let us consider the problems inherent in learning to tie a bow. The educator will facilitate this learning by helping the child to hypothesise and predict until the correct solution has been reached. As the child's knowledge and repertory of skills is increased so will her ability to utilise experience more effectively, thereby enabling more complex problems to be tackled satisfactorily. Adults, by intervening and talking through the problems, will help to establish the verbal skills necessary to enable the child to move into the mode of symbolic functioning. To me, it is one of the most important functions of the nursery school to ensure that children are supported in their acquisition of skills by the use of language which will provide them with coping strategies so necessary in later schooling, which is almost entirely word based.

The nursery curriculum, like that for older children, should be based on a process of growth and experience where the child is an active learner but where the adult provides the appropriate experiences to allow the child to develop skills and knowledge which form the basis of later learning.

Learning in the nursery years, as at every other stage of schooling, will only take place if the children are well motivated and display curiosity and interest in the world around them. This interest is present in the vast majority of young children who enter into early childhood institutions as, according to Vernon (1969, p. 23), at the age of three to three-and-a-half the child begins to experience pleasure in his personal competence to perform a specific task, and regret and shame if she fails. She turns less frequently to adults for help and support and the experience of competence brings its own reward. At four to five some children, instead of trying to overcome failure by greater effort, may resort to avoidance of the situation, or denial or concealment of failure.

The skills and competencies which young children develop during the years before formal schooling are of vital importance in their overall personal development. They will not only enable children to take a pride in their achievements but, through acquiring these personal skills, children can, with our help, perceive that they are effective and competent people.

DEVELOPING CURIOSITY

In this background section to the nursery curriculum I want to look at some of the ways in which educators can help develop curiosity in young children. From birth, the healthy infant spends much of her waking hours in exploratory, investigatory behaviour which, as language develops, becomes linked to the incessant questioning characteristic of many two-, three- and four-year-old children. These activities are important in providing the foundation for more complex behaviours such as reasoning, problem solving and social competence. Before suggesting how teachers might encourage curiosity in young children let us consider what is meant by a curious child.

Most people would agree that a curious child is one who:

1 reacts in a positive manner to new, strange and incongruous aspects in the environment by carefully observing, moving towards, manipulating and seeking information about them; and
2 persists in examining and exploring stimuli in order to know more about them.

A considerable number of theories have been put forward to explain why children are curious and although no one explanation seems to be all embracing, nevertheless each assumes that curiosity is important for the overall development of the young child. Theorists appear to agree that curiosity is a prerequisite to functioning as a competent, self-sufficient human being and that it is fundamental to any learning or problem-solving behaviour.

Curiosity, therefore, appears to be vital for the child's understanding and later development. However, we need to ask ourselves whether there are individual differences in children's expressions of curiosity, since such information could have far-reaching implications for educators who are attempting to engender curiosity by making classrooms interesting places and by providing opportunities for children to explore and inquire about the environment in which they live. A number of studies which have looked at children's curiosity have shown that there are considerable differences in their exploratory behaviour and in their reaction to novel stimuli. Studies of pre-schoolers have shown that some children rarely ask questions about novel objects presented to them, while others query and question constantly. This raises a major problem for teachers in attempting to determine each child's level of curiosity, as it is difficult to tell whether a child is asking questions in order to satisfy curiosity or merely to maintain a dependency-like contact with the adult. Likewise, quiet, unobtrusive children may be absorbing information from the situation or may be day-dreaming.

Curiosity and exploratory behaviour may also be related to the sex of the child. Maccoby and Jacklin (1974) showed that boys of nursery-school age are generally less reluctant to leave their mothers and explore objects and toys than are girls of a similar age. They have suggested, however, that it may have been the nature of the objects that accounted for the differences, since it could be that girls prefer to explore toys with faces or objects that are more social while boys prefer to explore novel fixtures and non-social toys and objects.

Further useful information for educators concerning individual differences and the development of curiosity comes from the work of Maw and Maw (1970) who postulated a negative relationship between authoritarian children and high levels of curiosity. They found such children to be intolerant of ambiguity, inflexible in their thinking and resistant to new information.

Awareness of this should enable educators to appreciate more fully why some children appear to be more resistant to novel and discrepant objects, information, situations or people than others, and programmes can be planned containing activities that help these children to become gradually more open to novelty, more flexible in their thinking and more creative in their approach to problem-solving situations. Curiosity will obviously be inhibited if children are fearful and anxious and an important role of the early years educator is to ensure that the nursery environment is as relaxed as possible.

White (1959), looking at the growth of the self-concept, showed that as children explore and learn that they have some control over their environment they correspondingly develop more positive self-concepts. Other researchers have also shown that children who exhibit the most curiosity also display the most positive self-concepts.

Research points to the view that by increasing children's overall curiosity and encouraging them to observe what is going on in the world around them we can have an effect upon their self-concept. There is a strong possibility that children who are both low on levels of curiosity and have a poor self-concept are less likely to cope effectively with the demands of nursery or school. Is there any particular type of educational programme which may be most stimulating in encouraging the development of curiosity in young children? Research by Miller and Dyer (1975) looked at a variety of pre-school educational programmes and concluded that although there was little or no difference in overall curiosity behaviour by the differing groups of children, it did show that well-planned nursery experiences coupled with sensitive reactions with educators and peers were more likely to stimulate curiosity development. The evidence suggests that children's curiosity can be optimised by providing a proper balance between novelty and familiarity. Novel objects and opportunities are welcomed provided that the children are with familiar people and situations.

One of the best ways in which children seem to develop curiosity is through modelling themselves on the behaviour of respected adults. Zimmerman and Rosenthal (1974) showed that modelling can be used to teach children to ask more efficient questions and to engage in more efficient problem-solving strategies. Overall it seems that adults who themselves are curious, questioning people and who value curious behaviour will encourage this characteristic in children in their care. Children do not appear to require extrinsic rewards for curious behaviour, rather they show that they are more attentive and receptive to information that stems from their own curiosity. There is also evidence to suggest that they will be able to recall and use this information more effectively at a later stage.

ENCOURAGING INTRINSIC MOTIVATION

Curiosity and intrinsic motivation seem to be inextricably linked and it is therefore important that teachers look at motivational and curiosity behaviours very carefully in their attempts to teach children how to learn. A number of theories have been put forward concerning the development of intrinsic motivation. One approach which is widely accepted in educational circles is the cognitive approach which takes the view that children are more likely to investigate, be curious and explore if they encounter something new, complex, incongruous or surprising because these experiences cause conceptual conflict which the child must resolve. Although exposure to a novel and varied environment should produce intrinsic motivation, the particular stimuli that produce intrinsic motivation differ for each child because cognitive conflict can exist only in relation to the child's current knowledge. The environment, therefore, plays a particularly important role in these theories. Another approach to motivational development is taken by White (1959) who argues that initially children seek to interact effectively with their environment and through mastery the child experiences a feeling of efficacy, which is an intrinsic motive. A third theoretical stance on intrinsic motivation relates to attribution theory. Proponents of this approach argue that the important point is how children perceive the cause of their behaviour. When children attribute the cause of their behaviour to their own efforts, competence and intrinsic motivation are likely to be enhanced. On the other hand, when children attribute the cause of their behaviour to external influences, such as reward for parental or teacher demands rather than their own efforts, their intrinsic motivation is likely to be diminished.

In recent years there has been a great deal of research into the ways in which intrinsic motivation can be fostered and maintained, and from the findings it would appear that a variety of stimulation encourages children's cognitive development. As with the development of curiosity, it appears that a discrepant, novel environment is likely to produce the level of intrinsic motivation required to reduce discrepancy and thereby advance the child's cognitive structures. Overall, it seems that children's experiences of mastery and effectiveness in the environment are important components in their developing intrinsic motivation. Although rewards do not necessarily decrease motivation as was once thought, there is a suggestion that they do not act as positive reinforcers, and often intrinsic motivation will diminish when the reward is no longer available. What we know from the research is that early childhood educators should attempt to develop all these aspects of intrinsic motivation: cognitive conflict, competence and attribution.

Although there has been little or no direct research to show the relationship between intrinsic motivation and education in the pre-school years there is no doubt that the environment should be as free from anxiety as possible, since it appears that higher levels of academic anxiety are associated with lower levels of academic intrinsic motivation. It has been suggested that teachers should stimulate cognitive conflict to develop children's curiosity and the best time for developing curiosity is during the pre-school years when evaluation is minimal. Some recent research has suggested that teachers who give children more choices and use information feedback as rewards will encourage children's motivation. In planning a curriculum for pre-school children, therefore, we should aim to provide an environment which:

- introduces incongruity, surprise and novelty in learning of new concepts
- provides experiences in which children can see that they can have a noticeable effect on the environment
- provides children with opportunities to investigate individual interests
- gives children choices
- provides an atmosphere of trust so that children can ask questions without fear of making mistakes.

Curiosity and intrinsic motivation are closely linked and there is no doubt they play an important part in helping children to develop positive attitudes towards learning. One of the main functions of the nursery is to provide a stimulating, enriching environment where children are encouraged to 'learn how to learn'. In preparing this book I have divided the skills and competencies into five broad areas which should form the basis of any curriculum for young children. There will obviously be overlap in each of these areas and in no way should one consider them as discrete groupings, but by focusing the educator's attention upon the various sections I hope to ensure that children are offered a wide range of experiences relevant to their needs. Over the last few years there has been an increasing awareness that young children have a greater understanding than we had hitherto imagined and it is imperative that pre-school years are not wasted with 'trivial pursuits' but that we channel the lively interests and curiosity of children into a positive approach to understanding themselves and their environment.

Many of the skills and competencies which will be discussed will be further developed and refined during the later years of schooling but it is hoped that the nursery curriculum suggested here will offer all children the opportunity to enjoy being 'three and four years of age' while laying down solid foundations for later learning.

3　Development of personal and social competence

One of the main aims of early childhood education is to help children become independent, autonomous adults. In *Desirable Outcomes for Children's Learning* (SCAA 1996b) stress is placed upon the importance of sound personal and social development including 'the development of personal values and an understanding of self and others'. Confidence to tackle new learning and show an awareness of the individual social and cultural needs of others is a fundamental part of children's development. This chapter will focus upon personal and social development and look at ways in which the educator can foster the growth of competence in these areas.

DEVELOPMENT OF PERSONAL AWARENESS

Probably the most important area of competence for the young child relates to personal awareness and self-awareness. What she feels about herself, and her ability to cope with the world around her, will have far-reaching consequences upon the skills and competencies learned during the nursery years and beyond. The child who is developing positive feelings about herself and her abilities is more likely to be curious and motivated to learn than one who has feelings of inadequacy and fear of failure.

The small child, though, not only has to develop positive inner feelings but must develop bodily and sensory awareness. As children gradually develop control over their bodily functions they become increasingly aware of what they can do with their bodies. They begin, through language, to express ideas on how they look, feel, sound and smell and to appreciate that their bodies change over time. From an early age they will have looked in the mirror and begun to identify themselves as individuals, but as many teachers learn to their surprise a large number of children enter school at three years of age with a very limited understanding of the relationship between the parts of the body. I recall talking with a three-and-a-half-year-old girl in a large nursery school about her appearance, and when we were discussing her necklace it rapidly became obvious that although she was aware of the words head, neck and shoulders, she was, as yet, totally unaware of the relationship between them.

During the two- to five-year-old age range children gain some understanding of the concept of inner physical space. Their ideas are often mixed up and confused but one four-year-old boy was some way towards understanding when he commented to his teacher that it was funny how the blood came out when he cut himself and yet most of the time the skin keeps it in all dry.

By around two years of age children begin to learn the appropriate use of gender terms – for example, boy and girl – as they become aware of gender differences, and one of the important functions of the nursery teacher is to help in the establishment of gender identity. Gender identity is concerned with children developing ideas and feelings about their biological sex, being a boy or a girl, and should be clearly distinguished from the development of sex-role stereotyping which involves cultural definitions of masculinity and femininity. It appears that length of hair and body build are the most important cues for four- to six-year-old children in establishing sex. In some cases we know that up to the age of four to five children are not fully aware of gender constancy and it is possible to ask, for example, a four-year-old girl who wears dresses all the time whether she would turn into a boy if she wore trousers and to get a reply which points to the child's uncertainty as to whether a clothing change could imply a sex change.

Once children have made decisions about their gender identity they quickly learn how they are expected to behave and the kind of sex role to assume. Even today, from birth, most children will have been exposed to traditional sex-role stereotyping and there is evidence to suggest that they have established a firm notion of their sex roles by the age of three. A study by Kuhn, Nash and Brucken (1978) showed that two- and three-year-old girls tended to assign positive aspects to their own sex (e.g. looks nice) and negative characteristics to boys (e.g. are mean, like to fight) while boys of the same age did the reverse (e.g. girls cry and boys 'work hard'). The same study also demonstrated that not all aspects of behaviour were stereotyped; for example, there was no sex preference for being strong. The development of this understanding that the world is divided into two genders and that there are appropriate behaviours which accompany them is the result of social expectations, particularly those of parents and respected adults; for example, a mother will correct her young child who points to a boy and calls him a girl.

Nowadays there are some parents in Western society who are trying to raise their children in such a way that there are fewer distinctions between boys and girls, particularly in relation to appropriate behaviour and aspirations for boys and girls. The task is not easy as the messages passed to children from their peers and other adults, as well as the media, may be very different. Statham (1986) interviewed parents who were trying to raise their children in a non-sexist way and found that although they had similar aims for their sons and daughters there was greater concern about traditional stereotyping from parents of girls than from parents of boys. Although the aims of parents of both boys and girls were similar in that they wanted children to be independent and caring, and have equal job opportunities, parents still felt it was less acceptable for boys to develop non-traditional sex roles than girls. These parents also believed that it was difficult to change attitudes within society, even though we should continue to try.

However, in some cultures there are more overt marked distinctions in the ways in which boys and girls are treated. Whiting and Pope-Edwards (1988) studied children throughout the world and found that in many societies the most obvious symbols of gender are the clothing and attitudes towards children helping in adult work (e.g. in Juxtlahuaca in Mexico the ears of all little girls are pierced during the first few weeks of life and all females wear earrings). Similarly, little boys would be willing to help their fathers but not their mothers. Such distinctions also occur in many of the various societies which are living in the UK. The socialisation process begins long before children enter school but we can only hope that by giving both boys and girls equal opportunities to play with a wide variety of toys and equipment they can be encouraged to adopt person rather than sex roles.

The child's self-image and feelings about herself are also affected by what the teacher deems to be attractive or unattractive. The teacher who praises a child, makes positive comments on attire, manners and so on will indeed be enhancing that child's self-concept, but it may also be that as a result of this, another child is inadvertently receiving negative feelings simply because the teacher says nothing about that child's behaviour.

The stereotype of attractiveness appears to emerge during the pre-school years and even at this stage attractive children are thought of positively in terms of being more self-sufficient and independent compared with children perceived as unattractive who are labelled anti-social (Dion and Berschied 1974). Although we do not know how children evaluate their own attractiveness at the pre-school stage, research has indicated that children as young as three years of age are more likely to select pictures of attractive rather than unattractive children. It appears, therefore, that attractive children start with a more favourable bias in their relationships with adults than those deemed to be unattractive. It is important for teachers to appreciate the implications of this since, even if children are treated equally, the less attractive child by the age of around four will have learned that she is less attractive than her peers and may have begun to develop a negative self-concept. The chance of developing negative self-concepts may be greater among non-white British children who may be faced with racist, derogatory remarks.

Although many teachers still state emphatically that there is no evidence of negative attitudes towards black children during the nursery years, there is strong evidence to show that children as young as two or three years of age recognise skin differences. Goodman (1952) was one of the first people to show that young children noticed ethnic differences and that prejudiced attitudes could develop at an early age. Katz (1982) has suggested that early observation of racial cues (skin colour, hair, facial features) start well before the age of three and can lead to the formation of rudimentary concepts about varying ethnic groups.

In a study of children in three London boroughs, Pushkin (1967) found that white children's preferences for their own group were present in this age range. Further, he found that by the age of six some children were racially hostile and that a substantial proportion of these children had mothers whom he also noted as hostile. The mothers and children displaying the greatest hostility came from an area where there was marked racial tension. This was in contrast to Laishley's (1971) study of nursery-school children carried out in areas which were not racially tense, which showed that the children were almost unaware of skin-colour differences. However, as Laishley has pointed out, her children were very young; older children might have displayed different reactions. Both Milner (1983) and Maxime (1991) showed that children learn positive and negative feelings about racial groups from an early age. Milner goes on to state that even very young children have an awareness of a racial hierarchy in line with 'current adult prejudices' (1983, p. 122), which places white at the top and black at the bottom. Educators must work towards ensuring that black British children arc clear in their ethnic identity since this affects their whole development and learning. Wright's (1992) research into the experience of black children in nursery and primary schools found disturbing evidence that it is not only the children who behave in a racist manner but some of their teachers. She found that teachers held negative stereotypes of South Asian children in particular and seemed unaware that their attitudes were disadvantaging many black children in these early years of schooling.

It appears, therefore, that some children will have learned negative attitudes towards black children even during the nursery years. Likewise, some black children will have learned negative attitudes towards white children.

Children as young as two may begin to notice physical disabilities and in the next two or three years query and question what attributes of self will remain constant. It is at this age that they ask whether they themselves will change skin colour or whether they will get a similar disability to their friend. Equally, the child with a physical disability may believe that in time it will disappear. It is often because of this personal uncertainty that children may taunt their fellow classmates. Any child who is different from the 'norm' is likely to cause discomfort and may therefore be rejected, although with sensitive adult support many young children are able to empathise with people with physical disabilities. Educators will need to work hard at ensuring that such children develop positive self-concepts.

The idea that the body changes with age (although certain disabilities remain) is a difficult one for children to grasp. Even those who have baby siblings and accept that they too will become boys and girls find it hard to understand that 'mother' or 'teacher' was once a baby. Concepts like growth, life and death develop very gradually and during the nursery years children attempt to deal with these complex issues by reducing them to very simple terms. For example, many young children associate death with stillness and for this reason may become afraid of bedtime.

So far, in this section, I have considered some general ways in which children begin to become more self-aware and understand some of the basic concepts related to this area of development. In the following few paragraphs I intend to identify some of the body-awareness knowledge which can be discussed with three- and four-year-old children. In helping a child to 'become somebody' the educator not only has to encourage the development of body and sensory awareness but has to ensure that the child has the appropriate language and cognitive understanding to make sense of the experiences given. It will probably be many years before the child is fully cognisant of all the implications of the skills and concepts introduced during the pre-school period but this should not preclude their introduction at this stage in the child's development.

What are the main skills and concepts that children can develop during the pre-school years with regard to body and sensory awareness?

1 Knowledge of the names of various parts of the body.
2 Ability to identify body functions, to realise that all living things have certain features in common, e.g. food intake and elimination.
3 Understanding that although individuals may differ in appearance, e.g. different coloured hair and eyes, different height, all human beings have physical characteristics in common.
4 Acceptance that all people have limits to what they can do, e.g. most human beings can walk and jump but none can fly. However, some

children at this age find it difficult to accept their limitations compared with adults and other children.

5 Ability to understand that the body is constantly changing and that physical growth has both a beginning (birth) and an end (death). Also understanding of sleeping and waking and the importance of these two in the life-cycle.

6 Knowledge of sensory awareness. The child needs to acquire the vocabulary to enable her to discuss taste, touch, smell, hearing and vision. She also needs concrete experiences upon which to base these discussions.

7 Understanding of the body's limitations, that it can become tired, sick, and so on.

The development of self-awareness is more than just understanding the development of bodily and sensory awareness skills. There is another aspect which is related to the emotions and inner experiences. For many years, influenced by the findings of Piaget, it was argued that young children are egocentric and therefore unable to take another person's point of view. Later research has suggested that this may not be so, an approach which has confirmed the feelings of many workers with young children who have long felt that three- and four-year-old children display feelings of empathy and understanding towards other children and adults. Even the liveliest group of nursery-aged children attempt to stay a little quieter if they are told that their teacher has a headache or does not feel well.

Healthy emotional development is vital for successful learning. By helping children to explore and share their feelings we can help them better understand themselves and others. Children need to learn that people respond differently to the same thing because they interpret it differently. For example, some people are afraid of mice and react by screaming or jumping on to a chair, others are frightened of spiders and react in an emotional way. In these instances, teachers have a positive contribution to make by helping children to understand the problems of others and/or their own anxiety responses to different situations. Teachers who help children to express and describe their own emotional feelings are helping them to build up a positive self-concept. Children also need to learn about emotions in others. They need to understand whether an adult's anger is directed at them or at other members of the family.

Young children display high levels of empathy with their peers. Borke (1971) demonstrated that from the age of three children could understand one another's feelings and share one another's point of view and that by the age of five all children shown pictures of adults and children in difficult situations were able to see things from another's perspective. There is also research which shows that children can take into account another person's perspective in terms of their likes and dislikes and how they perceive the situation. Harris (1989) has pointed out the value of pretend play in helping young children to take into account another person's point of view, and how it can encourage children to cope with strong emotional feelings. For example, the child, who is taking the part of an engine driver, falls over and hurts her knee but does not cry as engine drivers do not cry!

What are the emotional skills that teachers should attempt to develop and foster during the nursery years?

1 The ability to recognise, accept and talk about feelings such as happiness, sadness, anger, surprise. Shields (1985) has shown that quite young children are able to identify and describe their feelings. It is particularly important for their emotional development that children learn to accept that one is sometimes angry, annoyed, and so on.
2 The awareness that there is a relationship between emotions and social behaviour; e.g. children have to learn that hitting the person who has made them angry may temporarily alleviate personal feelings but there is a strong possibility that the action will provoke retaliation.
3 The ability to take action concerning emotional feelings without affecting others; e.g. at home, turning off the TV programme that is frightening or avoiding a risk-taking activity in the nursery if there is no adult around to help.
4 The ability to be sensitive to the needs and feelings of others.

By accepting that children have problems and that it is quite natural for them to react sometimes quite strongly in certain situations, teachers can do a great deal to help children's emotional development. It may be helpful in certain circumstances for children to realise that teachers can also be sad, cross or happy. In talking to children about how they feel and react in particular situations it should be possible to help them appreciate more fully the feelings of others. For example, a child may be acting out the part of a giant too realistically for her playmate who starts crying or shows fear or apprehension in some way. The teacher may find it necessary to interrupt the play and point out to the 'giant' the effect she is having upon her friend. Hopefully the 'giant' will take on 'gentle, kindly' properties so that the play can continue, otherwise it may be necessary to suggest that the game is either discontinued or played with another child. In either case, the child has been made to appreciate that her behaviour has provoked a distressing reaction from her playmate. Opportunities for helping children to become more emotionally aware occur at all times during the day and the sensitive teacher will herself be fully aware of the many openings that exist to help children understand themselves and their effect upon others.

DEVELOPMENT OF SOCIAL SKILLS

The second area of competence to be considered relates to the development of social skills. Socialisation is a process which begins at birth, and by the time children reach the age of three to four years they will have learned many skills from parents, siblings and other adult members of the family. However, as many children soon discover, the social skills and behaviour acceptable within the family may be very different from those accepted within an institutional setting. It has already been pointed out that children develop their social perspective-taking skills during play situations but in order to be socially competent the child must be able to adjust her social behaviour to different social contexts and have the ability to take into account the particular characteristics of her social partner, such as age and gender. This ability to take into account the age and gender of a person is an important skill and one of the major reasons why children of mixed age groups should be encouraged to play together at this stage.

From watching adults working in the nursery environment children will learn not only what is socially acceptable in such a situation, but ways to interact effectively with adults outside the family. Even more important, the nursery will provide children, maybe for the first time, with the opportunity to socialise with members of their peer group, with whom they can argue and learn so much about the world.

There should be opportunities for children to play together free from any adult interference. In those situations, where no one is in charge, children learn to cooperate, make concessions, learn to assert themselves and come to appreciate the dynamics of group interaction. At this young age, when friendship patterns are so ephemeral, children move freely from one group to another depending on whether they agree with what is going on. The two-year-old will probably want to stand and watch the older children, but many with older siblings will try to join in various play activities. All this is in marked contrast to their relationships with adults who are still seen as ultimate authority figures representing an ordered social reality in an adult-dominated world. In the main, it is the peer group which provides children with opportunities to nurture their social skills and by means of social comparison leads the way to further self-understanding. Relationships with peers are based on mutual respect and cooperation; children share the same feelings, problems and experiences – they understand each other, whereas adults 'don't understand'.

What then are the social skills which children need to develop and practise through their contact with their peers? In general terms when we talk about social skills we are referring to different kinds of strategy that are used when we attempt to initiate and maintain any social interaction. More specifically, social skills fall into three main areas: affiliation, which involves understanding the basics of social interaction, cooperation and resolution of conflict, and kindness, care and affection (empathic skills).

Affiliation skills

The ability to cooperate and work with others is a most necessary skill in our highly socialised society and although, as will be discussed later, the adult has an important role to play in helping children to develop these skills, it is through the peer group that most of the learning will take place. Affiliation skills involve children developing the ability to identify socially acceptable and unacceptable behaviours in themselves and others and to understand the consequences of such behaviours. For example, the four-year-old who continually tries to take toys away from her peers comes to appreciate that her actions will result in social isolation.

Another important set of social skills concerned with affiliation are those related to the rituals involved in social engagement. Every time the child in the nursery decides to join another who is already involved in an activity she has to have the following social knowledge:

1 She must know how to break into the situation.
2 She must know how to manage the encounter while it occurs.
3 She must know how to extricate herself in an acceptable manner.

Goffman (1972) has made a study of the 'access' rituals used by children to gain entry into an ongoing play situation. He observed that they may try to gain entry by smiling, using non-verbal gestures or carrying on a parallel activity and then gradually blending into the play of the other. The articulate child may ask, 'Can I play?' but that is a less likely approach from the two-and-a-half- to four-year-old. Those children who attempt to break into the game by simply being disruptive or just pushing soon learn from the comments of their peers that this is not acceptable behaviour.

Often the child who breaks into an activity quite successfully finds herself unable to sustain it. How often do nursery staff hear the refrain, 'Miss, she's spoiling our game,' particularly if she is much younger than the rest of the group. The new participant is deemed to be inept by the original player(s) and therefore a nuisance. Once the child has intervened successfully she must negotiate the activity and follow the rules laid down by the initiators. Assuming that the interaction has been successful the child has to decide how to end the play in a manner which will leave the others feeling that it was an enjoyable experience for both parties and that the relationship should be pursued on a subsequent occasion. Farewell rituals may include such statements as 'I'm off now' or 'I have to go home for dinner.' Thus, sustained cooperative play involves a high degree of social interaction, both verbal and non-verbal, and children who play well with their peers are firmly set on the road to later educational progress. On the other hand, the child who has not learned these rituals can very easily become a social isolate and will need adult assistance.

What is the role of the adult in encouraging social skills? First, we should be aware that, although children will need our help on occasions to resolve clashes during play sessions, nevertheless it is better, where possible, for children to cope with the problems themselves as through this they will be able to develop good negotiating skills. Naturally, we should not stand back and do nothing if we see a child obviously isolated and unhappy, but too great an adult involvement can mean that the child becomes totally alienated from her peers.

We also need to remember that just as there are individual differences among children with regard to physical and language skills, so there are differences with regard to sociability. Some children may be perfectly well adjusted but not necessarily desirous of large-group or even continuous peer-group involvement. Children also vary from day to day concerning the intensity with which they wish to become involved with their peers. Sometimes even the most socially oriented child needs to stand back and observe the situation. Understanding how children view their peers will help adults to understand their behaviour. Talking with children and encouraging them to explore their feelings about their friends is one of the best ways of helping children to understand at a cognitive level how they behave towards others and others behave towards them.

A practical way of encouraging this understanding is to provide opportunities for children to get to know each other, their likes and dislikes, wishes, and so on. However, there are always children who seem to be rejected or rebuffed by their peer groups and for these children teachers must offer understanding and support. Hartup (1979) carried out some research on the social isolate and found that they benefited from one-to-one play with younger children. When these children returned to play with their own age group it was found that their social skills had improved. This could be a useful technique for teachers to use, particularly if the child's unacceptable behaviour is due to social or emotional immaturity. Likewise, such traditional activities as storytelling and milk-time or lunch-time discussions all provide ideal opportunities for group affiliation.

Further specific games and activities to encourage social interaction are to be found at the end of this section.

In addition to understanding the rudiments of friendship and ways of achieving social contact, children also need to understand the concept of family life. By the time they enter school, children will be aware of the family in which they themselves live and its importance to them as individuals, but few will have fully appreciated that not all families are the same as their own. An appreciation of the differences between households and family lifestyles should enable children to accept more easily the cultural differences which exist in our society.

Cooperation and resolution of conflict

Once children realise that they can become part of a group and have learned the skills necessary for group allegiance they will wan* to influence the behaviour of others. Influence helps children feel that they have a sense of power over their own and maybe other people's lives: people will listen to them, ask their opinions, and involve them in decision-making processes. The child who is socially competent and feels in control of a situation is able to accept both leading and following roles, whereas the child who feels inadequate and that life is overwhelming is unable to m...'.e or accept decisions made by others and is likely to resort to aggressive behaviour in order to influence other children. As a result of this unsociable behaviour, the child's influence over others will decline even further, resulting in even greater feelings of incompetence.

Children's attempts to influence others inevitably leads to conflict, and, according to Piaget, conflict with peers is an essential factor in decreasing egocentric thinking. Children have to learn that even friends have their differences and that the resolution of these differences involves cooperation and adjustment to each other's point of view. Most young children resolve their conflicts in one of two ways: they either retreat from the situation or use physical force. The role of the teacher is to help children appreciate that there is normally a variety of alternative ways in which to settle a dispute. Several studies have shown that the child who has a wide range of strategies available to her in conflict situations is more likely to be effective in resolving the issues. At this age it is extremely difficult for young children to accept that if one person is to win, another has to lose, and that resolution of conflicts sometimes involves adjustment so that nobody wins or loses.

In what ways can adults help children develop skills of cooperation and conflict resolution?

1 Help children understand the reasons for the rules, regulations and constraints upon their behaviour, e.g. why there is a rule about only four people playing in the home corner at the same time.
2 Help children identify the causes of conflicts, to describe the possible alternative actions and consider their consequences. Discuss the values of sharing, compromise, and so on and the negative value of violence and aggression as a means of resolving issues.
3 Ensure that the child understands what is involved in the concept of cooperation. Small children need to be shown how useful it can be for two or more people to work together to solve a problem or complete a task.
4 Encourage children to look after others and to accept help in return.
5 Provide a learning environment which emphasises cooperation, caring and sharing, but also gives the children appropriate opportunities for 'rough and tumble' play. As Aldis (1975) has argued, rough and tumble play is natural for young children and may lead to cooperative behaviour; and the opportunity to display strength and to experience the strength of others may build mutual respect. Hartup (1976) has gone as far as to say that if we deprive children of the opportunity to display aggressive behaviour we may actually contribute to aggressive problems in children, particularly boys.

Kindness, care and affection

The ability to display empathy, care and affection contributes to the development of social skills. According to Schutz (1979), kindness is made possible by belief in our own worth, therefore it follows that children who perceive themselves as socially competent and respected by others are more likely to display acts of nurturance and support than those who regard themselves as insignificant and feel that they have nothing to offer. Kindness and a caring approach are taught by example and there is no doubt that children who spend their time in an atmosphere where adults are helpful and supportive will begin to adopt caring attitudes towards others.

However, although children may perceive the need to assist one another, they are often confronted by a situation which they find difficult to handle effectively. For example, a child may realise that her mother does not feel well; having made that decision she now has to consider whether it is appropriate to intervene and, if so, what action she should take. By the time the child finally displays her expression of concern and care she will have made a large number of decisions, each of which has involved a variety of problem-solving skills. Sometimes children's caring strategies are inappropriate and it is vitally important that when they demonstrate a sensitivity to distress, their help and compassion are accepted, even if their offer of assistance is unsuitable.

Young children frequently have difficulty in understanding the difference between sharing and generosity. Adults are often guilty of confusing children over these terms since we ask them to both 'share their sweets' and 'share their toys'. In the first instance we are actually asking the child to 'give' some of the sweets to another person, be generous, and in the second we are asking the child either to cooperate with another or lend the toy on a temporary basis. In helping children to show care and compassion to others it is important that they learn that true kindness is a sincere emotion. The young child who is forced to say 'I'm sorry' without any real understanding of the meaning of the word is being encouraged to display a false kindness and will be conditioned to believe that every transgression can be condoned the moment the magic words 'I'm sorry' are uttered.

Abstract concepts such as kindness, affection and cruelty are difficult for young children to understand but they will be learned most easily in an environment which encourages generosity, tolerance, respect and care for others. Earlier in this chapter it was pointed out that children regard adults as people to observe and learn from. It is therefore essential that there are models of altruistic behaviour for them to copy. Children, though, not only need to observe kindness and compassion but need occasions to be kind to each other. The environment in the nursery, therefore, should be one which promotes kindness and respect, gives social reinforcement in the form of praise and, above all, creates opportunities for children to be kind to each other.

In helping children to develop their social skills and awareness of the feelings of others through play we are, in my view, encouraging their moral development. Although there is a school of thought that says that children can be trained (indoctrinated) to adopt moral behaviours through rewarding, punishing, modelling, and so on, the majority of teachers of young children take the view of Piaget who argued that the child comes to understand the beginnings of morality through learning and appreciating the need for rules to the game. Damon (1977), whose work reinforces the stage theory approach to moral development, has argued that the development of the concept of positive justice is the central aspect of morality. Between the ages of four and eight years children gradually come to understand fully the principle that everyone should be given a fair share.

The evidence suggests that moral development is best facilitated by giving children the opportunity to understand principles and reasons rather than to teach specific actions which may be situation dependent. The nursery needs to be organised in a way that ensures that justice can prevail for everyone, each and every child being given the same chance to learn. The need for a structured framework was stated clearly by Wilson, Williams and Sugarman (1967) who wrote, 'To try to impose values is immoral, but to fail to create frameworks within which people can choose their own values is just as bad!' (p. 168).

The rules introduced into early years settings must be based on good reasons that take into account the needs of all the children and the adults. Children should be able to discuss these reasons so that they come to understand the principles upon which these decisions have been made. Although true negotiation is beyond the ability of three- and four-year-old children, the rudiments of compromise and understanding can be fostered during the pre-school years, and some nurseries provide children with situations in which they can learn to develop negotiating skills. Educators should remember that they are teaching moral values with every action, rule or statement they make.

DEVELOPING CULTURAL AWARENESS

At the same time as children are learning social skills they are also learning about the relationship between themselves and their environment. Teaching children how to participate in their culture is an important feature of early childhood education, as not only have they to learn that they are members of a family group but that they are part of the wider community. We live in a society with many different cultures and subcultures, but, owing to the geographical distribution of the minority groups, large numbers of our children grow up unaware that in many of our cities there are people from different races and creeds.

Sensitive teachers working in monocultural areas often feel that they are unable to introduce a true anti-racist, multicultural curriculum, arguing that young children cannot grasp the concept of different countries or the relationships and correspondence among different cultural groups within a country. Piaget and Weil (1951) found that children before the age of six could not relate the concept of town, state and country, stating that the attitudes of the young child are initially egocentric or personal. Nevertheless, in spite of children's inability to understand the spatial relations between towns and countries, they can still develop some understanding of different cultures and creeds.

It has already been shown that children as young as two or three years of age can begin to develop negative stereotypes, and educators in both multicultural and monocultural areas must try to integrate an anti-racist, anti-bias approach into the overall curriculum.

Learning to be a member of a multicultural society is more than just accepting that there is a number of different racial groups in that society. An approach which Demon-Sparks (1989) terms the 'tourist curriculum' involves accepting that there are both similarities and differences among all groups of people, including one's family and friends. This includes gender, race, culture and different physical abilities. The young child has first to come to terms with the various roles played by members of the family and the fact that not all families are alike. In learning about family relationships the child comes to realise that not everyone lives in a two-parent household and that some mothers stay at home, while others work outside the house. The concepts of grandparents, aunts and uncles also need to be developed and explained as nowadays many children are not in close contact with their relatives, who may live miles away.

The most effective way in which children can learn about the different members of the society in which they live is if they are in an environment in which they feel free to ask questions and make comments about the various differences between individuals. Learning about our society also involves children finding out about the jobs that exist in the community. The function of the early childhood educator is to know the resources of the community and to help children get to know individual workers where possible: for example, the local postman, dustman, milkman and policeman. Visits to the local shops will also help children become familiar with the role of the various shopkeepers.

From television exposure children will have absorbed some ideas about various occupations such as doctors and nurses or pilots but their interpretations will naturally be limited. By encouraging people from different walks of life to come into the nursery and talk about their jobs, children can be educated about the community in which they live. Town children, whether they are black or white, are likely to have a different cultural background from rural children who may live miles from the nearest cinema or disco. Some three- and four-year-old children may be aware of the differences between the two ways of life but the majority of town dwellers have no idea of what life is like in unlit streets, with the only shop being a small general store. Likewise, country children would be astounded by the noise and bustle of city life.

Children can acquire some understanding of the different lifestyles experienced in the town and country but it is very important that they are given a realistic view of the two cultures. Idyllic romantic settings are no more a true picture of country life than the idea that the streets of London are all paved with gold. Children need concrete experiences of life in the town and country by means of visits, looking at books and discussions. In spite of economic stringency it should be possible for schools to arrange visits to other environments so that children can begin to build up some concepts about the different ways of life.

By the time children reach the end of the nursery-school period they have begun to establish concepts about themselves, not only as family and community members but as part of a wider world. For the child brought up in a multicultural community, visual if not spoken contact will have been made between blacks and whites, unlike in the monocultural areas where children may not have had this experience. However, it is still possible to help children living in areas where there are no black minority groups to develop positive anti-racist attitudes.

FOSTERING MULTICULTURAL AWARENESS

Multicultural education is not a set of activities added on to the existing curriculum but embodies a perspective rather than a curriculum. Every decision that is made about materials, the organisation of the nursery, the role of parents and the approach to the curriculum reflects attitudes towards cultures.

The most important factors in developing a multicultural, anti-bias approach are the attitudes, skills and knowledge of the educator. It is often a salutary experience for the adults to review honestly their own cultural backgrounds, relationships with the larger society and their attitudes towards other people. However, it is crucial that educators recognise their own prejudices if they are hoping to develop appropriate attitudes in children.

What can educators do to encourage children to become more culturally aware?

1 Encourage activities which enhance self-awareness and appreciation of each child's feelings and competencies.
2 Encourage children to discuss how their lives are similar yet different. In this way children not only identify with their own culture but become aware of the culture of others. Positive discussions of this kind should help overcome the development of negative stereotypes about minority groups. In areas where there are few overt cultural differences children may be limited to discussing differences in physical appearance, family size and personal experiences, whereas in multicultural areas there are excellent opportunities to discuss differences related to physical appearance, dress, language, and so on.
3 Encourage children to appreciate that other people may have points of view and feelings different from their own. The evidence suggesting that young children are not as egocentric as was once thought implies that

this aspect of cultural awareness should be more feasible to teach than was once imagined.

4 Broaden the cultural basis of the curriculum to include discussion and activities related to different types of clothing, speech, music, food, and so on. In addition to the traditional festivals of Christmas, Easter or Hallowe'en, the children can be introduced to the celebrations of other cultures such as Diwali and Chinese New Year. Even in areas where there are no ethnic minority groups it is possible to introduce these activities, although they are obviously not as meaningful to these young children as they are to the children who see the differences in clothing and hear music from other cultures as part of the daily life in their community.

5 Create a visual environment in which there are pictures of the children and staff and their families, as well as those of ethnic minority groups in this country. Paintings, prints, sculptures and textiles by artists from different cultural backgrounds should also be part of the nursery environment.

Although young children will have limited conceptual understanding of different countries and race there are nevertheless many concrete and meaningful ways in which they can be exposed to a wide variety of cultural experiences. The purpose of multicultural education in the nursery years is not to teach facts and figures about the various countries from which black children and their families may have originated, but to help each child come to understand that she is a valued member of the community and that she in turn will value and respect everyone else. The development of true cultural awareness implies showing respect for others no matter what race, creed, religion or class. In a culturally diverse nursery children can experience this in a concrete manner, but although the concepts are more difficult to convey in a monocultural situation it is possible to produce tolerant, open-minded attitudes which, hopefully, the children will take with them through life.

High self-esteem and a positive self-concept are crucial to all children if they are to 'learn how to learn' and achieve their full potential, and practitioners have a vital part to play in helping children to develop their social and personal skills.

4 Development of communication skills

The ability to communicate with others through spoken language is a singularly human characteristic, but that is only one medium through which we can express our thoughts, feelings and ideas. Music, movement, drama and art are also ways in which we can communicate with each other, as are the non-verbal actions and gestures which we use. In this chapter we shall be looking at the ways in which educators can foster language and literacy development through story, drama, song, rhyme and talk. In Chapter Seven we shall be looking at communication through music and movement and art.

DEVELOPMENT OF COMMUNICATION THROUGH LANGUAGE AND LITERACY

Language is not only a means of communication, it is a tool for thinking. From a very early age the baby has attempted to communicate with its mother or primary caretaker by gestures and meaningful sounds long before there is spoken language. Bower (1977) and others have demonstrated clearly that the baby is not the passive recipient of information but that there is active participation and reciprocal involvement with adults from the first few weeks of life.

Although much of their speech is immature, the majority of children entering nursery school are able to convey simple information and understand simple instructions. In fact the amount of language children have learned in the first three years of life is most impressive. They also bring with them varied knowledge and experiences, as a result of which they have developed ideas and understanding. Nevertheless, language development will continue for several years to come, since, as Carol Chomsky (1969) has pointed out, even at nine years of age some children experience difficulty in expressing certain sentence forms.

During the nursery years many children will rely heavily on non-verbal gestures in their conversations, pointing or taking the adult with them to find something, rather than attempting to express their ideas in words. Speech at this stage is still immature and articulation may not be clear. Young children are likely to substitute sounds when talking: for example 'ming' for 'thing' and 'tar' for 'car'; and they may be confused in their use of pronouns, 'me do this'. Although the children appreciate the need to change tense when referring to the past, there is relatively little use of the future tense at this age. The tendency is to overgeneralise the rules, thus irregular verbs become regularised, for example, 'I catched the ball.' With the introduction of pronouns, prepositions and a few adverbs into their repertoire, children's speech begins to sound more mature, and girls in particular use a wide range of vocabulary with fluency. However, teachers need to check that the children are not simply imitating what they have heard and that there is a real understanding of the meaning of such prepositions as 'behind', 'up', 'down'. Frequently, children appear to use the words in what seems to be an appropriate context but, in fact, do not fully understand the underlying concepts. Failure to clarify these meanings can result in learning difficulties, particularly in solving mathematical problems at a later stage.

In spite of these immaturities, many four-year-olds are able to use clauses, change verb tenses and select pronouns so that by the end of their time in the nursery children should be able to initiate and extend conversations and, during discussion, be able to explain their own meaning when there is some misunderstanding.

Children's speech during the nursery years has been described by writers as 'egocentric' and for many years it was assumed that pre-school children are unable to take into account the listener's point of view. However, classroom practitioners are well aware that many children attempt to modify their language and approach based on the listener's perspective, even if it is not always entirely successful. A neat study by Menig-Peterson (1983) has demonstrated that some three- and four-year-old children seem to take into account the listener's knowledge of the situation being described. Furthermore, other research has shown that by the end of the nursery school years some children are aware that differences in perspective exist between the speaker and the listener.

The development of language is dependent upon the amount of practice children have in both speaking and listening, and interaction with good adult models is essential if children are to build up a body of language and develop an awareness of particular ways of thinking and of interpreting their own personal experiences.

Each child comes into school with a different background of linguistic experiences and although we no longer talk about children being 'language deficient' there is no doubt that some may lack the necessary confidence and appropriate skills to handle language in a classroom situation. Gordon Wells (1987) has demonstrated in his Bristol study that inarticulate children in the classroom can engage in conversations at home that show them to have considerable control over the language system. Likewise, Tizard and Hughes (1984) argued in their study of thirty girls that there was more talk and learning going on in the home than appeared to be happening in nursery school.

In the one-to-one relaxed atmosphere of the home children will talk more freely than in a noisy classroom but there are still many children who enter nursery school with a very low level of expressive language. For these children the adults in the classroom have a very important role to play. Such theorists as Bruner and Vygotsky have demonstrated the importance of the adult in providing a 'scaffold' for children's learning and this has been clearly shown in a study by Hughes (Hughes and Westgate 1997) which focused upon interactions by teachers and other adults in the classrooms. She showed that nursery nurses in particular used what Wells termed a 'supportive' style of interaction resulting in more meaningful conversations with the children, inviting the pupils to take more part in the direction of the discourse. She also revealed that there were considerable differences between the types of interaction of teachers and other adults in the classroom (assistants or parent helpers). Children are active participants in their own learning, but their learning will be enhanced by the support of an interested adult. Hughes' study suggested that as the teachers were so busy making cognitive demands upon the children they focused upon 'directed talk', allowing the children little time to initiate the conversations. It appeared in this study that the nursery nurses offered a more effective scaffold for the children.

Before looking at the ways in which educators can encourage language development in the classroom we need to define the elements that go to make up language communication skills. Language skills involve both listening and speaking.

Listening is a receptive system which involves:

• the physical aspect of hearing
• the attention of the learner
• the ability to process auditory information.

Speaking is an expressive language system which involves:

• the production of speech sounds
• the ability to produce meaningful sentences and use grammar
• the ability to use speech for a range of purposes.

This emphasis upon developing competence in both listening and talking is evident in both the National Curriculum and the guidelines to language and literacy in the *Desirable Outcomes for Children's Learning* (SCAA 1996b).

The work of Hughes *et al.* (1994) illustrated the ways in which adults can affect language development in the classroom and how it can be encouraged by the educator's own language and questioning strategies. Joan Tough (1977), as part of the Schools Council Communication Skills in Early Childhood Project, was one of the first people to identify different kinds of dialogue strategy that can be used by teachers in their interaction with the child:

1 Orienting strategies: these are utterances, questions and comments that direct the child's attention towards a particular topic and invite her to think in a particular way, for example, predicting, reasoning and imagining.

2 Enabling strategies: these are comments which help the child to move towards further discussion. These can be follow-through strategies, focusing strategies and checking strategies.

3 Listening strategies: whereas orienting and enabling strategies are used to help give the child ideas, these are strategies which provide information or ideas at the time when the child seems receptive to them.

4 Sustaining strategies: these are comments which are aimed at encouraging the child to continue talking. Frequently they are non-verbal, like a smile or nod of the head.

5 Concluding strategies: in order to leave the child with a feeling of satisfaction, the teacher needs to bring the dialogue to a conclusion and yet leave the way clear for later talk.

Many early childhood educators have found these strategies to be of considerable help in dealing with nursery- and infant-aged children but it must be remembered that not all talk should be teacher initiated. A number of earlier studies found that a greater number of exchanges took place in conversation with adults when it was child initiated and even longer exchanges occurred during child–child dialogue, while Bruner (1980) found that the most sustained, productive conversations came from a pair of children working or playing together. There is also evidence to show that children often make effective teachers, being able to explain quite complicated issues to their peers more satisfactorily than an adult.

What then is the role of the early years educator in helping children develop fluency and encouraging their ability to use language to verbalise concepts and express thought? Probably the most important factor in encouraging language development is the atmosphere of the classroom.

When this is relaxed, with emphasis on shared experiences with an adult, rather than an instructive approach which conveys the idea of the 'all-knowing' adult, it is more likely that children will converse freely. There are a number of ways in which children can be encouraged to develop confidence and competence in their use of language.

Listen to the children

One of the major differences between home and school is that there are a large number of children competing for the attention of one, or at the most, two adults; therefore children, in their dealings with adults, are more often placed in a listening rather than a speaking role. However, it must be very frustrating for the three- or four-year-old child to be told to listen attentively to the teacher if she feels that she is never given the opportunity to be heard. In a busy classroom it may be very difficult for a teacher to find time to listen to individual children, particularly if their speech is unclear and the content of the message confused. Nevertheless, the adult who takes time to listen and, if necessary, ask the child to clarify what she is saying will help the child feel that her contribution is worthwhile.

The importance of attending to what children say is not only appropriate when the child has initiated the conversation but after the adult has asked a question, particularly an open-ended one. Little children may take a minute or more to respond to an adult's question, especially if the reply involves trying to convey a complex idea, but too often hard-pressed teachers do not wait long enough and either answer the question themselves or make a further statement which can add to the child's confusion. If children encounter this reaction from educators on a number of occasions they will either withdraw completely or simply say the first thing that comes into their head. Neither response is conducive to productive language development.

Give children something to talk about

Asking and answering questions, sharing experiences, predicting and anticipating what will happen next and recalling past events are all important ways of developing children's language competence but if we want children to use words to express concepts and thoughts about what is happening, has happened or will happen we should make sure that we give them something real to talk about. Discussions should be an accompaniment to experience. It is no longer considered appropriate to assume that exposure to interesting material in a relaxed atmosphere is sufficient to produce growth in language and intellectual ability. Research has shown that unfocused attention is not enough. The educator needs to direct the children's attention towards salient features or objects and by careful questioning encourage discussion and understanding. In this way children increase their knowledge about the world and acquire relevant vocabulary.

Pictures make excellent stimulus material for discussion and can be used in a number of ways. One purpose would be to encourage children to abstract and report on the central meaning of a picture, a task which can entail considerable linguistic skills including hypothesising about the alternatives and possibilities available and using language to project into other people's feelings. Similarly, pictures can be used to stimulate the imagination, for example, 'What would happen if . . .?' Young children enjoy making up stories and expressing their feelings in a socially acceptable manner.

Visits to places of interest outside the nursery also provide children with valuable conversation points. With young children, even though they have been prepared for the visit, the discussions prior to the outing will be much less fruitful than those during or after the event. Describing to others what they have seen is an excellent way of helping children to express themselves fluently and coherently and to demonstrate an understanding of temporal order. Putting events in sequence is a challenge for young children and it is a most important skill for them to develop since it plays such an important part in logical and causal thinking. If these visits are also linked to some form of socio-dramatic play, language will be even further enhanced.

Structured discussions are another useful way of encouraging language development. For example, the teacher may be trying to help children understand concepts such as 'floating' and 'sinking'. The child who watches the stone go straight to the bottom while the cork bobs around on the surface of the water is more likely to grasp the meaning of the words 'sink' and 'float' if the appropriate vocabulary is introduced while the child is experimenting with the objects. Combining actions and words has been shown to be a highly effective technique to encourage children to form ideas and concepts. Bruner (1956) terms this 'active verbalisation', arguing that a mixture of actions and words is better than either actions or words alone.

Encourage conversation and dialogue

Children, like adults, will be more motivated to talk if the conversation has some relevance to their own real-life experiences. Researchers have found that one of the major reasons why children talk more at home is because there are so many more shared experiences which are fruitful to discuss.

When children are given opportunities to talk about topics of personal interest and immediate concern – for example the arrival of a new baby, the antics of the family pet, or new clothes – they are more likely to relax and express their ideas and feelings with fluency.

The majority of these types of conversation are child initiated and one of the difficulties for the teacher is to step down from her role as 'instructor' into one of 'sharer of experiences'. Any sense of prohibition or criticism in the teacher's reply is likely to cut short any further conversation immediately. The ability to toss the conversational ball back and forth is essential if the teacher is to prolong the dialogue. Milk and lunch times provide ideal opportunities for teachers to engage in fruitful discussions as in these relaxed settings children will talk freely and, hopefully, gain the impression that social conversation is an enjoyable pastime.

The best language does not necessarily take place when there is an adult present. When children work together in pairs or small groups, without an adult present, there may well be extended language and challenging discussions during which they are learning to take turns to listen to each other. This type of dialogue occurs very naturally in role-play situations when children are dressing up, engaging in improvised drama, or small-world play.

Children like to experiment with words and sounds through well-known rhymes and improvisations created by themselves, many of which will reflect their growing sense of humour and fun. Likewise, they imitate speech patterns and jingles, and practise new expressions. This is why it is argued by many that the nursery years are a good time to introduce a foreign language as children will repeat the new patterns and sounds with a total lack of inhibition. Listening to children of three and four imitating the speech patterns and accents of others can be a revelation, as they have such a wonderful ear for language at this stage.

Provide opportunities for listening skills

For a child to be able to communicate effectively she must be able to listen attentively so that she can hear differences in sounds and words. In many homes there is such a high noise level that children have learned not to listen and for them it is essential that they not only learn how to listen but learn the value of silence. One of the ways to try to achieve this is for teachers to select a time during each day when they and the children stand quietly to listen to the various everyday sounds around them. The importance of the 'quiet time' was brought home to me many years ago when I took a class of town children into the countryside for the day and a small boy came up to me and said, 'Miss, you can hear the quiet!' For him, it was the first time in his life that he had ever been in a situation where there was the type of quietness experienced regularly by those of us who live in less densely populated areas.

There are a number of ways in which educators can encourage the development of listening skills, some of which will be listed at the end of the book. However, the main medium is through listening to nursery rhymes, poetry and short stories. Children at this age delight in repetition of familiar rhymes and stories and a useful way of encouraging effective listening is to make intentional mistakes. There is genuine delight when the teacher's mistake is detected and undoubtedly children's concentration span increases during such activities.

When children are listening to stories they are not only learning to concentrate, but are learning the pleasure that can be derived from hearing good literature. Literature should provide children with happiness and pleasure but many of the familiar early childhood stories also pass on the values and attitudes of our society through the characters portrayed.

Help them to understand

Language and thought are inextricably linked and one of the main functions of the teacher is to help children understand what they are doing or saying. During discussions children often appear to use vocabulary appropriately, but careful observation of their actions may show that there is not a full understanding of the concept or idea. This is particularly noticeable with words dealing with spatial relationships. Outdoor activities and movement sessions may reveal confusion in this area.

Likewise, the educator eavesdropping on an informal play session may hear a child explain something to a peer in a way that indicates lack of comprehension. Although it would probably be inappropriate to intervene immediately, at a later stage an opportunity should be made to ensure that the misunderstanding is clarified. During the day, there will be many occasions when children have to follow instructions or simple directions which will reveal whether they can understand the basic language used in the classroom. Asking children to take a message to another adult in the nursery is a further way of discovering their level of understanding since this involves not only listening carefully to what is said, but interpreting the message accurately and then transmitting it to the receiver.

However, the fact that the message may not be delivered accurately is not necessarily due to lack of understanding or to poor listening skills, although it may be for one or both of these reasons. It could well be that the child has simply forgotten the details of the message. Although children have good memories, they have not yet developed appropriate strategies to help them to remember specific information accurately, as at this age they assume that if they listen, they will retain and be able to recall what they hear. Some writers have suggested that the teaching of simple mnemonic strategies could have a positive effect on children's ability to remember information, for example, repeating the message several times before asking them to deliver it. Although the rote learning of messages would seem to be a rather sterile exercise, if the child can understand the gist of the message, then ways of helping to memorise the salient features could be useful. This is a strategy which could be tried with children towards the end of the nursery years.

EMERGENCE OF LITERACY

Even at this early age the printed word is conveying ideas and concepts; long before the child is able to read for herself, she is becoming aware of print in a variety of forms. Emergent literacy is the current term to describe the beginning of reading and writing which we now acknowledge begins much earlier than we had previously considered possible. According to Goodman (1984) the 'roots of literacy' are to be found in what she terms 'functional literacy', that is, literacy which is to be found in real-life contexts and serves a real purpose, for example, the child sees adults reading the newspaper, instructions in a cookery book, books, letters, greeting cards, and so on. These activities support children's literacy development both overtly and covertly. The skills relating to reading and writing emerge gradually and without any formal teaching. All the research over the last decade has indicated that learning about literacy begins very early in life for almost all children in a literate society and often takes place without the adult being aware of it happening. The young child who at breakfast time asks what a W is on her Weetabix cereal packet is showing a real awareness of print. However, the amount of early reading and writing that evolves from the ordinary family environment will depend upon the literacy levels in the family. The child who has parents and grandparents who obviously read, and enjoy reading, is at a great advantage compared with the child whose family has no interest in print. The influence of family reading habits is long lasting as there is evidence that a child whose involvement in stories has begun well before the age of three is likely to be the best listener at thirteen. Just as storytelling improves with practice so does listening.

Children live in a world of print and the influence of the family in this development will be discussed more fully in Chapter Ten. For children who do not grow up in a language-rich environment it is important for them to see adults in the nursery involved in reading as it helps to convey the message that reading is a worthwhile activity. Supportive materials for role play, such as telephone directories, catalogues and newspapers, are all ways of developing interest in reading.

This awareness that literacy emerges gradually over a period of time means that we no longer sit and wait for children to become 'reading ready', as though there is a magic moment when children are ready to learn to read. The days when reading books were given to children on the results of reading-readiness tests are a thing of the past. Many of us knew that there were children who performed successfully on these types of test and yet were still not able to begin reading whereas others whose results were poor could tackle reading. Nevertheless, we know that some items on these checklists are associated with later reading achievement. For example, between the ages of three and five children who are aware of rhyme, similar-sounding initial letters and the sounds and names of letters which make up words seem to make better progress at reading than those who are not (Adams 1990; Goswani and Bryant 1990). However we interpret these findings, there seems to be no doubt that the informal learning experiences which the children have had at home and in the nursery will have contributed to their learning.

Although we are looking at reading and writing as separate skills, Ferreiro (1984) has pointed out that 'developmental literacy cannot be understood by isolating some of its components from others', although she admits that it is very difficult to analyse all the components at the same time and to the same depth (p. 154).

Storytelling is one important way in which children can enjoy print and later turn to reading themselves. Children at this age have lively imaginations and stories can open up a magical world of make believe. The book corner needs to be inviting, with books well displayed and accessible to children. From looking at books children learn other basic concepts about print: in our society we turn the pages from left to right; we start to read from the top left-hand corner and read across the page and from top to bottom. Children from other cultures may have to learn that they read from right to left or from the bottom up and for some children they have to learn both sets of rules if the writing system in the home is different from the school.

Although there are yardsticks against which to measure children's ability to learn to read, it is important to remember that learning about literacy will differ from child to child and will be affected by the experiences they encounter (Teale and Sulzby 1986). Goswami (1994) has argued that there is a strong connection between children's ability to detect and manipulate the sounds making up spoken words and their reading development. Bryant and Bradley (1985) had argued that 'phonological ability in pre-school children is one of the biggest predictors of later success in reading ability' (p. 32).

Why do some children appear to be 'natural readers' and appear to learn to read regardless of the help of the teacher, while others take such a long time to master this skill? The Sheffield Early Literacy Association (Weinberger 1996) investigated this question and identified some common features which helped to form 'natural readers'. These included:

• early immersion in language and print
• positive interaction and active sharing of books with an adult
• repeated reading of favourite stories
• 'talking like a book'
• memorising a story; lack of knowledge of the structure of a story has been found to be one of the most significant contributory factors in children who find reading difficult
• reading activities where the child is encouraged to take the initiative, with the adult taking a supportive role
• developing personal libraries
• having stories read aloud – not just until the child becomes a fairly competent reader, but beyond.

If these factors are important in encouraging children to develop an understanding of literacy, then it is essential that they are shared with parents who, in the main, are very anxious to help their children to learn to read.

EMERGENT WRITING

This is defined by Sulzby (1990) as 'the reading and writing behaviours of young children before they develop into conventional literacy' (p. 85). The onset of emergent writing is naturally gradual but Sulzby defines this as:

• writing that another conventional literate person can read conventionally
• writing that the child himself reads conventionally.

However, early writing takes on a number of forms before it becomes conventional including scribble, drawing, non-phonetic letter strings, copying of conventional print, invented spelling, abbreviations, and idiosyncratic forms of letters. From around the age of twelve months babies begin to make repetitive marks, often on furniture and walls. At first this is undifferentiated scribble, but gradually it develops into scribble for drawing and scribble for writing. Some children make up and down lines to denote writing and circular patterns for drawing. Harste *et al.* (1984) pointed out that scribble is not random mark making; from their research they found that a child whose name began with a linear letter such as K tended to use linear marks for writing, whereas one whose name began with an S would be more likely to use a circular pattern. Children use the same marks for different things: for example, a child may make scribble marks on paper when playing at 'shops' and this would definitely be a shopping list; however, what seem to be very similar marks to an adult could be representative of drawing. At this stage the main thing to remember is that the child has grasped an important principle: these marks can convey meaning.

It is generally around three years of age that letter-like features begin to appear. At the same time children learn to identify and name some letters, and discriminate between letters, sounds and words. Research has also shown that at this age many children are able to switch between cultures and appreciate the differences between two or more languages.

Generally the child's first name is among the first letters put together to form a word. In many instances the child starts with the initial letter of her name to indicate the name itself. For example, my granddaughter Katy used the letter K to indicate her name and only later did she come to realise that K alone was not the word for Katy. Two months later she was using four letters to denote her name.

Towards the end of the fourth year children begin to write strings of letters to denote stories. These letters bear no relationship to the message they are meant to convey but are 'writing' as far as the child is concerned. Children gradually move towards conventional spelling by using such strategies as:

- spelling the way it sounds
- spelling the way it looks
- spelling the way it means.

These strategies, identified by Harste *et al.* (1984), develop gradually but there are few children before statutory school age who can write and spell correctly, although some children towards the end of their third and in the beginning of their fourth year are able to produce conventionally spelt words, such as cat. However, there are some children who, by choice, spend considerable periods of time copying words, an activity which can help the writer's understanding and knowledge of the writing system.

Stages of emergent writing

Just as it is dangerous to put children's development of reading into rigid categories, so it is for writing. Children use a range of strategies to help them develop writing skills and young children are quite happy to mix letter strings, scribbles and conventional spelling together. Ferreiro argued that there are five levels through which children pass and they cannot be said to be writers before this occurs.

Clay (1975) identified six key principles which children use as they emerge as writers. These are:

- the recurring principle – when the child makes the same basic form to convey a message: e.g. a chain of Ks to convey a message
- the directional principle – until this principle is understood the child will put letters and signs anywhere on the page. Clay believes the child has to master the following: start top left; move right to left across the word; return down left and locate the next starting point
- the flexibility principle – i.e. the reversal of lines and letters, much to the concern of many adults, particularly parents: e.g. p and b or m and w
- the generating principle – the repertory of known signs is used to produce long 'letters'
- inventory principle – when the child takes stock of her own learning and writes lists of all the words she knows
- the contrastive principle – Clay considers that this principle is used when the children contrast shapes, letters and word meanings.

Children need to realise that there is a purpose for writing and this is clearly available in their play. Harste *et al.* (1984, p. 145) reported that 'children at three know that usually pens are for writing and crayons are for drawing'. Children get many opportunities to practise writing during natural pretend play and a number of studies have shown that if play areas are made into properly resourced print areas the children will actively explore print in ways which show clearly their interest and understanding of the function of print. Home corners with writing materials, diaries, telephones directories, books, catalogues and other print materials placed strategically are important in encouraging the development of writing skills. During these play sessions the child comes to understand that 'in learning to write the child must disengage himself (or herself) from the sensory aspect of speech and replace words by images of words' (Vygotsky 1978, p. 132).

Through the strategy of emergent writing associated with play, children can be encouraged to be creative and adventurous in their use of language. By the time children leave the nursery the majority should be able to use language to communicate effectively with both adults and other children; the more articulate may be speaking in full sentences, using conditional clauses and introducing some adjectives, adverbs and prepositions appropriately in their speech. Furthermore, many will be well on the way to becoming readers and writers.

5 Development of analytical and problem-solving skills

Children can be brilliant thinkers . . . . A child enjoys thinking. He enjoys the use of his mind just as he enjoys the use of his body as he slides down a helter-skelter or bounces on a trampoline . . . . If children can already think so well at this age, then surely the long years of education must develop this ability to a high level. Not so. At the end of education there has been no improvement in the thinking ability of children, in fact there has actually been a deterioration.

(De Bono 1972, p. 8)

It is not the place here to enter into a discussion as to why this occurs, if indeed it does, but to try to analyse the skills that young children need to develop during the nursery years so that they can reason, hypothesise and predict. We must not only analyse the skills they require but consider the types of concrete experience which will best facilitate the development of problem-solving skills.

The nursery period is an exciting time in children's cognitive development as although some children are still functioning at a sensori-motor level the majority coming into school will have reached what Piaget terms the 'stage of pre-operational thought'. This stage encompasses the period roughly from two, or two-and-a-half, to about seven years of age, the nursery–to Key Stage 1 phase of schooling. Earlier reference has been made to some of the recent criticisms of the work of Piaget, particularly with reference to his views on the egocentricity of young children; nevertheless, he still provides a useful guide to the characteristics of children in this age range.

WHAT ARE THE CHARACTERISTICS OF CHILDREN'S THINKING AT THE PRE-OPERATIONAL STAGE?

- Children's thinking is bound by perception. They believe what they see and can focus on only one attribute of an object at a time, usually the predominant feature. Piaget terms this 'centring' and argues that it prevents children from observing other properties of an object simultaneously. Nevertheless, it enables children to acquire physical knowledge about the object, and physical knowledge is a prerequisite for the development of logical thought.

- Children's thinking is not reversible. Children at this stage can focus only on the beginning or end state of a transformation, not on the transformation itself. For example, a child may understand that she is older than her sister, but she is unlikely to understand that, if this is true, her sister is younger than she is.

- Children are unable to conserve and as a result are not able to recognise the invariance of a number of objects when their spatial arrangement is altered. They also cannot compensate for changes in dimensions, e.g. length or breadth. Invariance relating to volume, area and weight (both liquids and solids) is not fully understood at this period but it is still important to provide early experiences through which understanding will eventually occur. Both Bryant (1974) and Bruner (1966) have queried Piaget's views on young children's inability to conserve, arguing that, if helped, some young children are able to conserve small numbers at least.

- Children's thinking is egocentric. Piaget argues that because children view the world from their own perspective it is difficult for them to imagine how an object or scene might look when viewed from positions other than their own. He also points out that egocentrism can lead to misinterpretations of natural phenomena. Not only has research such as that of Donaldson and her colleagues queried Piaget's views on egocentrism but more than fifty years ago Susan Isaacs questioned whether children displayed the inability to think logically to the extent that Piaget assumed.

When considering children's thinking at this stage, there are, in my view, two important points to bear in mind.

1 Although pre-operational children are unable to think logically, this does not necessarily mean that they are deficient thinkers. On the contrary, the children are busy exploring, questioning, comparing, contrasting, labelling and forming mental images, activities which are the foundation for the development of the ability to think logically.

2 This characterisation should serve only as a guideline since wide individual differences exist. Understanding of these individual differences is vitally important in dealing with children in all aspects of their development, but it is crucial in helping them to develop analytical and problem-solving skills. The essence of the pre-operational sub-period is

the growing ability of the child to use symbolic representation. It is the development of this ability which is vital to later logical thinking.

Before we look at some of the skills which children require in order to become logical thinkers capable of solving problems and analysing situations we need to consider whether young children have a real understanding of the concept of a 'problem'. As a working definition a problem can be said to exist when there is a discrepancy between the expected or desired and the outcome. For example, we notice that magnets do not pick up some metallic-looking objects. How likely is it that a child understands a problem in these terms? She may realise that something does not work but unless she has had experience of possible solutions, she will be unlikely to come up with novel suggestions. For example, a child painting may comment, 'My paint is too runny!' She will know from previous experience how the paint should be in order to achieve the desired effect on paper but is unable to provide the solution, to stop the paint from dripping. If the child has not had any previous experience of the type of problem, she may not even be aware that discrepancies exist. In this case, her attention will need to be drawn to any incongruities. Problem solving requires an inquiring mind and a natural curiosity, and in this respect children are natural problem solvers. Teachers need to provide the educational experiences to enhance these activities.

What are the cognitive skills children require in order to become logical thinkers?

OBSERVATIONAL SKILLS

The value of observational skills is well appreciated by early childhood educators but just as we have had to learn how to observe, so we need to teach children the same set of skills. It is only through close attention to detail that children become aware of differences and similarities, discrepancies and incongruities. Children should have practice in looking carefully at both two- and three-dimensional objects and be taught how to 'look'. Discussions centred on the observation of a specific object or objects also provide controversy and interest as children become aware that we do not all see the 'same thing', each person placing greater emphasis on different features of the observed item(s).

CLASSIFICATION SKILLS (SORTING)

When children first begin to group items together they start by making what Piaget terms 'graphic collections'. These are objects arranged together in a way that is meaningful only to the child and has nothing to do with their similarities and differences. Their first attempt at grouping according to consistent criteria is likely to be matching items that are exactly the same on every dimension. However, by the end of the fifth year many children can sort by their own choice of principle. For example, they may put doll's house furniture into rooms according to their function or sort a collection of materials by texture and explain the reasons for their choice. The latter development is a big step forward as it is far more difficult to justify the criteria one has selected for classifying in a specific manner than to sort according to the teacher's request.

The importance of these skills to children's overall conceptual development is emphasised by Bruner (1966) who argues that through categorisation children come to realise the complexity of the environment and to identify objects around them. In helping children to develop classification skills the teacher is enabling them to build constructs upon which later knowledge can be based, thus reducing the necessity for constant relearning.

How can children be helped to classify?

1 Give children the opportunity to investigate and describe to adults and other children the characteristics of various objects – size, shape, function, smell, sound, feel, taste. Both usual and unusual things should be offered for investigation.
2 Encourage children to describe ways in which materials are similar and different. Children require many experiences of sorting and matching before they fully understand the words 'same' and 'different'. Although it is usually easier for children to talk about similarities than differences many are confused by the ambiguity of the term 'same', i.e. identical (exactly the same) or similar (the same in some way). Children who experience confusion with these terms may well have later difficulties in their mathematical development.
3 Encourage children to determine grouping categories for themselves as in this way they are more likely to appreciate that objects can be used and described in different ways. In developing this skill they are laying the foundation for the next stage of development when they come to realise that items have multiple attributes and therefore do not belong exclusively to one class. e.g. a boy is not only his parent's son, but may be a brother, cousin, friend, and so on.
4 Help children to understand the difference between 'some' and 'all'. Children need many opportunities to carry out instructions and hear the words used in appropriate contexts before they can make a distinction

between these terms. Understanding of the concepts 'some' and 'all' is basic to the understanding of the differences between a part of something and the whole of it. Children also need a considerable period of time to understand the meaning of 'full' and 'empty'.

5 Relations. Mathematics is the study of relations but the concepts are often difficult for the children to grasp. Children need to understand how things are connected, e.g. family relations: brothers, sisters, father, mother, aunt, and so on. They also need to understand the relationships between numbers, e.g. 1 and 2 are connected by the relation 'less than', i.e. 1 is 'less than' 2. During discussions with adults and in their play children begin to understand these mathematical concepts. Play also provides opportunities to learn mathematical vocabulary such as above, below, next to, over, under and beside.

SERIATION SKILLS (ORDERING)

Seriation involves arranging objects in a logical order along some dimension such as weight, age or height. It is a general cognitive skill which, as with classification, is not fully mastered until some time after the nursery years. In order to be able to seriate effectively, the child needs to be able to answer the question, 'What comes next?' This question involves making comparisons and the role of the teacher is to give children opportunities to compare a wide variety of objects and materials so that they can learn to discern differences.

What are the specific experiences children need to help them develop the skill of seriation?

1 Opportunities to arrange things in order. Children should be encouraged to use the appropriate vocabulary – 'tall', 'taller', 'big', 'bigger' – when discussing size relations. Besides helping children to learn to grade objects according to size they can be encouraged to grade according to quality and tone. Grades of sandpaper can be provided so that children have opportunities to arrange them from rough to smooth, bells can be arranged from high to low, flavours can be offered that range from sweet to sour and colour swatches used to identify depth of colour.

2 Opportunities to make comparisons as they play with materials. Children need to involve all their senses when engaged in making comparisons as it is only in this way that a real understanding of the attributes of objects will develop. Differences between objects must also be obvious as children of this age cannot make subtle comparisons.

3 Opportunities to match one ordered set of objects to another. This is a more complicated task than arranging items in a single series since it involves arranging both sets of objects and then seeing the relationship between the two series. The classic example of this is 'matching dolls and beds' which Piaget used in his experiments, although more commonly children get this experience by attempting to fit saucepan lids to saucepans of different sizes or fitting together different sizes of nuts and bolts.

NUMBER SKILLS

In recent years there has been considerable discussion as to how children develop number concepts but it is generally agreed that they need experiences with counting, matching, grouping and comparing before reaching an understanding of number. According to Piaget, before children can understand any form of mathematical operation they need to comprehend one-to-one correspondence and conservation. Although most nursery-school-aged children are unable to conserve number, they begin to acquire some understanding of one-to-one correspondence, that is, they gradually realise that two kinds of object can be matched one to one (one knife with one fork). However, children do not understand that there is an equal number of knives and forks unless they are arranged in the same way, for example, in two lines of equal length. Watching a child set a table for lunch is an interesting way of seeing how well she understands one-to-one correspondence.

Ways of encouraging children to develop their concept of number

1 Counting objects. Children of three and four years of age learn to count and chant numbers but counting does not necessarily mean the same thing to them as it does to adults. They may be repeating numbers simply for the pleasure of saying them and are very likely to count in the wrong order. This is to be expected when one realises that most nursery-school-aged children cannot either conserve number or seriate correctly. Under those circumstances I believe it is better for the adult to accept the child's tally and at a later stage count correctly in front of the child who will imitate and eventually use the correct order.
2 Providing opportunities for children to develop one-to-one correspondence. Laying the table, helping to fit a straw into each bottle of milk or a brush into each paint pot are practical ways of helping children come to terms with this difficult concept.

3 Comparing amounts. Although it may be another year or so before children come to understand the meaning of the terms 'more' or 'less', there will be many opportunities for teachers to help them compare amounts of both continuous and discontinuous quantities. (Continuous materials are those which can be poured from one container into another: water, sand, flour. These cannot be broken down into countable parts. Discontinuous materials are those which can be counted separately: beads, sweets, cars. Children need opportunities for comparing both types of materials.)

In the *Desirable Outcomes for Children's Learning* (SCAA 1996b, p. 3) it is anticipated that by the time children reach the age of compulsory schooling they will be able to 'compare, sort, match, sequence and count everyday objects, recognise and use numbers to 10, as well as be familiar with larger numbers from their everyday lives'. They will also be expected to understand and record numbers and begin to show awareness of number operations such as addition and subtraction.

SPATIAL RELATION SKILLS

Ideas concerning proximity, how close things are in space, and separation, how far they are apart, are fundamental to a child's understanding of space. Young children are actively exploring space, taking things apart and putting them together again. They are beginning to come to terms with the idea of 'spatial enclosure' and use such words as inside and outside although not always accurately. Piaget and Inhelder (1969) found that four-year-old children could discriminate between objects with holes and objects without holes as well as between a closed loop of string with objects in it and one with objects outside it, although they still have a long way to go before being able to deal successfully with many spatial relations.

How can children be helped to develop spatial relations skills?

1 Give children ample opportunities to fit things together and take them apart. During these activities children become aware of the different ways in which things fit together, e.g. screw, clip, push, and how some fit together easily while others need precise manipulation. These activities also help children to develop fine muscle control.
2 Encourage children to rearrange and reshape objects and materials. Children at this age are guided by their perceptions and therefore may have difficulty in believing that the objects which they have rearranged or reshaped have remained the same, e.g. children will not necessarily

realise that the same number of bricks they used to build a fort can be transformed into a long chain across the nursery. Gradually, through experience, children come to realise that objects still retain their essential features in spite of repeated transformations.

3 Encourage children to observe things from a different spatial perspective. Young children enjoy getting themselves into unusual body positions and it is both fun and useful to talk to them about what the world looks like from that particular viewpoint. During such discussions it will be possible to try to help them understand how the world looks to a baby in a pram or a person who is confined to a wheelchair. This will also give teachers an opportunity to introduce vocabulary related to spatial positions such as over, under, on, off, beside, between. These are always difficult concepts for children to grasp and adults need to take every opportunity to ensure that they understand their meaning.

4 Help children to become more aware of their bodies and the different ways they can move.

5 Encourage children to look at and discuss drawings, photographs and pictures so that they can compare reality with pictorial representations.

Points 4 and 5 are discussed fully in Chapters Six and Seven, respectively.

TEMPORAL AWARENESS

The ability to recall or anticipate the order of events as they occur in time is called 'temporal ordering' and it is an ability which is present in elementary form at an early age. A two-year-old is well aware of the routines that occur in her life, as many parents will attest when they attempt to alter the daily routine. However, it is not until well into the fourth year that most children begin to realise that time is a continuum and to understand that things existed before now and will exist after now. Even then, young children have no real idea of the passing of time and even less as to how it is measured. Inexperienced teachers often find this aspect of working with young children very frustrating if they are trying to get a group of children ready for an activity or event at a precise time.

Although it will be a long while after the nursery years before children develop objective ideas about time, there are a number of ways in which temporal awareness can be fostered. These include:

1 Sequencing activities in which children are encouraged to describe past events and anticipate future events.

2 Discussing major events in the children's lives and in the calendar, e.g. birthdays, holidays, Christmas, Easter, Diwali, Ramadan.

3 Commenting on seasonal changes.
4 Exploring materials such as alarm clocks, egg-timers, metronomes, and discussing their uses as timers. Many activities can follow from the use of these objects which mark the beginning and end of time periods.
5 Warning children that they will have to stop their current activity and prepare for another event within a specified time (no more than five minutes ahead).

UNDERSTANDING THE RELATIONSHIP BETWEEN SIMPLE CAUSE AND EFFECT

Closely linked with problem-solving and analytical skills is an under-standing of the relationship between simple cause and effect. Although Piaget (1930) has pointed out that children do not develop clear notions of physical causality until much later, they begin to acquire this concept in the nursery years. Many of the cause and effect relationships are learned incidentally, for example, the child who spills her milk knows that she must wipe up the mess.

By four years of age children can begin to handle such cause-related questions as 'What will happen if . . .?' or 'Why do you think . . .?' Some of the finest examples of young children's understanding of physical causality are to be found in the observations made by Susan Isaacs at the Malting House School, Cambridge. Children need to know how and why things work and it is therefore most important that children are given opportunities to handle materials of different textures and types so that they can compare, judge and solve problems. Hopefully, they will then generate questions for themselves and, with the help of an interested adult, seek and find some of the answers.

SCHEMAS

Since the publication of Athey's *Extending Thought in Young Children* (1990) there has been a great deal of interest in the ways in which schemas are part of the development of children's mathematical and scientific ideas. Nutbrown (1994) gives numerous examples of the ways in which children use schema to develop ideas about rotation, height, capacity, tessellation and spatial order, all of which help to demonstrate how young children learn in an active, dynamic way.

Scientific skills and concepts such as making and recording observa-tions, identifying patterns, developing hypotheses and investigating and experimenting are best learned through exploratory play. In this way scientific interests are fostered with the help of an adult to talk with the children about what they have seen and help them test their ideas. Many of the science-based activities suitable for nursery-aged children will encourage an understanding of the relationship between simple cause and effect. To help the busy teacher, a selection of these will be found at the end of the book.

In this chapter, by concentrating on analytical and problem-solving skills, there has intentionally been little or no emphasis upon the subject areas of the *Desirable Outcomes for Children's Learning* or the National Curriculum. Through developing their problem-solving and analytical skills, children come to understand the environment and features of the natural and man-made world, both in the early years and later. The subject areas History, Geography and Science, as well as Mathematics and English, all involve these skills.

In discussing each of the major skills relating to the development of problem-solving and analytical skills I have tried to discuss ways in which they might be fostered. However, I believe that in order to help all children realise their true potential we need to organise the learning environment so that children maintain their sense of wonder and curiosity, there are ample opportunities for practice, including 'real' problems to solve, and the activities are enjoyable.

6 Development of physical competence

GROSS AND FINE MOTOR SKILLS

For many years pre-school institutions concentrated upon the development of large motor and fine manipulative skills through physical play, but with increasing pressure being placed upon early years educators by many parents to begin the teaching of reading, writing and number skills as soon as possible, more and more children are spending large periods of time sitting at tables. It is generally assumed that young children have plenty of time during the day to pursue the vigorous exercise they need in order to develop their movement abilities. Children may have the time, but do they always have the opportunity? With so many families living in high-rise flats or cramped accommodation where the television is switched on constantly to keep the children occupied, we should question whether there is sufficient room or opportunity for gross motor skills to develop fully. Furthermore, the increasing numbers of computer games and programmes available for this age range could prove an even greater incentive for children to gravitate towards more sedentary activities. The results of the Happy Heart Project which looked into the physical-activity patterns of primary-school children were disturbing as they found that 'overall children engaged in very little physical activity' (Sleap and Warburton 1994).

Many parents and educators assume that children automatically develop their movement abilities through maturation, but as Gallahue (1982) has pointed out, such an idea is absurd, as there is little evidence to support the notion that fundamental movement activities are developed automatically. In his view 'regular, systematic, quality instruction and supervised practice are crucial for most children if they are to develop their movement abilities to their mature form' (p. 20). An approach which is upheld by the American Alliance for Health, Physical Education, Recreation and Dance (AAHPERD) (1991) argues that children need to be active and that it is not acceptable to 'place children in long lines waiting to take turns, to seat them in circle games with only one or two children moving' (p. 21). It may be difficult for early years educators working in confined spaces to allow children the freedom of movement they require to develop effectively, but it must be recognised that these types of programmes are not substitutes for meeting the physical needs of young children. Children need the opportunity to explore the capabilities of their bodies within a carefully planned environment. Their ability to control their bodies can be encouraged by providing challenges such as avoiding obstacles, concentrating on using different body parts, changing speed and direction.

Motor movements are divided into two kinds:

1 Gross motor movements which involve the movement of the large muscles of the body and include such skills as walking, running, skipping, balancing (locomotor skills).
2 Fine motor movements which involve the use of limited individual parts of the body, especially the hands and fingers in the performance of precise movements, and include such skills as cutting, writing, pasting (manipulative skills). The main feature of fine motor control is that it involves a close functional relationship between the use of the eyes and the small muscles of the hands, fingers or feet.

By the time children enter nursery school at three years of age they have mastered the rudimentary movement abilities of standing, walking and grasping which form the basis for the development of what Gallahue calls 'fundamental movement patterns' which will be defined and extended throughout childhood and adolescence.

What are the basic movement abilities (locomotor, balance and manipulation) which children should be developing during the nursery-school years?

LOCOMOTOR SKILLS

1 *Walking* The mature walking pattern is usually achieved between three and four years of age. By this stage the child is able to walk in different directions – e.g. backwards, sideways – and vary the rate of walking. Experimenting, like walking on tiptoes or along a line, is often apparent during spontaneous play activities.
2 *Climbing* This is related developmentally to walking. Children will attempt to go upstairs even before they can stand alone but once walking independently will ascend the stairs in an upright position with support from an adult or, later, a handrail. This first attempt at climbing will involve using the same lead foot for each stage of the ascent, a pattern which will continue for several months, after which the alternate-foot

pattern emerges. However, the descent pattern is very different. Children usually first attempt to go downstairs by crawling down backwards and it is not until four or even five years of age that the mature pattern of descent becomes evident. Climbing apparatus in the nursery makes useful practice for this skill.

3 *Running* Children begin to run shortly after they learn to walk and most can do this by the age of five. It is an important skill for children to learn since without a good running pattern they will be unable to participate in many of the physical activities so enjoyed by their peers.

4 *Jumping* Both vertical and standing long jump occur at an early age, and although the mature standing horizontal jump is not mastered until about six years of age most children are able to jump vertically with a relatively high degree of proficiency by the age of five. Research by Halverson (1958) and others suggests that practice is an important contribution to the development of a mature jumping pattern. Three- and four-year-old children enjoy jumping over lines or very low obstacles, as well as jumping down from blocks of various heights.

5 *Hopping* This is a difficult task for young children as it requires the regaining of balance on one leg after jumping in the air. At around three-and-a-half years of age most children can hop one to three steps; by the time they are five most children can manage ten consecutive hops. Children in nursery classes should be encouraged to hop on either foot and on alternating feet as practice movements for skipping, a skill which develops later, usually in the infant school years.

6 *Galloping* Galloping is a combination of walking and leaping which is mastered reasonably well by the end of the fifth year. By then most children will not only be galloping proficiently but will begin to introduce patterns into their actions by, for example, moving backwards and sideways.

7 *Skipping* Very few nursery-aged children are able to skip as it is one of the last locomotor skills to appear. At around three years of age some children attempt a shuffle step which resembles a cross between a run and a walk. As proficiency in hopping progresses so we see the step-hop-step, half-skip which is characteristic of many four-year-olds, although movements are jerky and non-rhythmical. It will be at least another two or three years before a mature skipping pattern is achieved.

DEVELOPMENT OF BALANCE SKILLS

The ability to carry out effectively most locomotor skills depends upon establishing and maintaining balance. Although there is general agreement that balance performance improves with increasing age, it also appears that balance does not develop solely as a result of maturation but can be improved by practice. Two major characteristics of balance tasks seem to exist: static and dynamic. Static balance tasks require balance while standing still, whereas dynamic balance requires the maintenance of equilibrium while the body is moving.

Static balance

1 Standing on tiptoes.
2 Balance on one foot, then the other for short periods of time.

Vision appears to play an important role in balance with young children and Cratty and Martin (1969) found that under the age of six, children could not balance on one foot with their eyes closed.

Dynamic balance

1 *Beam walk* Children of three and four years of age can walk a two-inch beam using a follow-step with the dominant foot leading, but it is not until the end of the sixth year that most children can use alternate stepping action and are able to focus their eyes beyond instead of on the beam.
2 *Balance using an object* Children at this age enjoy walking with bean bags on their hands, backs, head, and so on. With practice they can become very skilled at this activity.
3 *Body rolling* Although this is a locomotor movement involving the body rolling forward, sideways or backwards it is included in this section since a great deal of balance control is required to carry out this task.

Like all other locomotor movements these have a developmental sequence and the mature level is not reached until well into the infant school. Tasks involving pushing, pulling and lifting also require the child to display balance skills.

DEVELOPMENT OF MANIPULATIVE SKILLS

In this section we shall be looking at two discrete categories of skills. First, those manipulative skills involving gross motor movements which nursery children, given appropriate practice, can master reasonably well, and second, the fine motor manipulative skills which involve the small muscles of the hands and fingers.

Throwing overhand

Children begin to throw overhand from a very early age – as many mothers know to their cost when the six- to eight-months-old child keeps throwing objects from the pram, but it is several years before they develop the mature throwing pattern in which they have some control over the direction of the object. This is not surprising as it is not until children have some degree of proficiency in basic locomotor skills, such as walking and running, that they have the balance and body control necessary to project an object while standing upright.

Catching

Catching is a fundamental motor skill involving the use of the hands to stop tossed objects. Like running, it is a most important skill for children to master since catching forms the basis of so many games and play activities. The first attempts at catching a tossed ball occur around three years of age when children put out their outstretched arms in a rigid position with the idea of pulling the ball towards the body as it contacts the hands and arms. As coordination and timing are poor the ball is frequently missed. Success at this stage is dependent more on the skill of the thrower than that of the catcher.

With practice and increasing maturity children are able to reach a fairly sophisticated stage of proficiency by the end of the fifth year; however, the size of the ball is an important factor in affecting catching performance. The classic study by Wellman (1937) found that children were more successful in catching a larger ball than a smaller one but large balls may not be as effective as smaller ones in eliciting the more mature catching response. It may be that the skill is best learned by using a ball that can be cupped in the hands but does not need the fine perceptual–motor control that, say, a tennis ball requires.

Another factor that can affect children's ability to catch is the speed at which the ball is thrown. Young children cannot make the necessary perceptual judgements quickly enough to adjust their body movements to catch a fast ball. Likewise, better catching performance tends to be achieved by bouncing the ball rather than throwing it to the child. Both throwing and catching usually require adult participation since the children are more likely to achieve success in the tasks if there is adult guidance and interest.

Striking

Hitting at an object with an implement causes children a number of problems. There is not only the movement of the body to take into account but the coordination of the movement of the implement with the body. Further, if the object to be hit is stationary, there is the problem of accurate positioning, but if the object is thrown to the child, then the issue is compounded since she now needs to take into account a number of things including the speed of the 'flying object' so that the striking response is appropriately timed. Striking is indeed a highly complex skill and one which takes several years to master, although many five-year-olds are able to strike a stationary ball with a fair degree of accuracy. Some nurseries have a soft woolly ball hanging from the ceiling on which children can practise their striking skills. (This is also a useful way of channelling aggressive behaviour if the ball is placed in a corridor away from the rest of the group.)

Kicking

The basis for kicking skills is the stationary kick and it is not until children have achieved some degree of proficiency at this that they can move on to kicking a moving ball, which involves extra perceptual demands. When attempting to kick a rolling ball, speed and direction have to be coordinated with the kicking response and although some children in the nursery display a high level of skill, it is not until the infant-school period that most boys and girls show mastery of kicking a stationary ball. Coping with a moving ball is not usually achieved until much later.

Bouncing

Relatively little is known about the development of this skill although Espenschade and Eckhert (1980) suggest that ball-bouncing skills originate when a ball is dropped accidentally or deliberately, causing it to bounce. The child will then tap the ball again in an attempt to repeat the action. Children find it easier to practise this skill on a large ball using two hands before progressing to using one hand only. Once they have mastered the skill of maintaining the momentum, the skill can be further developed by bouncing it to each other.

MANIPULATIVE SKILLS EMPHASISING THE USE OF FINE MOTOR CONTROL

One of the areas in which three- and four-year-old children make the most progress is in the development of fine motor control. This can be defined as the ability to coordinate the action of the eyes and hands together in performing skilful, adaptive movements.

There appear to be four major stages in the early development of this ability: static visual exploration; active visual exploration; use of vision in regulating fine motor control; and mature, eye–hand coordination behaviour. These are usually all established by the end of the second year of life. However, most manipulative actions require the use of two hands and/or limbs working together in harmony and need a great deal of practice. Bilateral motor coordination, as this is termed, follows a pattern of development which suggests that the system is maturing rapidly during the nursery years.

Some of the fine motor skills which can be fostered with two-and-a-half- to five-year-old children include:

1 Personal skills, such as undressing and dressing (particularly when buttons and zips are involved), teeth cleaning, feeding oneself.
2 Building with small blocks such constructions as a tower, road, steps. Also the ability to connect pieces of equipment together, e.g. Lego or Stickleback.
3 Using jigsaws to encourage eye–hand coordination and spatial ability.
4 Using tools in woodwork and cooking, preparing and serving food, laying the table.
5 Using pencils, pens, paintbrushes, scissors, needles.
6 Handling small animals appropriately.
7 Copying shapes, such as vertical and horizontal lines, circles, squares, triangles.
8 Pouring water to and from containers.
9 Threading and sewing.
10 Using computers and calculators.

Although children make great advances in fine motor control during the nursery years, there are wide individual differences and it is important that not too much time is spent on fine motor activities as they require a great deal of concentration and control and can lead to frustration, particularly in three-year-old children.

DEVELOPMENT OF PERCEPTUAL–MOTOR SKILLS

It is generally agreed that perceptual development plays an important role in children's cognitive functioning and that the greatest growth of these abilities occurs during the pre-school and primary years. It is also agreed that movement helps in facilitating perceptual development in young children, hence the use of the term perceptual–motor skills. This linking of the two areas does not mean, though, that both perceptual and motor abilities will develop at the same time and the same rate. What occurs is that some perceptual abilities develop earlier and are independent of movement, although they will eventually become paired during childhood. However, before we discuss the different perceptual skills and their relationship to later academic learning it is useful to define the term. Perception refers to 'any process by which we gain immediate awareness of what is happening outside ourselves' (Bower 1977, p. 1). We rely on all our various sense modalities (visual, auditory, tactual, olfactory, gustatory and kinaesthetic) to gain information about the outside world.

Visual perceptual skills

Marianne Frostig (Frostig, Lefever and Whittlesey 1966), a pioneer in the study of visual perception in young children, identified five areas that are of importance in the development of early visual perception. They are:

1 Eye–motor coordination: the ability to coordinate the use of hands and eyes skilfully.
2 Figure–ground perception: the ability to pick out a figure as distinct from a less clearly defined background.
3 Form constancy: the ability to recognise a shape as the same shape regardless of the context in which it is seen.
4 Position in space: the ability to recognise differences in the position of forms in space.
5 Spatial relationships: the ability to recognise the relationships between two or more objects in space.

Considerable controversy exists as to whether these five processes are truly discrete areas of visual perception, but Frostig's findings indicate clearly that children at the nursery-school stage show rapid development in visual perception skills relating to eye–motor coordination, figure–group perception and form constancy. Perception of spatial orientation seems to begin between three and four years of age and shows a steady progression until about eight or nine. In the nursery children begin to appreciate spatial opposites such as top/bottom, over/under, high/low and can readily distinguish verticals from horizontals: 'Miss, you've got the book upside down!' is a common cry from a three- or four-year-old. The next stage would be to be able to discriminate between horizontal and oblique lines, a skill which a very few children may attain.

Knowledge of how much space the body occupies is another problem encountered by young children. They need many opportunities to develop spatial awareness skills before they can finally orient themselves effectively in space.

Directional awareness is a perceptual skill which has important implications for later school learning. Although nursery-school children cannot label the left–right dimensions of the body, by four years of age they can recognise that the body has two sides (laterality) and are able to discriminate and coordinate movements of the two sides of the body. Only when children have adequately established laterality can they really understand directionality, a sophisticated extension of the left–right dimension.

An incomplete understanding of directionality may lead to children encountering difficulties in discriminating between various letters of the alphabet, with resultant problems in reading and writing. However, it is perfectly normal for the four- and five-year-old to experience confusion in direction and, in my view, this is a very sound reason for not introducing formal reading too early for the majority of children.

Opportunities for movement activities similar to the ones suggested in Part II (pp. 181–4) will help children develop directional awareness. Both depth and movement perception appear to improve with age but young children are unable to respond to moving objects in terms of adapting their own motor behaviour. It seems as though they are aware that the object is moving fast but cannot control their reactions effectively. Further understanding of this aspect of children's perceptual–motor development could be useful to adults who are responsible for their safety. Visual perception not only appears to play an important part in the development of motor skills, but research has suggested that there is a significant relationship between cognitive development and visual perception in young children, although the relationship diminishes by the age of six (Belka and Williams 1979).

Development of auditory skills

Although the auditory system is perhaps the most intricate of all sensory systems, very little is known about the development of auditory skills. The nature of the development of auditory localisation is not known, but by the age of three, children are able to localise the general direction of a sound.

Children of three and four are able to carry out simple auditory discrimination tasks, as has been discussed in Chapter Four, but these skills continue to improve until children are at least twelve or thirteen years old.

Development of tactile–kinaesthetic abilities

This is another area about which little has been written, although tactile experiences play a very important part in young children's lives. What is known, though, is that by the age of five, tonal discrimination is well developed. If a tactile stimulus – a pencil point, for example – is applied to the hand and forearm of a child who is blindfolded she is able to point to the exact spot were she has first been touched. Ayres (1978) and others have shown that there is a high correlation between level of touch discrimination development and the ability of children to perform complex motor activities.

Research on the development of perception of taste and smell is even more sparse than that on hearing and touch. However, we know that children react to smells and taste, developing quite strong preferences by the age of three.

Fostering perceptual–motor development

The skills that have been described in this section all require repeated practice and teachers can enhance perceptual–motor development in two main ways:

1 Provide opportunities for practice in the specific skills that have been outlined.
2 Encourage perceptual–motor development through creative activities and self-expression.

The importance of sensory experiences and the development of perceptual–motor skills cannot be overemphasised. Although there is insufficient evidence to support the claim that practice in perceptual–motor activities will enhance academic achievement, there is no doubt that competence in these areas enhances children's feelings of self esteem and self-confidence.

Children's physical play needs to be safe, challenging and stimulating, and must provide children with the opportunity to be adventurous and inventive. The well-planned programme for physical development will include both outdoor and indoor activities and provide sensory experiences such as working with materials such as sand, water, dough and clay. Adults need to guard against allowing stereotypical gender differences creeping in – girls need to be encouraged to be as active as boys on the large apparatus and boys need to have opportunities for fine motor development by sewing, threading, and so on. All children need constant opportunities to move and practise all the skills which will help in their perceptual and motor development.

7 Development of creative and aesthetic abilities

To be creative you have to dare to be different.

(Claxton 1984)

Although this is the last of the areas of learning which will be discussed, in no way should it be considered the least important and therefore be given less attention. Rather the opposite, as at a time when schools are being urged to 'return to basics' in the curriculum and four-year-old children in many parts of the country are entering classrooms with poor adult–child ratios, there is a very grave danger that children's aesthetic and creative development will be overlooked. Developing creative and aesthetic awareness involves helping children to communicate and express their feelings through music and movement, art, drama and storytelling, as well as developing a sensitivity to the world around them.

Our technological age needs creative thinkers who can approach problems with a fresh outlook but it also needs people who have an awareness and sensitivity towards the beauty around them. As Reed (1956) has pointed out: 'for education to fulfil its purposes, the cultivation of aesthetic sensibilities and the development of the means of self-expression are of fundamental importance. By learning to perceive, understand and react to the aesthetic accomplishments of others we are enabled to create, perform and respond in a more artistic and thereby holistic way to our environment' (p. 61). Developing creative and aesthetic skills in young children needs teachers who are professionally committed to such an approach and who themselves have an appreciation of the beauty in the world around them.

DEVELOPMENT OF COMMUNICATION THROUGH ART

From a very early age children enjoy scribbling and making marks on paper. At this stage the child is not trying to represent anything, but is simply enjoying her own actions and effects. There has been considerable discussion as to whether at this early 'scribbling stage' (the name given to this stage by Lowenfeld and Brittain (1975)) children simply enjoy the act of making the marks or whether it is the scribble marks themselves that children find satisfying. Gibson and Yonas (1968) found the answer to this question by providing children at the scribbling stage with two different writing implements. One made a mark and the other did not. Children who were given the non-marking stylus quickly abandoned the activity, so it appeared that the fun seemed to be in seeing the mark, not the motor action. Those working with very young children will be well aware that if a toddler picks up a pencil which is broken or a pen which has no ink, she will soon lose interest and drop the object if it fails to make a mark.

Once the child discovers the pleasure of making marks on paper she will practise and practise, her scribblings progressing through a recognisable sequence. Rhoda Kellogg (1969), whose work will be familiar to readers, identified twenty basic scribble patterns made by children of two and under. The basic scribble patterns include circles and squares and become the foundation for later representation. However, not everyone would agree that it is possible to identify all the scribble patterns of Rhoda Kellogg. Cox (1997), in referring to her own research, suggests that not all children 'scribble' and has pointed out that scribbling is not a necessary step in drawing. She has stated that there is no evidence that there would be a problem if children missed this experience altogether: 'there are examples of children in our society and in others who have not had the opportunity to draw but later, when provided with pencil and paper, have produced recognisable figures often within the first half-hour of experimenting with paper and pencil' (p. 6). Cox refers to the work of the anthropologist Alexander Alland (1983) who found that there was little evidence to suggest that the normal early drawing development followed by Western children happened at similar ages in other societies. He also found that the drawing of circles and mandalas was not universal as Kellogg had suggested.

The child's first attempts at representation will occur around the age of four, although some children who have had ample opportunities to use pens, crayons and paints may begin earlier. Matthews (1984) argued that children's scribbles may be representational even though they are not recognisable to adults. This second stage of development, termed by Lowenfeld the 'pre-schematic stage', generally persists until the age of seven and coincides with Piaget's 'pre-operational stage'. Before children develop an awareness of symbolic representation they will only be frustrated if well-meaning adults try to teach them how to represent something.

However, once young children realise they can create whatever they wish, they will often spend long periods of time at an activity and make several drawings on the same topic; and although the representation may be quite unintelligible to others, they know that their drawing symbolises something real. It is not until the pre-schematic stage is reached that the child is willing to talk about her drawings and often asks the adult to write a name or sentence beneath the work. At this stage the child is aware that the drawings are representative of her thoughts and feelings and she can communicate these to others either verbally or in the written form. The ability to represent the world around them symbolically is a very basic and important skill and one which represents a big step forward in children's thinking. It can be a most important form of communication for children with language difficulties or for those for whom English is a second language.

For many years it has been the tradition in Western societies for adults to stand back and not intervene in children's drawings as it was argued that it stifled children's creativity. Franz Cisek and others in the late nineteenth century argued that children's artwork should be allowed to develop without any adult interference, a view which was upheld by Lowenfeld in the mid-part of this century. Eisner (1972) challenged this *laissez-faire* approach as did Robinson (1982, p. 16) in *The Gulbenkian Report* when he wrote that 'the task is not simply to let anything happen in the name of self-expression or creativity'. It has been pointed out that in such societies as China and some Eastern European countries the level of painting and drawing by young children is very high. In China there are teachers who work with children as young as three years of age teaching the skills and techniques necessary before the children can express their ideas. Likewise, in Bulgaria and Hungary artists are invited into the kindergartens to work alongside the children. Painting is considered a worthwhile occupation. I am aware that few pre-school settings can afford to invite artists into the classroom but as Cox has suggested, teachers should draw or paint alongside their children. Children need to see adults drawing and painting in exactly the same way as they see adults reading and writing.

Children's use of three-dimensional materials also goes through various stages of development. Just as they scribble before pictorial representation, so children touch, bang, mould and squeeze materials like dough, clay and finger paints before they try to make representational objects. Here again, it is the process that is important, as while manipulating the material the child is finding out what it is and what can be done with it. During this manipulative period, children are learning about colours, textures and other attributes of the materials; they are also gaining practice in fine muscle coordination, an essential skill when they reach the symbolic stage and want to shape the materials into specific forms.

Most children enjoy exploring the possibilities of different art materials and will spend long periods of time in the art area. Copple, Sigel and Saunders (1979) suggest that there are three reasons why this occurs:

1 Children enjoy having an effect and making marks or building things that bring immediately visible results.
2 They will work at an emerging skill until they have mastered it.
3 They seem to have a natural desire to represent aspects of the world and one's experience of them.

However, there are a few children who through fear of criticism (someone unwittingly or wittingly has laughed at their artistic efforts) or through fear of getting dirty will ignore this part of the classroom. These children will need help from a sensitive adult if they are to learn the pleasures to be obtained from being involved in art activities.

Communication through art enables children to express new ideas and feelings and for some it is their most effective way of informing others of their experiences. Children's pictures portraying a visit or outing can often tell more about the trip than close questioning or discussion. There are two groups of children for whom art is a particularly useful form of communication: those for whom English is a second language and children who are suffering from emotional difficulties. Children for whom English is a second language are often highly articulate in their own tongue and must find it most frustrating when they are unable to express themselves fluently to their teachers. Often, through art, they are able to convey emotions and ideas which at present they cannot do in the English language.

The therapeutic value of art has long been accepted and for children who are suffering from emotional stress, painting or working with plastic materials is an excellent way of alleviating some of the tensions.

FOSTERING COMMUNICATION THROUGH ART

There are four main areas of art experience which we can offer children to encourage them to express their ideas and feelings:

1 Drawing: with fat crayons, chalks, felt pens, pencils.
2 Painting: with brushes, fingers or feet.
3 Modelling: with clay, dough, plasticine, mud.
4 Collage work: using a variety of materials including scrap materials, leaves, shells, stones, boxes of various shapes and sizes, ribbons, pine cones, sticks, beads, rice, paste, and so on.

Each of these areas needs constant use so that the child can gain mastery of the skills involved. Only when the child has begun to master the techniques will she become more self-confident and therefore more creative.

Some of these art experiences lend themselves to group activities and by the end of their fifth year children may be ready to work together on a common enterprise. Working together not only encourages cooperation and sharing, but will involve the children in discussions as to how to plan and organise the work. Educators are often surprised at the high level of achievement reached by groups of two or three children.

In all these activities the role of the educator is crucial. Children should feel free from pressure and interference from the adult, yet feel able to share their 'work' with the teacher if they wish. It is often difficult for teachers to refrain from giving technical advice, for example, when they see that the child has made the paper too wet or the paint too runny. My own view is that one intervenes only if the child turns to the adult for advice, otherwise it is better to make a practical suggestion on a subsequent occasion before the same thing happens again. Effective communication through art will only occur when the environment is relaxed and secure and when the teacher displays sensitivity and awareness to the needs of the children.

DEVELOPMENT OF CREATIVE AND AESTHETIC AWARENESS THROUGH ART

For most people the development of aesthetic skills is seen as art education, but the interpretation used here is concerned with the awareness of beauty and with a gradual awakening of discrimination and taste. Aesthetic experiences, however, should not be totally passive; there is no doubt that when children are encouraged to be active in a creative and expressive way they will be more likely to become creative and aesthetically aware. They will be helped to appreciate beauty in the things they hear, see and feel.

Young children naturally like to draw and there has been a great deal of research into the way they progress from scribbling to recognisable figures. We have already discussed how children use drawing as a form of communication and the need for educationalists to recognise the value of their early and unique efforts. However, there has been relatively little investigation into young children's responsiveness to works of art. The few studies that have been carried out suggest that in talking about works of art, or in sorting/matching tasks using visual stimuli such as polygons, painting reproductions or photographs, young children prefer art objects with bright and contrasting colours, familiar subject matter and unambiguous spatial arrangements.

When talking to young children about paintings or art objects, researchers have found that they may be given idiosyncratic responses. It has been suggested that these replies are due not to the children's lack of attention or inability to perceive the relevant characteristics but to the children's inability to verbalise satisfactorily. Taunton (1984) found that four-year-old children were able to match painting reproductions to expressive description, but were unable to give their reasons for matching.

A number of researchers have suggested that if children are encouraged to talk about the aesthetic qualities of pictures and objects, and given some of the appropriate vocabulary to express beauty of line, colour and shape, then they will use it when discussing among themselves. So it appears that children can develop aesthetic awareness skills in relation to art at an early age but their ability to communicate their feelings and ideas to others may be hampered by inappropriate language. Furthermore, other studies have shown that when teachers are themselves interested in artistic concepts and discuss what they see with the children, awareness is likely to be increased. These teachers will also encourage the children to perceive the subtle aspects of the visual arts, such as style and expressiveness. Children need opportunities to discuss what they see when they look at beautiful objects and to learn to state what 'they like or dislike'. In this way, they not only increase their vocabulary but come to realise that language can be used to share expressive meaning.

When we talk about the need for children to be active in a creative and expressive way, what exactly do we mean by 'creativity' when referring to the activities of young children? An accepted definition of creativity implies an end product; an idea which is novel is related to reality and stands the test of being 'worthwhile'. Few of the activities of young children can be included in this type of definition but if we consider that it can also mean using previous experiences to make something new then this is, I believe, a useful working definition of what children do when they play imaginatively with expressive materials, solve problems and generate new ideas about how to manipulate materials.

Children enjoy exploring materials of different shapes, textures and sizes, and need to be given the opportunity to create visual patterns and pictures. They need to experiment with chalks, crayons, pencils, pens, charcoal and paints as well as pieces of material which can be pasted, cut or glued on to either paper or other pieces of material. Creating visual pictures and patterns also includes three-dimensional art and this involves not only making models from a wide variety of waste materials – there are other materials besides egg boxes, yogurt cartons and cornflakes packets! – but also the use of clay, wood, dough, mud, plasticine and building blocks. There is a tendency to think of building blocks as purely for constructions, with children becoming aware only of their spatial and other mathematical properties. However, to the child who is building a wall, she is not only trying to replicate the real thing, but is very aware of the symmetry and form involved. Building blocks are important to the child in several aspects of development. Not only do they help develop mathematical and scientific awareness, the use of motor skills and creative awareness, but they encourage problem-solving abilities: which block will fit this gap? How many do you need to form a secure base for a tall tower?

In developing their aesthetic awareness children should not only be encouraged to look at and talk about objects and pictures which are generally accepted as attractive and beautiful, but should be allowed to touch and rearrange and everyday objects. Here again our Eastern European colleagues are more aware of the importance of allowing children to have first-hand experiences of beautiful paintings and sculpture. In the Communist period their artists and craftsmen were employed by the state and therefore were more willing to let little hands touch and hold their works of art. We could do more to encourage artists to share their work with young children in a similar way.

Closely allied to awareness of colour and form is an appreciation of texture. Dressing-up clothes made of different fabrics will provide children with opportunities to handle a variety of materials and teachers can help develop awareness by talking to children about the sensations they experience when touching such materials as wool, velvet and tissue paper. Not only will these experiences help to heighten aesthetic awareness but they will encourage perceptual discrimination which has an important role to play in later learning.

DEVELOPMENT OF COMMUNICATION THROUGH MUSIC, MOVEMENT AND DANCE

Long before they have established language, children communicate non-verbally, expressing their emotions and wants through gestures. Even quite young babies engage in 'conversation' with adults, indicating through their early vocalisations that they understand the rudiments of turn-taking and communication. When children enter nursery school around three years of age they have learned to use language in a form which is quite near to that of the adult, but, even so, much of their communication is non-verbal. Indeed, expressions of emotion are much more likely to be motor than verbal responses at this age.

Although young children frequently express their emotions non-verbally, they are not necessarily able to distinguish them in others. Shields and Duveen (1986) showed that three- and four-year-old children did not distinguish between sad and angry feelings very well, seeing these as part of an 'upset state', although all their subjects were able to identify happiness.

It is not only emotional cues that children need to be able to interpret. Every close-knit group of people, such as a family, have their own forms of non-verbal communication which their members have to learn, and children are no exception. From a very early age they learn to interpret the non-verbal cues that indicate that mother is to be avoided this morning and big brother is willing to read a story.

However, when children enter school, they have to learn another set of non-verbal cues relating not only to their peers but to the adults in the classroom, whose gestures and expressions may be very different from those they meet in the family. The nuances and subtle gestures that each of us uses to convey our inner feelings, even if, on occasions, the words we speak are expressing different sentiments, make up part of an elaborate non-verbal communication system based on movements which children have to learn. Person-perception skills do not develop until later in childhood but the opportunities for expressive movement offered in the nursery help children begin to understand the gestures which tell adults so much about one another.

ROLE OF MOVEMENT AND DANCE IN DEVELOPING AESTHETIC AND CREATIVE AWARENESS

Traditionally, when we are talking about movement in the curriculum in relation to the expression of feelings and ideas, it is associated with music. Young children enjoy the possibility for self-expression that occurs during music and movement sessions as it not only stimulates the child's imagination but offers many openings for emotional release. It seems that moving to music can involve the child's entire body and produce satisfying emotional experiences that cannot be found in other ways. Although the majority of children enjoy participating in music and movement, there are some whose cultural background may positively discourage dance – for example, certain religious groups – and for those children it is important that the wishes of their parents are respected.

Movement plays an important role in children's aesthetic development as it is one way for the child to gather impressions of the world. Creative movement involves both mime and dance. In mime the performer uses facial expressions and natural body movements to convey to the audience feelings, action and situations: meaning of some sort is being communicated. On the other hand, dance may not necessarily convey a message or story; it may just be for the pleasure involved in moving in certain ways or in watching others carry out aesthetic movements. For the young child, movement is a pleasurable experience, and moving to music in particular can involve the child's entire body and produce satisfying expressions of emotion and pleasure. Gardner (1983) pointed out that in human development musical intelligence emerges earlier than other kinds of human intelligence – we know that babies can respond to music as early as two to three months and in providing them with a love of music we could be providing them with a lifetime of pleasure.

Movement is particularly valuable in helping children to understand the meaning of various ideas and concepts. For instance, children may find it very difficult to cope with such words as 'high', 'low', 'behind' and 'under' and a creative movement situation will help them realise fully the meaning of these words as well as helping the educator see which children have a real understanding and which require further explanation. Likewise, dramatic movements can help the adult discover whether children know the exact meaning of such words as 'sleepy' or 'sleeping'.

Whenever the child pretends to be another person or object, whether it be in movement sessions or during free dramatic play, she is faced with a number of intellectual challenges. She has to think carefully about the characteristics of the subject and then must consciously modify her body to achieve the desired result. For example, if asked to 'pretend to be an elephant', the child may portray four-leggedness by getting down on all fours, or may use her arms to convey the idea of an elephant's trunk. In this way, she would be attempting to capture the qualities of the animal's appearance, whereas others may choose to imitate the animal's slow ambling gait, thereby trying to convey the qualities of the movement of an elephant.

Imitating involves a considerable number of mental transformations as the child attempts to translate the action and/or appearance of what is being represented into body movements. Minimal transformation is required when the child is requested to imitate a human action – for example, scoring a goal in football – but the thinking becomes more and more difficult if the child is being asked to pretend to be an animal, bird or fish.

Teachers can help children to focus on these representational aspects of movement by asking questions about how they think the subject of their imitation looks, feels and behaves. In becoming more aware of the subject's characteristics the child is increasing her understanding and knowledge. Closely linked to movement is dance, an activity which is enjoyed by the majority of young children. Dance may take the form of free expressive movement to music with the child spontaneously moving to the rhythm or it may be movement which reflects the stimulus of a story, poem or instruction given by an adult.

Traditional action singing games such as 'The Farmer's in his Den' or 'Ring-a-Ring-o'-Roses' involve other forms of self-expression as well as an opportunity to develop cooperative and social skills. Most nursery rhymes involve some form of creative movement and during discussions teachers can talk with the children about the appropriateness of the rhythms and action used – for example, does the rhythm of 'The Grand Old Duke of York' suggest soldiers marching past?

Activities involving movement and dance have many benefits for young children including:

- personal satisfaction – they enjoy finding out what they can do with their bodies
- opportunities to increase their movement vocabulary
- spontaneity and concentration
- identifying and solving problems, e.g. finding your own way of moving like a snail
- responding to others
- recalling and memorising.

Even very young children can respond to markedly rhythmic music. A child of around twelve to fifteen months will sway to the rhythm, but it will be at her own tempo. Toddlers bob up and down in response to rhythmic music, and this repetition will help them to develop a relationship between music, the beat and movement, as will improvised hand clapping. Four-year-olds take an interest in acting out and dramatising ideas through music and in learning movement patterns, such as those of singing games and simple dances. By five they are beginning to identify and express the beat in music, helping them to understand further about tempo, beat, patterns and metre. Music is an ideal medium for communicating ethnic differences and the special qualities of various cultures. In Britain it is generally felt that nursery-aged children are too young to learn the traditional folk and country dances of a culture, but this is not the accepted view in many parts of the world. I have watched young children in South America, Eastern Europe and China carry out complicated dance routines with accuracy and pleasure. In Britain we have almost lost the tradition of dancing and therefore our children are not exposed to the traditional country dances.

However, even if we now believe that the dance steps are too complicated for four-year-olds, they are certainly not too young to listen to the different sorts of music and to feel the rhythms of East and West. Classical dance from India and Pakistan, kabuki music of Japan, Irish jigs and African music all have different rhythms and can convey to children some feelings about the quality of the cultures they represent. Some of these will contrast strongly with the Western 'pop' culture to which the children are regularly exposed!

Music should be viewed not as a subject to be taught to children but as an experience to offer them. Maybe we should consider it in the same way as the Nigerian definition of music, 'egunu', which encompasses more than just music – it is costume, dance, drama, ritual and the whole nexus of activities. Children should not only listen to music but be encouraged to make their own, as they enjoy exploring sounds and rhythms not only with instruments, professional and homemade, but with their voices. Good experiences with sounds and rhythms provide training in aural discrimination which will have positive value in other areas of learning. ·

DEVELOPING AESTHETIC AND CREATIVE AWARENESS THROUGH MUSIC

Music, like art, is a form of communication and for some children it is an important medium for them to use to express their emotions. However, whereas art activities are present in every nursery, music does not necessarily feature strongly in the curriculum for some two-and-a-half- to five-year-old children. The traditional nursery rhymes and songs may be present, but in general there is little evidence of the presence of music in most early childhood settings.

Just as in art children need to create pictures and patterns for themselves, so in music they need opportunities to make up sound patterns as well as listening to a variety of tunes. Practice in certain basic musical skills is necessary before they can create or even appreciate music. However, young children are by no means musically naive. They are well able to arrange sounds on the basis of one dimension – for example, fast–slow, loud–soft, high–low – and can group sounds at levels, that is, all loud sounds, all fast sounds, and so on. It is interesting to note that teachers in infant classes often spend time concentrating on these discriminating skills which children are well able to perfect in the nursery years.

Most children like to sing and have a wide range of pitch and tones at their disposal. From the research it appears that there may be critical periods in learning to sing or use an instrument. For example, three-year-old children are able to sing earlier learned songs in the same key that they first heard and learned them. Children seem to be best able to imitate pitch accurately when they are imitating a woman's voice and worst when they are trying to imitate a piano, a finding which should encourage more teachers to sing to and with the children. Three- and four-year-old children appear to be able to learn to sing, develop attentive listening habits, play musical instruments that do not require fine muscular coordination, and engage in creative movement to music.

Some teacher-directed activities are necessary and valuable but the music curriculum for young children should be child-centred and concentrate on personal involvement, as it is only through participating in the basic experiences of listening, performing and creating music that young children will begin to develop their own concepts about music. If you look at the backgrounds of many singers, there is a history of family interest in singing and playing music.

Young children often sing spontaneously during play, imitating the sounds they have heard and making up songs or tunes. A child dressing a doll may use the doll's name as a trigger for a tune, repeating the name over and over again. Many enjoy chanting and will put tunes to words they have heard, while others prefer to repeat melodic patterns. Experimenting with tonal sounds and having musical conversations with others, particularly adults, seem to be very satisfying emotional experiences for young children during the nursery years.

In listening to music children show a distinct preference for pieces with a strong beat, 'pop' music or traditional jazz being more popular than classical music. With appropriate listening experiences children of three and four can identify individual instruments such as the violin, clarinet, cello, French horn, flute, oboe and trumpet, and from hearing various passages of music they can appreciate the type of 'story' effects which can be made by the different instruments. Children can also follow a musical story and such pieces as *Peter and the Wolf*, *Carnival of the Animals* and *The Sorcerer's Apprentice* are great favourites, as, of course, are the traditional nursery rhymes and songs that have been handed down through the ages.

What is the role of the teacher in shaping the music environment?

Through music, movement and drama children can communicate their thoughts, feelings and desires to others. The role of the teacher is to provide adequate experiences for children to help them develop their confidence and skills in expressing themselves. This can be achieved in a number of ways:

First, by providing selections of pieces of music which are appropriate for both listening and group singing the teacher can help children to become more musically aware. The musical listening experience should cover a range of all types of sound, in a variety of different tempos, tones, qualities and rhythms. Children need to be given an opportunity to discuss what they hear and to acquire the appropriate musical vocabulary which will help them to describe the musical characteristics of the different passages. Group singing activities should be highly pleasurable experiences for young children, and will help to develop and reinforce some of their early musical skills.

Second, awareness can also be created by providing music-making materials to enable children to explore sounds in a variety of different contexts. The teacher should make available diverse instruments and sound-producing media such as wooden and metal objects of different kinds, for example, jars containing buttons or rice, as these lend themselves most readily to exploring and learning about different musical aspects. Just as textures and colours of various art materials provide children with creative visual ideas, so the presence of different sound-producing materials help develop musical ideas. Conventional instruments such as pianos, drums, triangles, tambourines, cymbals and xylophones have an important part to play in developing musical awareness, but such home-made sound instruments as jars containing different amounts of water and drums made of different depth and diameter may be more useful in helping children to understand the effects of tone and pitch.

Third, awareness can be created by providing opportunities during the course of the day for children to listen to music whenever they wish. A growing awareness of various types of music, of likes and dislikes, will not be fostered in an environment in which music is only provided at specific times by the adult. It should be possible to provide nurseries with earphones and tape-recorders so that children can sit quietly and listen to music selected according to their mood.

Zimmerman (1975) has suggested that without rich musical resources to nurture and maximise the child's potential throughout her development and especially when she is most susceptible to learning a particular skill or concept, it is likely that her potential will remain unfulfilled. Most music specialists argue that broad exposure to musical stimuli and experience is not enough. Detailed training and practice are necessary if the child is to develop both listening and performing skills. Young children enjoy listening to and making music and there is no doubt that the most influential ingredient in developing musical awareness skills is the teacher's own sensitivity to sound as well as to other interesting and beautiful events around her.

Closely linked to music and movement is drama, which in the nursery curriculum should mainly take the form of dramatic play, although there may be occasions when it is appropriate to act out a familiar story such as 'The Three Billy Goats Gruff' or a traditional nursery rhyme. During socio-dramatic play, which will be discussed more fully in the next section, children learn that people play different roles in our society, and can come to terms with mastering skills and competencies away from the prying eyes of adults.

DEVELOPING AESTHETIC AWARENESS THROUGH STORIES, POEMS AND RHYMES

During the pre-school years, stories and poems play a big part in helping children understand the world around them. In selecting appropriate prose or verse the adult is aiming to help children discriminate between good and bad material. One has only to look at the faces in a group of children listening to a well-written story to realise that they are well able to differentiate between good and poor literature.

In selecting stories for three- and four-year-old children, the teacher has to remember that although they need to stimulate the children's interest and imagination, they need also to foster feelings of self-confidence and security. The attention span of the average two-and-a-half- to three-year-old is shorter and therefore stories which may be highly suitable for the older children in the nursery may lead to restlessness among the younger ones. Younger children will like stories with a great deal of repetition and will often insist upon some being retold and reread word-for-word without change. The four-year-old continues to enlarge her understanding of real situations by enjoying longer and more complicated stories and her developing interest in words will result in the enjoyment of nonsense rhymes and humour in stories and poetry, especially rhyming poems. At this age children like to create stories with silly language and plays on words. They also enjoy open-ended stories which are left for them to finish.

Dramatising of stories or poems is also possible, particularly the more well-known literature, and although certain characteristics of the original story will be retained, the interpretation of any one particular role will vary from performer to performer. For some children who find they are unable to cope with creative drama the use of puppets is ideal. Under these circumstances the child is able to take on a number of roles without feeling shy or embarrassed. In classes where the teacher is relaxed and able to make up interesting stories herself, it is quite possible to find three- and four-year-old children handling ideas and creating stories for themselves. These may be recorded for future use either on tape or in a book. Although these are activities more normally associated with children in infant classes, there is no reason why this form of creativity should not be encouraged in the nursery.

Other creative activities can be stimulated as a consequence of stories and poems read to the children. Painting, drawing, modelling in dough or clay, or model-making with wood or junk materials may be triggered off by a literary or musical stimulus. The most likely creative response to a story or poem will be in the form of socio-dramatic play. For the young child, play is a positive way of fostering creativity. It has been written that 'play is the way a child learns what no one can teach him' (Hartley 1971, p. 32), a statement with particular relevance to play and creativity. Play enhances the child's creativity by providing situations where the consequences of one's actions are minimised and where there are many opportunities to try out combinations of behaviour that under other circumstances could never be attempted. The young child is able to identify with other things and people without direction from adults.

By the end of the nursery years, dramatic play will have become increasingly cooperative, each child being able to sustain his or her own role for a prolonged period of time. However, dramatic play does not always need to be group oriented; children require opportunities to try out their ideas alone and it may well be that a four-year-old who is engaged in solitary play may be reaching a mature level. Rubin (1977) has pointed out that there are varying levels of sophistication in solitary play and while some of it takes place at a sensori-motor level some may be of a high order involving a great deal of storytelling and dramatic play. For example, the four-year-old who is playing with a farmyard and animals may be assigning appropriate roles and language to the farmer and his helpers and building a complicated story around the activities of the farm.

There is increasing evidence from research studies that play, particularly imaginative play, encourages not only healthy, emotional development, but divergent thinking. During play situations, children are given the opportunity to develop alternative ways of reacting to similar situations and although the teacher may have, on occasions, to accept the somewhat chaotic quality of creative play, it is nevertheless one of the ways in which children acquire problem-solving strategies and begin to think constructively about the world around them.

Dramatic play is rich in symbolic activity, involving as it does the transformation of self, objects and situations into characters, objects and events that exist only in the imagination. When children are engaged in socio-dramatic play they are involved in cognitively complex behaviour, their play patterns are highly organised and consist of sequences of related ideas and events which need careful manipulating if the theme is to be maintained. Children need plenty of time, freedom and choice of materials if they are to engage in imaginative play and one of the most important functions of the educator is to ensure that children are free to move from one activity to another and have access to a wide range of materials.

Socio-dramatic play takes place in many instances by chance, but I am also suggesting that this should not always be the case. The introduction of a story which stimulates the imagination, the production of props that lend themselves to certain types of play activity or a visit to a place of interest are all opportunities for encouraging socio-dramatic play. There are few activities in the early years curriculum which are so effective in encouraging the development of social, linguistic, emotional and cognitive skills as socio-dramatic play, but the level of their effectiveness will depend upon the involvement (either overt or covert) of an adult.

Shefantya and Smilansky (1990, p. 22), in supporting their arguments for the benefits of socio-dramatic play, stated that six elements must be present for it to take place.

1 Imitative role play: the child undertakes a make-believe role and expresses it in imitative action and/or verbalisation.
2 Make believe with regard to toys: movements or verbal declarations and/or materials or toys that are not replicas of the object itself are substituted for real objects.
3 Verbal make believe with regard to actions and situations: verbal descriptions of declarations are substituted for actions and situations.
4 Persistence in role play: the child continues within the context of the play episode.
5 Interaction: at least two players interact within the context of the play episode.
6 Verbal communication: there is some verbal interaction related to the play episode.

Play of all types is essential for children's overall development and is the main approach to learning in early years education but socio-dramatic play is one of the most effective means of developing creative awareness.

8   Play and the learning environment

Children are active learners and if they are to develop the skills and competencies which have been discussed in earlier chapters they must be able to work and play in a safe and secure setting. Workers in the field of early childhood education refer to the need to provide children with a well-prepared learning environment, a need which is interpreted by some as simply making a wide range of materials and apparatus freely available and placing little or no constraint upon their use. As a result it is possible to go into some nursery classes and find children so overwhelmed by the wealth of equipment that relatively little learning is taking place, whereas other nursery settings will be similarly equipped but the material has been organised in such a way that opportunities for learning and discovery are maximised.

What are the reasons for the differences between these two environments which on the surface appear similar? Why is it that one situation is highly challenging and the other a place which provides ammunition for our critics who argue that the children have nothing to do except 'play all day'?

In this chapter an attempt will be made to analyse some of the main features of a 'well-prepared learning environment' and consider ways in which the organisation and deployment of staff can help to produce a fruitful and stimulating setting in which young children can explore and develop their individual interests. The first prerequisite of any learning environment is that it meets the needs of children, needs which are similar for all children between the ages of two and five years.

PHYSICAL ENVIRONMENT

In an ideal world all the buildings and surrounding play areas would be purpose built to meet the needs of young children, but in reality most early years workers find that there are some disadvantages to their particular nursery environment. However, the most unpromising building can be vastly improved with imagination and foresight. One of the most important features of the nursery environment is that it must be both physically and psychologically safe and secure; ideal equipment and materials are of little value if the children do not feel emotionally safe and relaxed to explore and move around freely. However, a safe, secure environment must not preclude opportunities for appropriate challenges according to the age and abilities of the children.

A basic need of all young children is space. The space to move freely within the environment is of particular importance for children living in urban areas where many are housed in high-rise flats or in cramped conditions with little or no outdoor play space. I would argue, though, that space is an essential need of all children which schools are finding increasingly difficult to meet when they are catering for four-year-old children in primary classrooms. The four-year-old is at a stage of development where she needs many opportunities for large motor movements and sitting at a table for long periods of time is both emotionally and physically undesirable.

Another basic need of children is the time to function at their own pace. In the nursery setting there should be as few time constraints as possible, as young children are frequently victims at home of the rush and bustle characteristic of so many households. Concentration and an increased attention span can only be achieved if there are opportunities to carry out and complete tasks at one's own pace.

INDOOR NURSERY ENVIRONMENT

Although the inside and outside areas should be viewed as total learning environments, for the moment we will consider each separately. In the recent past many nursery-school buildings have been designed as large, open-plan areas in which there is barely enough storage space and little opportunity for children to play away from the eyes of adults. In such buildings it often requires imagination and ingenuity by the staff to arrange the available space in such a way that there are carpeted quiet areas, corners where children can hide away, messy areas and spaces where children can construct and manipulate equipment undisturbed. Storage is often a problem in these situations since ideally all equipment should be visible and accessible to the children, who need to be able to choose and return apparatus freely and unaided. The opportunity to make choices and decisions for themselves is crucial for children's overall development. Where storage involves the utilisation of high shelves it is almost impossible to allow the children open access to the apparatus for fear of them falling and hurting themselves. When this occurs and children require constant help to reach equipment, one of the fundamental goals of early childhood education, that of encouraging independence and self-help, may be lost.

Quiet, carpeted areas near the bookshelves where children can sit and look at books or gather together for a story are a feature of every nursery, but not all nurseries have hidey-holes where children can play undisturbed by adults. The importance of these private areas was highlighted by the Oxford Pre-School Research Project which demonstrated that high-quality and prolonged bouts of play most frequently occurred when two or more children played together apparently hidden from adults. For those who have two-year-olds in their nursery settings it is even more important, for 'to be able to withdraw and be alone, and to experience a sense of privacy, intimacy and solitude is essential for one's identity' (Sebastian 1986, p. 96).

An important feature of the learning environment is the home corner, the source of so much imaginative play, the importance of which has already been discussed. This part of the setting should be large enough for children to play in, but secluded enough for the children to feel free from the prying gaze of unwanted adults. While not totally decrying the traditional commercial house, my own view is that an area of the nursery which is screened off but which is larger than the standard piece of equipment makes a better home corner and allows the introduction of varied pieces of furniture and apparatus as props. Among these props will be included dressing-up clothes which need to be kept near to the home-corner area. They are best hung on a rail rather than housed in a box since in this way they are not only more easily accessible to the children but it is easier to keep them clean and well preserved. When dressing-up clothes are washed and well cared for children will feel that adults value their imaginative play activities.

Although role play is a major activity in the home corner, some children use the area as a place to explore and use the various tools and utensils. Many children indulge in cooperative play, but others spend their time filling saucepans, stirring, mixing and sharing in an effort to perfect their skills. It may well be that there is a pretend element attached to their activity which develops after they have explored and come to terms with this aspect of their environment.

Imaginative play will also emanate from the 'block corner', an area which should be large enough to allow children to leave out their constructions overnight without fear of interference. This can present problems when the nursery is open for two sessions daily and the children go off and leave their work, but in spite of the difficulties it is important that children have an opportunity to continue with the construction on a subsequent occasion.

The block area provides excellent opportunities for problem solving and mathematical learning. It provides possibilities for the exploration of concepts such as number, shape, quantity, length, area, weight, spatial awareness and volume as well as presenting children with real problems to solve. They have to plan, make judgements and work together. As Gura and Bruce (1992, p. 79) write, 'part of the attraction and value of unit blocks is that the design enables children to judge, as they go along, the appropriateness of their own actions, relative to their intentions'. The following is an example of how block play can incorporate so many areas of learning.

A group of four-year-olds is playing with the blocks and has decided to build a multistorey car-park. They are arguing as to how they should build the slopes up to each storey and how the cars are to come down again.

During the discussion one child starts talking about how his mummy is learning to drive and how difficult it is for her to change gears. Another child intervenes with comments about parking and traffic wardens. After a while, a corner of the original structure topples over and suggestions are made by one child as to how they can stop the blocks from falling to the ground. This leads to an argument in which the child who has made the suggestion says that her father is a surveyor. At this point all conversation relating to the 'multistorey car-park' is stopped and the children begin to discuss the work of their mummies and daddies. One child's mother is a radiographer: she cannot explain her mother's job to the satisfaction of the other children and the help of the teacher is sought.

The conversation with the educator lasts for some five minutes, after which one child wanders away no longer wishing to construct the car park. The remaining three children go back to their block building and with the help of a picture and some advice from an adult eventually construct a garage. Once this has been completed to their satisfaction they start playing with the cars and make up a 'game' which lasts for more than fifteen minutes and would have continued longer had it not been the end of the session.

When the adult came to analyse the learning that stemmed from that particular play bout she realised that the children had worked in cooperation, explored their knowledge and understanding of the world, discussed various mathematical ideas, used their creative and problem-solving abilities and performed both fine and gross motor skills. All the areas of learning laid down in the *Desirable Outcomes for Children's Learning* were met in that one activity, besides developing the children's concentration and memory skills. There are many other instances which early childhood workers could cite to demonstrate the learning that can take place during block play.

What other features of the physical environment are important for children's learning? High on the list of priorities is the 'messy area' where activities such as sand and water play, clay, painting and junk modelling can take place without fear of chastisement because of spillage. Most children take great pleasure in playing in this area of the nursery, particularly as these are activities which can seldom be indulged in fully at home.

Play with sand and water is regarded by most nursery staff as highly desirable for young children, both for satisfying their emotional needs and for the mathematical and scientific concepts which can be learned. However, if the value of sand and water play is to be exploited fully then the provision must be organised so that it will enable children to extend their learning through play. There are many ways in which this can be done, but not by filling the sand and water trays with so much equipment that one can barely see the raw materials. Take sand play, for instance. Although some schools are fortunate enough to have a large outside sand area which children can use during fine weather, the majority of sand play takes place around fairly small trays and the number of children playing in the area at any one time must naturally be limited.

Many schools have trays of wet and dry sand so that children are able to experience the properties of this material under different conditions, but almost all schools use the same type of sand. Sand not only varies in colour and texture but in density, and children's understanding of this basic material could well be extended by introducing them to other varieties and by providing appropriate equipment which would enable children to discover for themselves the similarities and dissimilarities between the types. The presence of an adult who is able to introduce the appropriate vocabulary and to point out possible uses of the equipment will help to ensure that children obtain full benefits from playing with sand.

Just as the sand trays constitute a valuable addition to the learning environment so does the water container. Once again teachers need to ask themselves what is the value of water play for young children. Playing with water is a highly pleasurable experience for most children (and adults) and for some it may be therapeutic. For these children it will be necessary for them to dabble their hands in water for long periods of time, repeating an action in an apparently aimless fashion while they work through their anxieties and tensions, but for the majority, endless repetition of an activity is unnecessary and can only lead to boredom.

The water trough is more than a piece of equipment from which children can derive a great deal of pleasure; it is also an important part of the learning environment. Through experience with water children can develop their physical knowledge of the world and begin to discover some of the basic concepts associated with volume and capacity. However, if play with water is to be of real value then the equipment placed in or near the water tray must be part of a programme which has been well planned by the nursery staff. Most water trays have their articles that float and sink, but more use could be made in most nurseries of funnels, siphons and hoses from which children can become aware of some of the properties of water. Introducing bubbles and vegetable dye to the water is another way of maintaining interest in this area of the nursery. Some children whose concentration span is very limited will spend prolonged periods of time blowing bubbles and watching the way they float through the air. Planning the ways in which the play in the sand and water trays can extend children's learning is crucial if there is to be progression and continuity in these areas of the programme. Adults working with or near the water and sand trays can also introduce new and appropriate vocabulary to the children.

A third component of the 'messy area' is the part of the nursery where children can indulge in painting, collage and junk modelling, and so on. All these activities require access to sinks and water and a floor covering which will tolerate spillage. Most art areas have easels, but I would also make a plea for the wide use of flat surfaces since many young children find it frustrating when their paint continually runs down the paper as they stand at the easel, marring the effect they are aiming to achieve.

Although it is important for children to find out for themselves the effect of mixing various paints together, there is also justification for adult intervention on appropriate occasions, since by limiting the colours available children may learn how to achieve the desired effect more quickly. Children can be disappointed in their efforts simply because they are unaware that the addition of a certain colour would change the whole effect. Likewise, children need help in mixing paints with other material in order to achieve different textural effects. Frequently three- and four-year-old children have very firm ideas as to what they wish to achieve but need adult help to execute their ideas. An instance of this is four-year-old David, who was standing in front of an easel, crying bitterly. When approached by the adult and asked why he was crying, he replied, 'Cos I want to paint what I saw on my walk with my daddy but I don't know how to do it.' Here was a child demanding to be helped to make an accurate representation of what he had seen.

Through junk modelling children learn to fit different shapes together, take them apart, cut, rearrange and transfer them, all activities which will help them in their understanding of mathematical and spatial concepts.

Some will then use their completed model in pretend play, while others are only interested in the process not the end product. Well-prepared art corners must be equipped with boxes and papers of different shapes, sizes and textures to help facilitate the children's learning experiences. The foundations of design and technology are to be found in the nursery as the problem-solving skills and strategies required in making models are fundamental to later learning. Nurseries where children attain high standards in their modelling are generally those which not only provide children with a wide range of different raw materials but where the staff make sensitive suggestions and sometimes work beside the children, making models themselves. As in other areas of the arts curriculum it may be necessary to help children achieve an end product, but normally with two- to five-year-old children the process is everything: they are not concerned about the final result. Adults have to distinguish clearly between the need of the child to produce a product and the need of the adult to ensure that the child produces something to take home at the end of the session to please the parents.

The 'messy' area of the nursery is also the place where the clay table is located, although high costs and its extreme messiness has resulted in many nurseries making it available to children on very few occasions. I suspect the situation has changed little since the survey carried out in 1977 as part of the Social Handicap and Cognitive Functioning in Pre-School Children Project, where it was found that in only a small percentage of their nurseries was clay to be found on a regular basis. Many nurseries substitute playdo or dough for clay to give children three-dimensional experiences, but in spite of the high cost I would hope that all children are given some opportunities to work with this most satisfying material.

Just as the 'messy areas' need to be placed on the tiled-floor areas adjacent to the sink and water, so the woodwork table needs to be kept apart from the general play areas. For obvious safety reasons, children using carpentry tools need to be protected from others who are moving rapidly throughout the nursery. The woodwork table is an important part of the learning environment as it is here that children can develop new skills using real tools and real wood. Many nursery teachers are very apprehensive about the use of tools in the classroom and obviously careful supervision of the area is required. However, from my own experience, children who have regular access to this equipment soon become highly proficient at using the tools and treat them with the care and respect they require if there are not to be any serious accidents.

It is important that the woodwork table is adequately equipped and that construction materials such as glue, rubber bands and wire are readily available, as well as nails and wood. Children need to know that every tool and piece of equipment has a special place and that they must return them after use. This is another area where adult intervention is required if children are to progress beyond knocking a nail into two pieces of wood. If the nursery staff do not feel that they have sufficient expertise to develop the children's competencies, assistance can generally be sought from among the parents.

A new 'corner' in the nursery is the computer area. Although early years educators have expressed concern over the presence of the computer in the classroom, it is now generally accepted that this is another area of experience and learning for young children. Many develop good keyboard skills through practice, and improve their hand–eye coordination. The use of the computer will encourage not only cognitive skills, but concentration, memory and recall. Furthermore, it can be very helpful in encouraging cooperation and patience while the children wait their turn.

A well-planned indoor learning environment will also include child-sized furniture, table and chairs where children can sit and work at puzzles, games and other table-top toys. Many children will, of course, take these table-top toys into the carpeted area and stretch out on the floor rather than sit at the tables. A number of educationalists have queried the value of this equipment in the nursery but Sylva, Roy and Painter (1980) found that puzzles and other task-orientated activities were rich in intellectual challenge and demanded greater bouts of concentration from the children. The satisfaction of completing a task cannot be overemphasised as many children take great pleasure in carrying out activities which have an end product.

An area where children can listen to sounds and make music is another essential feature of a well-prepared learning environment. Many nurseries have a piano but access to a record player which children can operate themselves enables them to explore and compare sounds and rhythms. Listening skills are an important factor in later learning and although many nurseries provide children with opportunities to listen to music in groups, few have their rooms arranged so that individual children can listen to or make their own music on either commercial or home-made instruments. It is interesting that teachers who make a feature of the music area are often surprised at the high level of musical skill achieved by many three- and four-year-old children.

A rich learning environment will include aesthetic considerations. Smith (1989, p. 14) stated that 'the aim is to generate an atmosphere in which concern for aesthetic quality becomes deeply ingrained'. This will include ensuring that any curtains or drapes are clean and properly hung and the whole room is tidy and aesthetically pleasing. This is an aspect of the learning environment which is frequently overlooked.

A permanent feature in every nursery should be an area where there are animals and plants. Young children need to learn to feed, water and care for living things as it is only by observing how plants and animals grow and change over time that they will come to understand natural phenomena. Health and hygiene regulations have prevented the inclusion of pets in classrooms but they can still be kept outside. The value of keeping pets in a nursery setting cannot be overestimated for the timid, insecure child.

A well-prepared learning environment will include other areas of interest beside those mentioned already. Most nurseries have 'interest tables' on which children and staff place articles brought from home which relate to topics which have been dealt with in the classroom. These provide opportunities for discussion and investigation and should be changed regularly. There may also be a table with old clocks, radios, and so on that children can take apart to find out about their workings, while other tables may be covered with articles and equipment designed to develop such awareness. The opportunity to explore and experiment with materials and equipment is an important feature of children's early learning.

The number of these 'discovery' tables will depend to a large extent upon the amount of space available in the nursery. Many early years educators feel that not only is there insufficient room, but it may be educationally undesirable to have all the areas operating simultaneously, and therefore select from the various activities available, changing the equipment on a regular basis.

In discussions with students on provision for young children the question often arises as to how frequently rooms should be changed and equipment moved around. It is obviously necessary to make changes in any classroom if after observing the children's use of space it is found that one area is never used while another is overcrowded. Also children become accustomed to materials and equipment being always in the same place. For some children, a change will be upsetting but for the majority an altered environment will create challenges and provide stimulating experiences. The adult will need to observe the children, and any who are very timid or anxious, or those with special needs, will require help from the staff to settle into the new environment, but if they have been involved in the discussions concerning the alterations and actually helped to move the materials and equipment then they will enjoy the new challenges.

Outdoor play area

The physical organisation of the indoor space is important but no nursery environment is complete without taking into account the outdoor area since together they make a total learning environment which caters for every child's interests and provides materials that will be appropriate for the level of development of each and every child. Many of the skills and competencies which develop during these early years are learned from the outdoor natural environment. Children will gain more from digging in the garden and watching worms and insects than they will from looking at pictures.

The value of an outdoor play area has long been appreciated. Early educationalists such as Margaret McMillan and Susan Isaacs were well aware that there must be places where children can dig and watch things grow and die. The need for outdoor play areas was expressed very clearly by Lady Allen of Hurtwood (1968) who wrote: 'children seek access to a place where they can dig in the earth, build huts and dens with timber, use real tools, experiment with fire and water, take really great risks and learn to overcome them. They [children] have an irresistible urge to build houses and dens, dig holes, make gardens, trot after pets, make bonfires and cook meals out-of-doors. These are all delightfully messy occupations and they make the planners, who are mostly tidy-minded people, unhappy' (p. 16). As space in the home environment becomes more limited for many children so the outdoor facilities of a nursery become even more important.

What are the main requirements of an outdoor play area to facilitate learning?

Primarily it must be safe and secure with ample space for the children to play freely, preferably with trees, flat grass areas and bushes where children can hide-and-seek and play in the mud. If the nursery is attached to an infant school then it is most important that the play area is separated from the rest of the school so that children can move freely without fear of intrusion from the older children. This need for a separate outside play area is one of considerable concern to many early childhood educators now that so many four-year-old children are entering reception classes. The outdoor equipment should provide children with a wide variety of opportunities for active physical experience. Wood, boxes, crates, planks, and so on will enable children to build interesting structures which will serve as triggers to imaginative play. Even an asphalt playground can become a positive learning environment with the aid of an imaginative and ingenious staff who provide interesting materials with which the children can play. I have seen highly stimulating outdoor play going on thanks to the creativity of the staff in a nursery class where the playground is on a steep slope cut into the edge of a mountain.

Apart from play experiences the outdoor area should also provide children with opportunities to learn about their natural environment. A garden where children can dig, plant seeds and watch things grow is an important part of a well-prepared learning environment, particularly as for many children it will provide their only opportunity to enjoy the pleasure of the cultivation of the soil. Such an environment needs also to be aesthetically appealing. A well-prepared physical environment, both indoors and outdoors, should be spacious enough for children to move around freely, but at the same time provide ample opportunities for 'getting away' from the adults. Above all, it should have a relaxed, calm atmosphere so that children can develop fully the skills and competencies appropriate to this age range.

The organisation of the physical environment both indoors and outdoors will play an important part in helping children to acquire the skills and competencies associated with nursery provision but the most important facet of the prepared learning environment is the adult. In the next section I want to look at the role of the adult in helping children to gain the greatest advantage from the materials and apparatus available in our modern nursery schools and classes.

THE ROLE OF THE ADULT

There will be more than one adult in the majority of nursery settings and in most there will be at least one qualified nursery nurse and possibly parent helpers besides. Within the education system there will be at least one teacher and nursery nurse, and more in the larger nursery units. In all early settings, whether they are educational establishments, day nurseries or playgroups, the successful planning and organisation of the daily routine will depend upon a team approach where all the adults involved discuss together the implementation of their aims and objectives. Each adult will bring to the situation her own particular strengths and skills.

The role of the early years educator, like that of all educators, is a diverse one, but above all it is that of a leader of a team, who works to ensure that the environment is planned to meet the needs of each and every child. In deciding the layout and organisation of the particular nursery setting the educator will have to take into account not only the aims and objectives of the nursery and the skills and competencies considered to be most appropriate for children to develop at this stage in their education, but the community in which the children live. It is this aspect of planning which is sometimes neglected.

Although the overall aims of nursery education are the same for all children, the emphasis within the learning environment will change according to the individual needs of the children. For instance, a learning environment planned for children who come from high-rise flats will place greater stress on developing gross motor skills and unrestricted movement within both the outdoor and indoor play areas than one planned for children who all come from homes where there are large gardens and places to run freely. This is not to say that the latter environment will not provide opportunities for climbing, running, and so on but rather that the emphasis may be different.

The educator must ensure that the children are offered a wide range of multi-sensory materials and activities which will both stimulate and challenge. However, if the children are to receive valuable educative experiences rather than a haphazard set of activities then it is imperative that they are presented with materials and ideas based on systematic planning. This can only occur when the nursery staff are clear in their goals and have a sound knowledge of each child's stage of development based upon an individual objective assessment.

Children vary in the rate at which they develop various skills and competencies and it is the role of the adult to ensure that progress is appropriate to the needs of each child. For some children the next step must be small and very carefully introduced, while for more able children it may be possible to offer greater challenges; this is a crucial problem for teachers aptly expressed by McVickers-Hunt (1961) as 'the problem of the match'. Too great a move forward can produce a 'boomerang effect' resulting in negative responses, but, equally, too small a progression can lead to boredom and indifference.

The activities not only need to be matched to the individual abilities of the children but to be structured in such a way that children can develop further skills and understanding. In encouraging the extension of the children's abilities the adult also acts as a facilitator and enabler. For example, the strategic placing of a particular piece of equipment near a child or group of children engaged in imaginative play may well help sustain the play episode and introduce a further dimension so that the fantasy is enhanced. Likewise, the child who is having difficulties in making a model will be helped if the adult suggests the use of a certain type of glue or shows the child how to use a particular implement.

The educator may act as facilitator simply by encouraging children to carry out their own investigations. An example of this is instanced by an incident reported by Susan Isaacs, one of our eminent early childhood educators. The school rabbit had died and on the following day there was strong speculation and curiosity as to what would happen to the animal's fur, claws, and so on after death. Where would they go? Would they change colour? In order to satisfy the children's curiosity and pose an element of scientific inquiry, Isaacs encouraged the children to do the only possible thing – dissect the animal (Isaacs 1930, pp. 243–4). Young children have a healthy curiosity and since they are more likely to learn from their own experiences than from second-hand information, Isaacs, by making it possible for them to find out for themselves what had happened to the animal, was actively facilitating their learning about the physical environment. Given a safe setting, children will explore, query and question, drawing pleasure from the feelings of competence which result from their explorations.

As the children carry out day-to-day activities in the nursery, the role of the adult is to guide and help them to plan appropriate strategies which will result in experiences being extended and links being made between past and future events. The importance of this form of adult help is demonstrated in the High Scope programme. This programme, which is one of the few to have been evaluated over a long period of time and shown to be effective, stresses the importance of guided play. The adult helps the child to plan her actions, consider the various options and then review the outcomes. Bruner (1980) suggests that in this way the adult provides the 'scaffolding' or framework within which the child can make choices and decisions. It is not only at the planning stage when adult involvement can be valuable. Frequently, a situation arises when a child makes a 'discovery' and spontaneous adult intervention can result in the educational content of the activity or experience being developed. Intervention of this kind, though, requires skill and sensitivity if the child is not to be robbed of the feeling of wonder and curiosity; there are occasions when the adult must accept that this is a moment to be savoured by the child and stressing the educational message is highly inappropriate.

Although child-initiated activities are normally those in which children engage for longer periods of time and display the greatest interest and level of concentration, there are occasions during the nursery day when adult-imposed activities are both necessary and desirable. There are certain skills and competencies to which children need to be introduced in exactly the same way as the infant- and junior-school teacher presents new information to the older-aged child. Having shown the child what to do the teacher will then provide opportunities for the newly acquired skill to be perfected through practice in play situations. The Plowden Report (1967) stated that 'play is the business of childhood' and few would argue against the view that play is the basic medium for learning during early childhood. But we need to ask the question whether adults should intervene in children's play and what is the effect of their intervention. Sylva, Roy and Painter (1980) demonstrated in their research that playing with an adult was intellectually more stimulating for three- and four-year-old children than playing with another child, although the best social setting for elaborated play is the pair.

Corinne Hutt has suggested that children's play be divided into two categories, epistemic or exploratory play and ludic play. She argued that children learn during exploratory play and it is this type which lends itself most readily to adult intervention. When the child is exploring and solving problems associated with the challenge of a new experience or piece of equipment, help may be needed from the adult to understand the full potential of the object. However, once the child has come to terms with the challenge and begins to fantasise and make up imaginary situations using the apparatus, then, according to Hutt (1970), very little further learning is taking place. Imaginary play which is less purposeful is termed ludic by Hutt and, in her view, is less responsive to adult intervention. The following is an example in which an adult-initiated challenging experience was turned by a group of four-year-old children from a problem-solving situation into a fantasy one after they had mastered the challenge.

The children were confronted with a hole in the ground about two metres wide, half a metre deep and some five metres in length. They were told by their teacher to imagine that this was a very deep river which they had to cross and which was too dangerous for them to swim. After being presented with the challenge the children began discussing the issue freely, each one entering fully into the spirit of the activity. By 'chance' the teacher had placed near by a collection of ropes, pieces of wood, tyres, and so on which might be helpful in solving the problem. During the next forty-five minutes the children worked diligently, seeking ways to cross the river and referring to the adult when appropriate. The teacher never allowed the children to become frustrated but helped only by guiding them to make their own 'discoveries'. Eventually the children solved the problem and an appropriate bridge was constructed using two of the wooden ramps provided for the wheelchair of a physically handicapped child. These ramps were almost exactly the width of the 'river' and so the children were able to walk across their bridge and successfully reach the far bank.

What followed was a perfect illustration of Corinne Hutt's theory. Once the problem was solved and the children had all crossed safely to the other side of the river, the concentration, the elaborate methodical and scientific discussion ceased and the bridge turned into a 'boat'. Some pieces of wood became oars and the children 'paddled down the river' singing nursery rhymes as they went. The new activity gave rise to much merriment, more language, but of a very different kind, and considerable fantasy play. The 'boat' remained the centre of imaginary play on several subsequent occasions during the ensuing weeks.

What contribution did the teacher make to the learning of these children and how did she intervene? In the first instance the whole idea was adult-initiated. Both the hole and the story stemmed from the teacher, although had the children failed to show any interest, the project would have been abandoned. However, after firing the children's imagination the teacher stayed in the background, answering questions and discussing ideas when appropriate. Her role was that of facilitator. The teacher's presence also had a positive effect on concentration, since the children felt that her involvement with them in their task implied that she valued the activity. However, once the bridge was built and the children had shared their success with the adult, her presence was no longer necessary or appropriate in the fantasy play which followed.

That is not to say that fantasy play should always be free of adult intervention. Traditionally, early childhood educators have stood back and followed a policy of non-intervention in children's fantasy play but there is now some evidence to suggest that adult involvement in the form of play tutoring may be of value, particularly to socially disadvantaged children. However, the intervention demands extreme sensitivity as we are all aware that an inappropriate remark or action can ruin an imaginative game.

One of the earliest advocates of 'play tutoring' was Sarah Smilansky (1968), working with socially disadvantaged children in Israel. She demonstrated that intervention strategies in the form of arranging carefully selected materials, questioning and discussion with the children, increased the level of socio-dramatic play which she argued has a positive effect on later learning ability. However, even in Israel, where teachers were able to see the positive effects of their work for themselves, there was reluctance to intervene in what they regarded as 'child's business'. Play tutoring involves broadening the teacher's role from that of facilitator to participator. As facilitator, the adult is structuring the environment by providing materials and experiences to trigger the imagination but in the intervention role the teacher becomes part of the play activity, assumes a role and models appropriate play behaviour. Adults have long been spontaneous participators in children's fantasy play, for example, when they have been invited to drink endless cups of tea. So what is the difference between this type of spontaneous involvement and that of play tutoring? In the intervention model the adult is trained to observe systematically children's play to determine what crucial elements are missing. How much knowledge do the children have of the imaginary roles, are they utilising the appropriate props effectively, do they use the vocabulary associated with their particular play theme?

If, after careful observation, the teacher considers vital play elements to be missing then she will intervene in order to clarify and expand the play and promote content and appropriate action. In becoming part of the socio-dramatic play activity the adult has the opportunity to assume a role and model that type of behaviour. Work of several researchers has shown that intervention in fantasy play can facilitate language learning and problem-solving activities. Overall there seems to be evidence to support the view that adult involvement in children's play can contribute to the development of young children in the cognitive areas as well as in areas of social and emotional development. If this is the case, then there is a need to include play training for educators of young children in their initial training courses so that they can enhance the quality of children's play in a sensitive way and approach this delicate area of intervention with perception, sympathy and insightful understanding.

The adult in the nursery has another, maybe even more important, role to play, in addition to that of facilitator and provider of materials and ideas. It is that of speech and social model. From listening to the adults' spoken language children not only learn correct grammatical models and appropriate vocabulary but become aware of the importance of intonation and how to cope with various social situations. In hearing the adult praise, accept and criticise they learn what is acceptable behaviour in different situations.

As Susan Isaacs pointed out in her pamphlet on *The Educational Value of the Nursery School* (1954) children needed skilled help not only in finding the right play material but, more important, in their own efforts to learn and understand the world around them and to cope with their own anti-social impulses. Young children are frequently frightened by the strength of their own feelings of anger and hostility and need the reassurance and calming effect of an adult to assure them that they are not evil and wicked.

The conduct of the nursery staff and parent helpers towards the children and each other should provide a model and standard of social behaviour which both respects and sets an example to children thereby helping them cope with the various situations they encounter during their daily lives. Where the adults in a nursery offer the children consistent behavioural and speech models even the most difficult child will gradually come to accept the limits imposed and begin to adjust her behaviour accordingly.

The role of the adult in the learning environment of young children is, as I have demonstrated, a very crucial and demanding one. It is almost a quarter of a century since Parry and Archer wrote the following description, but it is as valid today as it was then:

A teacher of young children obviously needs to possess certain qualities if she is to face well her responsibilities which are complex in nature and highly demanding of excellence of many kinds. She needs to be someone who is essentially human; someone who likes people, especially children, and is not only full of warmth and goodwill towards them but determined to do right by them. To achieve such ends she needs to be perceptive, sensitive, sympathetic and imaginative. She needs to be highly educated personally and professionally in those areas of knowledge, understanding and skill which she will be conveying to children, albeit indirectly at their stage of development and in those spheres of learning which are essential to her understanding of children and adults and to her skill in dealing with them.

(1974, p. 139)

Critics of this statement have argued that such a paragon does not exist, but many workers in the field of early childhood education would qualify for such a description.

The learning environment must be prepared to meet the needs of individual children, challenging enough to ensure that there are opportunities for even the most able child to be stretched and stimulated, yet secure enough to meet the needs of the most timid. Opportunities for guided play, and time and space to explore and talk about the environment, will enable children to learn how to learn. Currently, early childhood educators are being pressurised to ensure that children achieve the learning outcomes advocated by the SCAA document (1996b) and as a result many are being tempted to offer children a formal approach. Such an approach is entirely unnecessary and inappropriate as the outcomes will be achieved by most children by the time they reach statutory schooling if they are allowed to learn at their own pace, and value is placed upon the process of learning, not the end product.

9   Record keeping and assessment

An important aspect of our educational system is the evaluation of children's learning. Over the last decade, more and more emphasis has been placed upon the need for teachers to be able to show, in concrete terms, the progress that their children have made. The assessment of pupils' progress has always been a part of a teacher's role, but the introduction of the National Curriculum and the Standard Assessment Tests (SATs) at seven has led many teachers to argue for assessment of children on entry into primary school. If teachers are to be held accountable for their pupils' progress at seven years, then there must be some form of baseline assessment which can help to measure what a child has learned since school entry. The 'value added' factor is an important element in current educational thinking. As a result, the informal assessments of children before statutory schooling has become commonplace and those working with children under compulsory school age are required to assess their children's progress and to prepare records which, if necessary, can be used and made available to a number of people.

The introduction of SATs at seven years and with it the notion of increased accountability has led to a proposal to introduce a National Framework of Assessment for children shortly after they enter school. In spite of the protests, the idea of baseline assessment is not a new one as one of the first assessments was carried out by Isaacs and her colleagues during the 1930s when the Institute of Education, in conjunction with Wiltshire LEA, produced and used an 'infant admission card' for children entering school at five. Assessment has always been part of the early childhood education process, but has in most instances been formative not summative, based on judgements not statistics, and building on children's strengths rather than identifying their weaknesses.

Nursery schools and day nurseries have kept records for many years but these were individually prepared, not standardised. There have been many changes in approach since Walker (1955) carried out her survey, revealing an almost total absence of official nursery records, only nine authorities making any reference to nursery education on their official record forms. These nine nursery forms ranged from records almost identical to those used in infant schools to a brief line in which the only space available was for the name of the nursery. A large part of the records was concerned with the child's health and physical development and few were as complicated as those in existence today. Furthermore, few of the private nurseries or playgroups in the voluntary sector kept any records. However, just as political public interest triggered off a Schools Council project on record keeping in primary schools (Clift, Weiner and Wilson 1981), so at the same time money was being given for funding two projects which were to produce assessment materials for the three- to five-year age range.

As part of an SSRC-funded project based at Keele University, Stephen Tyler (1976) produced the *Keele Pre-School Assessment Guide* (PSAG), while between 1975 and 1978 a team of researchers at the National Foundation for Educational Research (NFER) worked together to produce a *Manual for Assessment in Nursery Education* (Bate *et al.* 1978). The authors of the *Keele PSAG* recommended that records should be designed specifically for individual schools and are convinced of this procedure, whereas the Bate *et al.* manual, because an attempt has been made to standardise the items and produce reliability and validity, warns against adaptation to meet the needs of the individual nursery school or class. Instead, the authors produced a shortened version which, it is suggested, is used on the majority of children, the lengthened form kept for use only with those children whom the teachers feel require extensive assessment. Other records and assessment procedures have been developed over the last decade which will be referred to later. However, before discussing the types of records which may be most appropriate to pre-school education there are a number of issues to consider concerning assessment and the whole concept of evaluation and keeping of records at the two- to five-year-old range.

There are four basic questions which need to be asked with regard to assessment and record keeping in early childhood:

1 Why assess?
2 What aspect of the child's progress is to be assessed?
3 How should we assess children under the age of five years?
4 When and how frequently should assessment take place?

Before tackling our four questions, let us first consider what is meant by the term 'assessment'. In the general sense the term implies 'evaluation', but in most definitions the monetary meaning relating to taxation is implied. I am sure that it is this meaning which hangs over many teachers when they think of assessment as closely linked with accountability, since implicit in the concept of accountability is the idea that children's learning can be demonstrated objectively and convincingly, an idea fundamental to the nineteenth-century system of 'payment by results'. While accepting that teachers need to be accountable for their actions, there are, nevertheless, many special problems in assessing young children so that their knowledge is accurately revealed. Later in the chapter we shall be looking at these special problems in greater detail.

The process of assessment is an integral part of teaching since it provides continuous feedback between educators and learners. In fact the report from the Task Group on Assessment and Testing (DES and SCAA 1988) stressed the fact that assessment was a meaningful part of a child's learning activities. Many of the problems, such as which aspects of the learning process should be focused upon and how they should be measured, are common to education of all age ranges, but they become more complex when the three- to five-year-old range is being considered.

WHY ASSESS?

Let us now return to the question, why do we need to assess children? There are a number of reasons why teachers should want to assess children of any age range. These relate to assessment for the benefit of the child, the school and external agencies.

1 A diagnostic reason, e.g. what is the child's present state as a learner? What are her strengths and weaknesses? How does she cope with any given task, and, even more important, if she cannot cope with the task, what are the reasons for her failure?
2 To match learning opportunities to children's development. Children with special educational needs, including those who are gifted, may be identified and an appropriate programme devised.
3 To find out what children have gained from a particular course of study or activity. Educators may have introduced new teaching methods and strategies in the classroom and wish to know the efficacy of their changes. These changes may have simply involved rearranging the classroom at no extra cost to the school, but some innovatory ideas may be expensive in terms of new materials or pupil–staff ratios, and therefore it is important that some attempt is made to evaluate them.
4 To keep a balance in all areas of the curriculum.
5 An early years educator may need to evaluate either the individual child's progress or a classroom effect, in order to be accountable to the head teacher, parents, school governors, the local education authorities or management committees.

6 To pass on information to other teachers, either in the school or between schools. Pre-school educators need to keep sound records of children's progress in order to have appropriate information ready to transfer with the child when she enters infant school. The importance of comprehensive records is vital in pre-school situations where the children may proceed to several different infant classes and it is difficult to maintain close contact between nursery and infant school. It has been found that some children were not always offered appropriate sequential materials so that they made effective progress in their learning because of lack of forwarding information. In some instances children were found to be repeating activities in the infant classes which they had carried out successfully in the nursery. Longitudinal records should enable teachers to achieve continuity in the children's education.

7 To assist in staff development. It has been suggested in the *Keele PSAG* that individual records can be used as a means of self-evaluation by nursery staff keen on assessing the effect of innovations in materials and on teaching styles.

It is important that these assessments are carried out over a period of time and used to review and evaluate the provision made for the children so that the assessments can form the basis for further assessments. Assessment and record keeping during the years before statutory schooling is for: diagnosis, curriculum planning, liaison and continuity, and staff development.

WHAT SHOULD BE ASSESSED?

With these reasons in mind, let us now turn to the second issue. What should be assessed, and what information should be contained in the records? Should all the records kept by the class teacher/early years worker be transferred to the next teacher in school or should a basic profile be drawn up for long-term information and the nursery-school teacher retain other information for personal use? Should the records be based on standardised tests or should all assessments be criterion referenced, that is, based on the individual child's own performance? Before answering these questions the early years educator needs to decide what skills and concepts the children can be expected to learn by the time they reach compulsory school age, (the term after their fifth birthday). The introduction of the *Desirable Outcomes for Children's Learning* (SCAA 1996b) as a basis for the curriculum in early years settings has provided workers with a focus for their assessments but they are only guidelines and need to be used in a flexible manner.

Early years workers must have a very clear picture in their minds as to what particular information they wish to record about the children's behaviour and performance, and the potential readership. Unless early decisions are made on these issues the records kept are likely to become cumbersome and inefficient. There are few records which can fulfil a number of purposes simultaneously.

Most early years educators, when asked what they wished to record about a child, will reply that they want to build up a profile which shows overall development and includes both the strengths and weaknesses of the child.

Although it is generally agreed that a record on a child should be made from the time of entry into nursery which will be passed on to the next teacher, there is evidence to suggest that nursery staff are justified when they argue that primary schools frequently disregard their carefully thought-out records. Many receiving infant teachers openly state that they do not look at children's records until they have made their own personal assessments. In some ways it can be argued that this is a valid approach but it will most certainly entail repetition and the possibility of periods of boredom for children who may be insufficiently challenged, besides wasting valuable teacher time.

Records made in the pre-school institutions are not solely for the receiving teachers but may be read by parents, governors, management committees and other agencies concerned with the welfare of the child. In deciding what to record about the child's behaviour and performance it is important to remember that the assessments themselves must not dictate the curriculum.

Baseline assessment

In order to meet the curricular needs of their children more and more local education authorities have been introducing some form of baseline assessment so that teachers can understand the children's learning needs and provide a starting point from which their progress through Key Stage 1 can be measured. As a result about half the LEAs in England and Wales undertake some form of baseline assessment. The type of evaluation varies enormously throughout the country and in order to standardise procedures the School Curriculum and Assessment Authority (SCAA) proposed some national frameworks for assessing children on entry into full-time schooling. After a period of consultation it is intended to introduce baseline assessment in 1997.

The SCAA document (1996a) states that the purpose of baseline assessment is to:

- identify the child's strengths and weaknesses
- enable the teacher to plan appropriate teaching and learning activities to meet the child's needs
- identify the child's individual learning needs, including special educational needs
- provide information that will inform discussion with parents about their child's learning and progress.

Not only will this help to assist with curriculum planning and aid accountability but it will form part of a 'value-added' measure.

However, there can be difficulties with baseline assessments, particularly if they are too closely linked to curriculum programmes. Doubts associated with this approach were raised by Maureen Shields, writing in the introduction to the NFER *Manual for Assessment in Nursery Education* (Bate *et al.* 1978) when she pointed out that:

> it is a recognised danger that assessment, instead of producing useful information about children's development and performance, may come to determine what is taught. A central purpose has been to serve the needs of teachers, not to impose external standards on them.

Curricular planning, assessment and record keeping go hand in hand but the principles of the curriculum must be settled first if the danger pointed out by Shields is not to become a reality. Nevertheless, in curriculum evaluation when the aims and objectives have been defined, a record-keeping schedule is a highly effective form of monitoring children's progress on the programme. Schools must therefore decide carefully what information they require and then ask themselves the form in which they wish to have the new information. Not all early childhood educators believe that an aims and objectives model is an effective way of planning an early years curriculum as they believe that this offers the children too restrictive a model; nevertheless, they accept that the institutions must have principles to guide them in their planning.

HOW SHOULD ASSESSMENTS BE CARRIED OUT?

Should they be in the form of a checklist? Should they be in the form of a 'diary description' based on observation of the children, thus building up a profile of the child, or should standardised tests be used?

Before considering which form of record-keeping schedule is the most appropriate for working with the under-five age range let us consider whether there are specific problems relating to assessment of young children. A look at this issue may help towards providing an answer to the 'how' question. Young children are notoriously changeable and although there are problems inherent in assessing children in any age range they are particularly pertinent to assessing children at the pre-school stage. What are these problems?

1 First, there is one major difficulty associated with assessing pre-school children and that is rooted in their stage of development. Many young children show by their behaviour and general understanding that they have a far greater knowledge than their language enables them to express. Therefore, teachers and experienced testers often encounter a situation where the child makes an incorrect response to a question because she has not yet acquired the appropriate language tools to be able to reply correctly.

   Likewise, failure to comply with the requirements of the test may be due to the child's lack of understanding the question, not a lack of understanding the task. Teachers frequently report that children fail to carry out a task, not because it is beyond them intellectually, but because they have misunderstood the instructions. For example, if a four-year-old is asked to 'put all the red beads into the box', she may be perfectly capable of performing the classification exercise that is required, but may not know the meaning of the word 'red' or 'beads' or 'box'. At this stage of development it is very difficult to ascertain accurately the state of the child's knowledge.

2 This is also a period when there are serious limitations in children's thinking, much of which would be considered idiosyncratic by adult standards. If the child fails to see the point of the question, she may refuse to reply, or alternatively respond in a manner which is consistent within her own terms of reference, but may be incorrect as far as the tester is concerned. There is no way of knowing whether she has refused to answer the question because she does not understand, or because she just does not want to reply. This is a very real problem at this stage.

3 Even the most cooperative three- to five-year-old will suffer rapid fatigue and boredom effects in a test situation if it continues for more than a few minutes. The small child has a very limited span of concentration, particularly for tasks that are intellectually demanding – a factor which many test constructors seem to forget.

4 Variables such as the time of day, whether the child is hungry or came to school after a very late night will also affect test performance and although many teachers try to take these into consideration, nevertheless, it is impossible to produce the ideal assessment situation for every child.

5 If the tests that the pre-school child are given are of the formal kind, then there is always the chance that inhibition may occur through fear or

anxiety. Tester effects are discernible even in the most sophisticated adults so one would naturally expect small children to react to a strange tester in an atypical manner. This is why it is very important for assessment of young children to be carried out by their teachers or someone with whom they are very familiar, in spite of the dangers of subjectivity.

6 Other factors, such as the child's own personality or the emotional instability present in the home background, will also affect the emotional state of the child. As educators, we can help the child to relax in the school situation but cannot alleviate stress due to external factors beyond our control. For example, we may have given Mary the same amount of educational input as John, but if her thoughts are centred upon the distressing scene that she had experienced the night before, then it is hardly surprising that there are differences in the two children's educational output.

7 One of the most important variables to affect a child's performance in school, either in a learning or a test situation, is the teacher. There is increasing evidence to suggest that expectations of the early years worker are closely linked to pupil performance. Her relationship with individual children will be a major factor in their progress. This is true of children of all ages, but it is particularly relevant to the nursery-aged child, for whom the adult is, in many instances, a 'mother-substitute'.

In earlier chapters I have discussed how young children learn and the importance of child-initiated learning and this needs to be borne in mind when assessment is taking place. The work of Donaldson and her colleagues (1978) demonstrated the difficulties associated with summative testing, while such theorists as Bruner and Vygotsky have demonstrated the importance of the adult's role in assessing children's development. The 'zone of proximal development', which Vygotsky (1978) termed the difference between what the child can do unaided and what she can do with help, is crucial in planning teaching programmes which will help develop children's skills and concepts.

It is also important to take into account the effects of interaction with other children when assessing children's learning. Research has demonstrated the value of children working together in pairs or small groups and how a much truer estimate of the child's ability can be found when assessing under these conditions rather than when the child is alone. This is particularly true of assessing children's conversational abilities, which is why experienced early years educators attempt to assess children's language skills through structured play or integrated learning situations.

What type of record should be kept?

One of the first questions that needs to be asked before deciding on the format of the record to be used is will the assessments be norm based, that is, will objective standardised tests be used, or will they be criterion referenced? Is the assessment to be seen as formative or summative?

Developmental checklists provide broad norms for children between the ages of two and five and can be regarded as a measure of children's progress over a period of time. The difficulty with this type of summative assessment is that it is not linked in any way to the curriculum. It will provide a broad measure of a child's understanding, but fails to take into account the social context. However, a number of criterion-reference tests have been devised for use with children with mild or moderate learning difficulties. These types of tests, unlike developmental tests, when drawn up by teachers in the schools for a specific school population, are more likely to be linked to the curriculum. Hopefully, schools which are offering children opportunities to develop the skills and competencies laid down in the *Desirable Outcomes for Children's Learning* will devise some form of criterion-reference assessment which relates to the curriculum.

Observations

In the early years most practitioners rely, quite properly, upon observational techniques to help them in the assessment of young children. The early pioneers made extensive longitudinal observations on the children in their care and it was as a result of the careful scrutiny made by Susan Isaacs on the children at Malting House School that she was able to develop an understanding of the psycho-sexual development of children. Assessment based on observations during the daily routine is the most powerful assessment tool available to nursery and infant educators. However, good observation is a skill which has to be learned; it is 'taught not caught'. Many early years workers, after short in-service courses on observation, have been agreeably surprised to see how their appreciation of their children's skills and competencies has changed as a result of careful observation. The child whom you thought worked quietly on her tasks may in reality be one who sits still but does relatively little, whereas another who gives the impression of being a flitter, rushing hither and thither, could be a child who completes many small tasks and is very bright and capable, the reason for the continuous movement being that the child is understretched and as a result completes lots of activities efficiently and competently in a very short space of time. However, in order to ensure that the observations are relevant and of value, it is important that they are structured and placed within a relevant framework.

Some very sound advice was written for teachers wanting to improve their observations of children by the Schools Council project on *Record Keeping in the Primary School* (Clift, Weiner and Wilson 1981).

1 Determine in advance what to observe but be alert for unusual behaviour.
2 Observe and record enough of the situation to make the behaviour meaningful.
3 Make a record of the incident as soon after the observation as possible.
4 Limit each anecdote to a brief description of a single incident.
5 Keep the factual description of the incident and your interpretation of it separate. Use only non-judgemental words in the description.
6 Record both negative and positive behavioural incidents.
7 Collect a number of anecdotes on a pupil before drawing inferences concerning typical behaviour.

The value of assessment by observation in early childhood education cannot be overemphasised as it is only through observation that the teacher can begin to ask the very pertinent questions – can the child do this particular task and how does the child go about the task so that it can be seen why that particular end result has been achieved?

The ways in which observations are recorded will differ from nursery to nursery. In one they may use the 'specimen description' approach such as that advocated by Lesley Webb (1974), whereas in others it may be felt that this descriptive-narrative approach is too lengthy and the 'target-child' approach used in the Oxfordshire Pre-school Project may be preferred. The target-child approach devised by Sylva, Roy and Painter (1980) enables the observer to focus on one particular child and chart her actions, language and behaviour with either adults or other children in a systematic yet straightforward manner. I have found that using this method with teachers on diploma courses has led to them focusing much more appropriately on the behaviours, language and activities of individual children. Some institutions prefer to develop their own schedules, but it must be remembered that any instrument which is too elaborate will not only take up more staff time but will produce minutiae irrelevant to the normal assessment requirements. Nevertheless, in using any observation schedule, staff should be aware that the instrument itself will focus their attention on specific behaviours and they need to use their present knowledge of the children to complete the profile.

Individual child profile

In drawing up a profile of each individual child, the teacher needs to consider the various skills and competencies that they would expect to be acquired during the pre-school years. Many schools are now producing checklists based on the areas of learning recognised by the DfEE in their guidelines: personal and social development; language and literacy; mathematics; knowledge and understanding of the world; physical development; and creative development. Others are basing their assessments upon links with the National Curriculum (e.g. *Baseline*, Wandsworth LEA (1993)).

An individual profile will not only include information on the child's performance in the curriculum areas, but must contain information on the child's health and something of her family background, factual information which will be helpful to future teachers, as well as examples of the child's work. The types of profiles suggested in the *Keele PSAG* (Tyler 1976) and the early learning model of Curtis and Wignall (1980) may also be helpful to teachers. The latter concentrates on helping teachers diagnose strengths as well as weaknesses with practical suggestions as to how to support children's learning.

All about Me (Wolfendale 1990)

This is a record of development and progress used in many nurseries and early childhood institutions which enables parents to note down and record their children's developmental progress. It is essentially a record for the family and provides parents with a basis for discussion with a teacher in nursery or infant class, a nursery worker or playgroup leader about their child's progress. It covers seven main areas of development in children from two to six years of age including language; playing and learning; doing things by myself; physical development; health and habits; other people; and how I behave, moods and feelings. It is designed to be used either as a baseline for entering school/nursery or as part of a continuous profile involving parents, early childhood education workers and children. As its title implies, *All About Me* is written from the point of view of the child.

Early Milestones (Waller and Brito 1992)

This is another checklist, derived from *All about Me*, which is intended to be completed by parents and child, covering the following areas: getting to know me and my family; everyday I learn something new; getting ready for school; more about my child. It was originally prepared for a specific school but has now been published by Letterland.

Profiles based on teacher descriptions have been developed in a number of LEAs in conjunction with experienced teachers and nursery staff. One which is particularly useful is the early years profile produced by the Kensington and Chelsea Education Department, which has close links with the National Curriculum and the DfEE areas of learning. This profile encourages focused observations of children's behaviour combined with sensitive recordings of key 'moments of learning'. The profile is divided into sections: background information; settling in; emotional and social development; physical development; communication, language and literacy; mathematical development; scientific and technological development; creative and spiritual development; moral and spiritual awareness; attitude and approach to learning.

A number of LEAs have experimented with child-assessment profiles in which the children's likes and dislikes, activity preferences and routines are recorded along with an assessment of their skills. One example of this is the early years profile produced for Walsall (Wragg 1991) in which the areas noted are: self-help and independence; play; fine motor; number; reading skills; gross motor; nursery/classroom routine; problem solving; organisational ability; listening skills.

Another example of an early years record developed in conjunction with an institution of higher education and an LEA is the classroom observation notebook and parent discussion record (Steirer 1991). This identifies six broad areas of children's learning which should be the focus of the classroom observations. These are: investigation; use of strategies; representation; communication; interaction; and attitudes. The parent discussion record places emphasis upon discussions with parents being 'real conversations' in which parents and staff share their understanding of the child's development. It is intended that these observations and discussions should form the rationale for a summative record of the child's development and provide a 'baseline' at five against which it will be possible to chart progress at the end of Key Stage 1. Records which ask about children's likes and dislikes are often very revealing for both parents and early years staff, as frequently parents discover that they do not know their child as well as they thought they did.

Even though the nursery vouchers have disappeared, the inspection of nurseries and playgroups will continue and all early childhood institutions will be making some form of assessment of their children. However, the actual type of record-keeping system used in a particular nursery will depend upon a number of factors: whether there is a standard local education authority policy; the relations between the pre-school and the primary institutions; and the attitudes of the staff towards assessment and curriculum. As was pointed out earlier, there is a link between the curriculum and the content of the assessment schedules. It follows, therefore, that where a standard record-keeping system exists throughout a local education authority one can make implicit assumptions about the structure and content of the nursery curriculum in that area. Records based on tight checklists are likely to be associated with nurseries in which fairly organised and structured programmes take place. Nurseries which accept that some form of structuring is necessary during their day use their records as a continuous basis upon which to plan their work programme, assessment by observation being particularly helpful to teachers in their evaluation, not only of their own programmes but in seeing what the children can actually do, and not what the staff assume the children can do.

When and how often should children be assessed during the pre-school years?

Assessment seen in terms of evaluating the programme is a continuous process; the feedback received by the teachers will continually affect their reactions to the curriculum being provided. However, assessment which is part of the child's total profile which is recorded and passed on to the next teacher in school should not be carried out too frequently. Most assessment guides recommend that no attempt to evaluate progress should take place until the child has been in school for at least half a term, and the NFER *Manual for Assessment in Nursery Education* (Bate *et al.* 1978) suggests six-monthly intervals between assessment. The recommendations of SCAA for baseline assessment of children entering reception classes is that assessment should be carried out within the first half-term of a child entering primary school even though the child may still be attending only part time, the argument for this being that any delay in assessing the child could result in the teacher being unable to plan effectively for the child's learning needs. The majority of early years workers would agree that assessment should not take place too soon after a child has entered an educational setting and many, like myself, are concerned that for children entering the primary school at barely four years of age the first few weeks of term is too soon to assess them, particularly if they have come straight from home. In the SCAA document it is recommended that it is good practice for assessment information and records taken during pre-school provision to be used in conjunction with the baseline assessment information. If this occurs, then this should satisfy some of the complaints of early years workers that the receiving schools ignore their records.

Reliability in assessments

When assessments of children are based solely on observations it is important to be aware that we may be biased in our perception of individual children. We may perceive some children as being more cooperative, linguistically able, and so on than others, and for this reason it is valuable to involve more than one person in assessing children. This is relatively easy in nursery schools and classes, but may prove more difficult in playgroups and other early childhood settings. Gipps (1982) found that there were considerable discrepancies between nursery teachers' and nursery nurses' perceptions of children's behaviour and abilities, a factor that must be taken into account if assessments based on observation are to have any reliability. Furthermore, joint assessment in a nursery can lead to fruitful discussion and clarification of views of various aspects of the children's performance and of the curriculum.

IN CONCLUSION

In this chapter I have attempted to raise and answer questions concerned with record keeping in the pre-school years. Issues related to why, when and how we should assess children in this age range have been considered before discussing the type of record which might be the most appropriate in the early years of schooling. As has been pointed out, there are special problems and difficulties associated with record keeping and the monitoring of performance in pre-school classrooms, and before drawing up a schedule or profile the early years worker needs to consider:

1 What aspects of the child's development should be measured.
2 The form of assessment to be used.
3 Whether help should be given in making the assessment in order to ensure reliability of observations.
4 What she intends to do with the information gathered.
5 How frequently the assessments are to be made.
6 What, if any, changes need to take place in the classroom in order that the children can progress more effectively.
7 What form parental comments should take.
8 Whether children's views should be taken into account.

Records which take into consideration these factors will be of value not only to the staff in the early childhood settings but to the receiving infant teachers, and should ensure continuity of progress for all children as they pass from non-compulsory to compulsory schooling.

10 Parents and their children's learning

One of the most important changes that has taken place since the first edition of this book has been the introduction of legislation which has given recognition to the role of parents in their children's education. However, the awareness of the importance of parents, particularly mothers, in their children's education is not a new phenomenon.

Over the centuries the influence of mothers in young children's learning has been recognised. More than 300 years ago Comenius was writing about the 'school of the Mother's lap', arguing that parents should systematically educate their children during the first six years of life. He advocated that mothers should tell stories and rhymes to their young children.

For many years, parents, particularly mothers, have been involved in the education of their children at the nursery-school stage; however, in the years before the Second World War much of the advice was related to health and hygiene. The Hadow Report on Nursery and Infant Schools (Consultative Comittee 1931) noted with satisfaction the benefits of teachers talking to parents about health and hygiene, the official view being that many homes were lacking in knowledge and understanding of these issues and needed support and information from the schools.

As Docking (1990) pointed out, parents were traditionally seen as problems. The original elementary schools had been set up to ensure that the children of the poor were saved from parental moral decadence and in the early years of the twentieth century teachers were urging parents to adopt the values of the school, particularly with regard to moral and physical welfare.

Although there were still many teachers who saw parents as clients who needed the support of the professional, during the 1960s two important events occurred which were to influence the attitudes of early years teachers towards parental support and learning. The first of these was the publication of the Plowden Report (Central Advisory Council for

Education 1967) which gave the first official recognition in this country to the importance of the parental contribution in their children's schooling. In the report it was written that:

> One of the essentials for educational advance is a closer partnership between the two parties (i.e. schools and parents) to every child's education.
>
> (Central Advisory Council for Education 1967, para. 102, p. 37).

The second event was the founding of the playgroup movement. The introduction of Circular 8/60 (Department of Education and Science), which banned the expansion of nursery-school places, prompted Belle Tutaev to write her now famous letter to the *Guardian* newspaper in 1962 encouraging mothers to get together to provide play opportunities for their children either in or outside the home. From this beginning the playgroup movement grew into an elaborate organisation, now called the Preschool Learning Alliance. At its inception parents were always practically involved in their children's play but over the years there has been a gradual movement away from involving parents on a regular basis and towards the establishment of playgroups employing full-time supervisors and regular helpers. The playgroup worker is no longer an amateur voluntary helper, but is fast becoming a qualified early years worker. However, in the majority of playgroups there is a high level of parental involvement in the day-to-day activities of the children.

In spite of this official recognition of the parents' role, the belief still existed that parents did not support the school or share its values. In the 1970s parents were blamed for the impoverished language used by their children. Research such as that of Tough (1977), Bernstein (1971) and the Bullock Report (Department of Education and Science 1975) advocated that teachers should try to influence the language used in working-class homes and attempt to 'improve' children's language in the classroom by providing appropriate models. This approach, which will be discussed more fully later in this chapter, is based on a 'language-deficit' model which has been challenged by the work of Wells (1984; 1987) and Tizard and Hughes (1984) who looked closely at the language used in the home and the school by parents from different social-class backgrounds.

The Head Start programmes for the disadvantaged children in the USA, and others in the UK and Europe, were set up to enrich the language and cognitive skills of children from disadvantaged homes. However, it was soon recognised that without parental support and involvement the programmes were ineffective as the children failed to maintain any of the progress they had made. Once there was parental involvement there was a greater possibility of children maintaining long-term gains from such programmes.

These programmes, as with those in Belgium and Holland, demonstrated how the effects of education are likely to be more positive once the child is considered in the context of the family and community.

In spite of evidence to the contrary, a 'language-deficit' approach is still held by many early years teachers whose attitude to many children is, 'What do you expect? They come from that estate.' Many children have poor language skills when they enter primary schools, but this may be due to such factors as television and video rather than poor parental language. There are many middle-class homes where the television/video is on all day and very young children are seated in front of it for hours at a time and their language is not always at the level anticipated by teachers of middle-class children.

Official recognition of the role of parents in their children's education was given in the Education Acts of 1980, 1981, 1986 and 1988, all of which refer to aspects of the relationship between home and school such as choice of school, involvement in assessment, representation on governing bodies and access to information. Side by side with this increase in the involvement of parents with their children's education, these Acts introduced the concept of 'accountability' of schools to parents. All schools now have parent representation on the governing bodies; and early childhood institutions in both the public and the voluntary sector have management committees which include parent representation, as do many private institutions.

In spite of government legislation there are still educators who hold the view that parents are problems. Even in the playgroup movement, where parents and educators have traditionally worked together, there are workers who prefer to cope with the children without parental interference, an approach which can be found in all sections of early childhood provision. There still exists a wide gulf between the official government view of parents as consumers and the reality. Legislation cannot change attitudes overnight.

However, just as there are differences in the attitudes of early childhood workers towards partnership with parents, so there are differences between parents and their expectations. Hughes *et al.* (1994) found that not all parents wanted the close cooperation with the schools advocated by government legislation. The consumer model does not necessarily satisfy all parents.

The Elton Report (Great Britain Committee of Enquiry into Discipline in Schools 1989) focused upon the importance of parental involvement as a useful mechanism to improve the relationship between home and school and recommended that 'parents should take full advantage of all formal and informal channels of communication made available by the schools'.

However, this advice, sound as it is, still places the emphasis upon the parent rather than the school, which seems to be the official approach.

WHAT IS PARENTAL INVOLVEMENT?

Before we look more closely at the role of parents in their children's education any further, let us consider what is meant by parental involvement. For parents to be involved in their children's education they need to be seen as partners not clients.

Wolfendale (1983, p. 15) was one of the first to raise this issue and discuss it at length. She pointed out that parents have traditionally been viewed and dealt with as clients and not as partners.

She argued that the client concept implies that:

- parents are dependent upon experts' opinions (paid professionals, books, official sources of information)
- parents are passive in the receipt of services
- parents are apparently in need of redirection
- parents are peripheral to decision making
- parents are perceived as 'inadequate, deficient'.

In contrast the partner concept includes these characteristics:

- parents are active and central in decision making and its implementation
- parents are perceived as having equal strengths and equivalent expertise
- parents are able to contribute to, as well as receive, services (reciprocity)
- parents share responsibility, thus they and professionals are mutually accountable.

The concept of reciprocity, a central issue in Wolfendale's argument, is one which goes further than much of the government legislation which sees parents as consumers to whom schools should be accountable. All the studies that have looked carefully at the effect of involvement of parents in their children's education demonstrate the effect of mutual benefit. It is not only helpful to the educational institution for them to understand and know about all aspects of the child, it is also valuable to the parent to be able to understand the aspects of their child's life which take place within the institutional setting. Reciprocity involves mutual involvement, mutual accountability and mutual gain, all seen within the wider context of the community, the society and culture in which the child lives.

In practical terms this view of partnership is about professionals respecting the knowledge and understanding that parents have of their children and about parents acknowledging that staff know about children and their development. Children can only benefit when each partner talks and listens to the other. Many working in early childhood institutions complain that it is very difficult to involve parents when they are working. This can pose a problem, but it is one which must be overcome as, increasingly, early childhood institutions will find themselves in situations where both parents are working, either full or part time. One way of making closer links between home and school is to organise workshops/ meetings for parents in the early evening. If the nursery provides crèche facilities they may well find that working parents will come with their children. Another obvious way is the use of the newsletter, although this is not as useful as face-to-face contact.

PARENTAL INVOLVEMENT IN PRACTICE

At a basic level it can be just bringing and collecting the children each day and passing pleasantries with the staff member. This type of meeting enables the staff to discuss the daily activities with the parent and to focus upon strengths and weaknesses. A valuable link between home and school, but is this enough?

There are a number of ways in which parents can become involved in their children's education. The most usual are the traditional approaches of fund raising; helping on outings and day trips; cleaning paint pots or tidying up at the end of the session (children should be doing most of this themselves); reading stories to children; helping in the classroom and working with small groups for such activities as cooking or clay modelling.

With the introduction of Baseline Assessment in Primary Schools and the focus upon the *Desirable Outcomes for Children's Learning* (SCAA 1996b) there is the possibility that more and more early childhood institutions will aim to involve parents in the curriculum as they try to explain how the various nursery activities help to underpin the knowledge content required by the government guidelines. The concept of parental involvement is a complex one and one which requires staff in early childhood institutions to think hard about how they can support parents and ways in which parents can support them.

More recently, various Acts of Parliament have formalised an informal structure and legislated first for parents to be on the governing bodies, and then, with the changes emerging from the 1988 Education Act, gave parents the opportunity to be partners in the business of running their children's schools. Such a partnership, although in theory ideal, has not happened to any great extent in practice as the vast majority of parents have been deterred from becoming involved not only because of the amount of time required, but because many are unwilling to take on the legal responsibility involved in becoming a school governor. At present, in spite of a major recruitment campaign by the Department for Education and Employment (DfEE) there is still a severe shortage of parent governors. This shortage of parent involvement is common not only to the state school system but to many sectors of early childhood: where many parents pay, they do not want to become involved in any way in the running of the institution.

The idea of parents as consumers of education may be difficult to accept for parents and teachers involved with children of statutory school age. But in the early years sector workers are well aware that the parents are consumers: a philosophy which may well be alien to many working in that field.

There are, though, parents in the second half of the 1990s who still think in the same way as the mother interviewed by the Newsons in 1977 who, when asked if she helped her child, replied:

> Not since going to the school and talking to the teacher. I found out that we were doing the wrong thing, teaching him in a different way you see, so it's best to leave it alone.

> (Newson, *et al.* 1997, p. 145)

I know only too well the feeling of that parent. When in the 1960s I first took my elder daughter to school and dared to tell the head teacher that she could read, his reply was, 'We will be the judge of that!' His words and the tone he used have been with me ever since, a salutary reminder of how not to treat parents.

Even if parents may not want to get involved with the day-to-day running of the school they are still very concerned about knowing what their children are learning.

PARENTS AND THE CURRICULUM

Government documentation has legislated for parents on governing bodies and it is therefore likely that there will be parents on subcommittees looking at curriculum issues. They will certainly wish to be kept fully informed about the inspections which all early childhood settings will be receiving in the future and in the self-appraisal forms which all institutions outside the state education sector are required to complete. In state nursery schools and classes parents as members of the governing body may meet with the OFSTED inspectors and receive the final reports. OFSTED inspectors may well want to discuss curriculum issues with parent governors.

It is interesting to note that in Denmark, where there is no central curriculum for early childhood education, there is a tradition of educators working in cooperation with the parents and the children to create their own curriculum. In Denmark every year the educators, in collaboration with parents, have to formulate the 'plan of activity', the only centralised document which exists.

In other European countries, such as France and Belgium, parents are encouraged to participate in their children's early education but their role is restricted to committees; few parents actually participate in classroom activities. One of the changes that has come about in the Eastern European countries in the last few years relates to the amount of involvement which parents can have in their children's education. Prior to the political changes parents had little or no say in what happened within the kindergarten as there was a very centralised curriculum. Nowadays, however, according to Graziene (1995), there are more individual learning programmes and the voices of parents may be heard. For instance in Lithuania, where there have been sweeping reforms in the approach to early childhood education, the kindergarten has changed its functions: it has become a family helper, not the opposite, as it used to be before the reforms when the kindergarten system seemed to exist just for its own benefit. Now the parents can suggest things, express their requests and thoughts. Parents decide when to take the child to the kindergarten; they may refuse to take meals and not pay for them; at their request, their children may not be put to sleep at bedtime; if a child misses a day parents do not pay for that day and so on. Parents as partners in the educational process is also becoming part of life in the Polish kindergartens, where teachers trained under a different philosophy are finding it difficult to cope with the changes afoot.

THE ROLE OF PARENTS IN THEIR CHILDREN'S LITERACY DEVELOPMENT

There are few areas of development which raise as much concern for parents, teachers and governments as the development of literacy skills. Research studies in the 1960s and 1970s suggested that many children were coming into school with a 'language deficit' with little or no understanding of early literacy development. Questions were asked as to why some children came into school highly verbal and enthusiastic to begin reading while others wanted to learn to read but had few of the prerequisite skills to enable them to start to 'learn to read'.

This prompted research into the factors in the home which contributed to children's literacy development. One of the most important studies of this kind was the Bristol Longitudinal Language Development Research Programme under the direction of Gordon Wells. As part of this research Moon and Wells (1979) carried out a study of twenty children over two years prior to their entry into school to find out what literacy practices and events the children and their parents were involved in at home. They found that there was a close association between parents' interests and provision of resources for literacy and teachers' assessments of children's reading. There was no doubt that children's knowledge about books and literacy before school was largely acquired through what parents and children did together at home, and this correlated highly with later reading ability. Throughout this longitudinal study it was the level of parents' encouragement for literacy that most fully explained the differences in children's progress in reading.

As part of the study, Wells also looked at language development (Wells 1987). He studied thirty-two pre-school children over several years and found that differences in oral language ability declined in importance once the children reached school age, but children's abilities associated with written language (both reading and writing) were most significant. He found that the understanding of written language was acquired by young children through experiences at home. Wells contrasted the number of stories read to two children from the study; one child had at least four stories read to her every day, while the other had none at all. Just reflect upon how many stories the first child would have heard before entering school by the age of five compared with the second child. Equally, even if both children had been at a nursery where stories were the norm, it is unlikely that the second one could go any way towards catching up, partly because the child accustomed to stories at home is more likely to demand stories from the nursery staff than one who has never been exposed to stories and therefore is only likely to hear stories in a group situation, not in a one-to-one relationship.

Wells' work, as with that of others, showed clearly that children with limited pre-school literacy experiences had less understanding about print and the purpose of literacy than their peers from more literate homes, and the more children know at the beginning of school with the help of their parents and families the more likely they are to cope with lessons in school.

Another study which looked at the effect of parental influences upon children's literary development was carried out by Tizard *et al.* (1988). They studied children from inner London, many from disadvantaged homes, and found that the best predictor for reading at the end of the infant school was the children's ability to identify letters when they were nearly five years old. The children had not been taught their letters by rote, but investigation showed that the parents of these children provided them with more exposure to print through having books and papers in the home which they read to the children. They also had a positive attitude towards helping their children. This led to the children scoring highly on reading and writing tests.

Similar findings were produced in the USA where Snow (1991) investigated the achievements of disadvantaged children and found that the most powerful predictors of word recognition and vocabulary were the literary environments and the mothers' expectations. Likewise, Hannon *et al.* (1991) showed similar findings from the Elmswood study.

Weinberger (1996, p. 30) has summarised some of the important processes developed by parents in the home which have a direct bearing on later literacy development. These include:

- the availability of literacy materials in the home
- parents creating literacy learning opportunities outside the home
- parental encouragement of literacy
- parental expectations of their child and their child's schooling
- frequency with which parents read with their children and teach them about literacy
- parental contact with school and knowledge about school
- frequency of library visits
- extent of book ownership and the variety of print materials in the home
- the literacy environment generally of the home and parents reading themselves
- the children's knowledge of letters pre-school
- the frequency of storytelling at home.

Other factors included: social class; parents' educational level; and family income.

There have been a number of other studies which have indicated that an understanding of letter names is positively associated with early literacy development. Ehri (1983) found that in the USA kindergarten children who could name eight letters had no problem in learning letter–sound associations, but it was impossible to do this with children who could not name eight letters. She also found that many children acquired this knowledge of letters before they started school. They had not been taught systematically but had gained the information incidentally through general language, asking questions and seeing print around the home. Researchers have also found that there is a relationship between phonological awareness, knowledge of nursery rhymes and children's subsequent reading achievement. This implies that parents who repeat nursery rhymes to children on a regular basis in the home are helping their children to acquire literacy skills.

Overall we can see that there is a link between parental interest in literacy and children's ability to become literate. There is also indication that parents have an important part to play in encouraging children's writing development. The Tizard *et al.* study (1988) has also shown that parental help with writing at the pre-school stage is related to children's handwriting at school entry. Almost 50 per cent of the parents in this study had taught their children to write their names and other words, while 40 per cent had taught them to write their names only.

HOW DO PARENTS HELP THEIR CHILDREN'S LITERACY DEVELOPMENT?

The vast majority of parents are interested in their children learning to read. Ask any parent what they want most from a nursery and it is almost always that their child learns to get on with others and learns to read. Many parents are keen on developing numeracy skills, but the vast majority will tell you that the most important thing is for children to learn to read. This can put pressure upon nurseries and playgroups to ensure that children are not being hot-housed into reading too early, raising the question of whether children should begin to read before they start primary school. The skills and competencies that young children need before they are ready to read a book develop gradually. It is the role of the early years educator to help parents understand the importance of their role in developing these skills and competencies.

From the early childhood educationalist point of view the study by Weinberger (1996) is one of the best in demonstrating the role of parents in their children's literacy development during the pre-school years. In this study an attempt was made to look at the differences between the literacy experiences that children gain at home and those obtained at school. The Elmswood study, which was based on sixty children, all aged three, whose parents were visited in the home, found that there are three main ways in which parents support their children's literacy development.

First, she found that parents provided resources and opportunities for access to print. The major resources included print in the home in the form of books, mail-order catalogues, comics, newspapers, magazines and printed materials that arrive unsolicited through letterboxes. Almost all the children had access to children's books at home, some they owned, others were borrowed from the library. It was also interesting that many parents did not see their cookery or gardening books as reading material. Much of the reading material was very different from what children would expect to find at school, although it was still reading material.

Some parents told their children stories, keeping to the oral tradition of storytelling; this was particularly true of children whose mother tongue was not English. Here, the parent often told a story in the mother tongue to maintain the cultural heritage. Other resources found in the home to foster literacy development included drawing and writing materials, games and resources linked with literacy, including: matching and sorting games; animal-sound games; flash cards; alphabet cards; pictures with words underneath; jigsaws; magnetic letters; post-office sets; cutting and sticking, including old catalogues; computers and toy computers. Many of these games were seen as entertaining and not as ones which encouraged literacy development.

The second way in which parents supported their children was to act as models for literacy. Just as parents are models for other behaviour so they are for reading and writing. When children see their parents reading and writing they are unconsciously absorbing lessons about what it is to be a reader or writer. A home where reading and writing is part of family life and where newspapers, magazines and books are left around will have a positive effect upon children's literacy development. Parents generate a lot of writing at home including: writing shopping lists, directions, crosswords, keeping a diary and making appointments, notes, cheques, bills, letters, word processing and writing for work, filling in football coupons, DSS forms, cards and accounts.

Children will copy their parents' behaviour and therefore, as professionals, we must provide material of this type at nursery in the writing corners so that children can bring the ideas from home and realise that we, as educators, do the same things as their parents.

The third area in which parents were found to encourage literacy development related to the literacy practices and events in which they engaged with their children. Weinberger found that the most common was to read to their children, normally at bedtime, although many parents will also read to their child after lunch or during a mid-morning break. Children have their favourite books and many learn to memorise the text and try to act like a reader; from this they frequently begin to see themselves as readers from memorising the text. Many a two-year-old will sit with a book, often turned upside down to 'read' the story which is known off by heart. Children of three or four will 'read' to their younger siblings at bedtime. Parents who run their fingers along the text as they read to their children may well find their children doing the same. It is from hearing stories read to them that children learn the conventional phrases that start stories such as 'One day' or 'Once upon a time'. At this stage in their literacy development children do not read the text, but what they have is an understanding that text conveys meaning, one of the first stages in learning to read.

Many parents find themselves teaching their children to read unintentionally, as through being talked and read to, the child has started to read without any formal instruction. There are, of course, some parents who try to teach their children to read, but these are in the minority. Similarly, in the nursery school some children will have learned to read but it has not been a conscious act by staff as when a planned and intentional method is used to teach children to read in primary school.

Developing writing skills is not something that most parents want to do and certainly most schools do not wish it to occur, although it is valuable to a child if they are allowed to develop writing naturally. In the Elmswood study many parents, if they did help their children to write, encouraged them to trace letters and guided their hand to follow dots to complete a pattern. The effect of lack of information can lead to many misconceptions about writing and it may well be that we should be giving parents more information on how children develop writing skills and help them to understand that the early scribbles play an important part in learning to write.

ENVIRONMENTAL PRINT

Most people would agree that children need to learn to read environmental print, but as yet there is no firm evidence to suggest that reading environmental print has a positive effect upon later literacy although common sense would suggest this to be so. Another way in which Weinberger found that parents teach reading and writing is through environmental print. Advertising logos and copy are among the most common. When they are out shopping the parent is likely to say to a child, 'Can you go and get me a packet of Weetabix from the shelf?' Children first identify the packet by colour and picture, but gradually will begin to recognise some of the letters.

This study, as in other studies carried out into children's literacy development before school, showed that young children have learned a great deal about literacy before joining the nursery and therefore well before the start of compulsory schooling. If, as the evidence suggests, parents are able to offer such a rich literary environment then it is vital that the children in institutional settings before the age of three are given the same type of language-rich environment.

Along with literacy development, many children begin to develop basic mathematical and scientific concepts at home. The role of the professional is to build on this knowledge and to encourage parents to work with the school in the best interests of the child. What can early childhood institutions do to engage the fullest support of parents and what do parents want?

Nursery education has a long history of working closely with parents in a positive and constructive manner. Earlier in this chapter the concept of partnership was discussed and the need for reciprocity was stressed. In the *Desirable Outcomes for Children's Learning* (SCAA 1996b) it is pointed out that to be a successful partnership there must be a two-way process, with opportunities for knowledge, expertise and information to flow both ways. Some of the key features underlying sound partnerships between early childhood institutions and parents include:

- parents' fundamental role in their child's education is acknowledged by staff in the institution
- recognition of the role that parents have already played in the early education of their child and that their continued involvement is crucial to successful learning
- parents feel welcome and there are opportunities for collaboration among parents, staff and children
- recognition of the expertise of parents and other adults in the family and this expertise is used to support the learning opportunities provided within the institution
- adults working in the institution give parents access to information about curriculum in a variety of ways
- parents contribute to and are kept fully informed of their child's progress and achievements
- admission procedures are flexible to allow time for discussion with parents and for children to feel secure in the new setting
- opportunities for learning provided in the institution are sometimes provided at home, e.g. reading and sharing books, and experiences initiated at home are sometimes used as stimuli for learning in the institution.

Few would disagree with these guidelines to good practice as the child will only develop her full potential when school and home work in close collaboration. Studies such as Elmswood help to make practitioners aware of the positive support that children can receive from language-rich home environments, but they also highlight the potential problems that face children coming from impoverished literarcy environments.

PARENTS AT TRANSITION

When children move from pre-school institutions into statutory schooling, parents have a vital role to play. At all transition stages the role of the parent is important, but it is particularly so when children enter into the primary school. In the next chapter we shall be looking at this in greater detail.

11 Continuity: from pre-school to statutory schooling

The transition from pre-school to compulsory schooling is one of the most important changes that will occur in a child's life. The attitudes adopted by both children and parents to the new environment are likely to have far-reaching effects upon later educational progress. In a country where there exists such a wide variety of pre-school services it is inevitable that there will be differences in ethos and approach between the various pre-school and primary institutions. Awareness of these differences and the possible effects upon the children and their families has resulted in research studies both in Britain and elsewhere looking at the issues arising from this break in the child's life.

In 1977 the Council of Europe made a survey of the twenty-one member states which resulted in recommendations being produced which stressed improving 'vertical continuity', that is, trying to offset the discontinuities which occur when the child transfers from pre-school to primary education; the recommendations are still to be effected. The issue of continuity is one which continues to exercise educationalists throughout Europe.

The Department of Education and Science commissioned a study carried out by the NFER to look at the importance of these breaks in the child's life. This study (Cleave, Jowett and Bate 1982) indicated clearly that vertical discontinuity existed for children transferring from pre-school education to the first phase of schooling. What is more, it demonstrated that, unless the transfer is carried out smoothly, children can, and do, experience anxiety and stress, ingredients likely to produce negative effects on the children's learning at the beginning of primary education. From our knowledge of the way children learn and develop new strategies and understanding we are all aware that discontinuity can play a valuable part in learning. However, the problem has been well expressed by McVickers-Hunt (1961) when he pointed out that one of the major difficulties encountered by the teacher was the 'problem of the match'.

Discontinuity in the form of a new stimulating experience within a secure framework is an excellent way of extending the child's learning and understanding but to obtain optimum benefit the incongruity must not be too great, otherwise it will produce a 'boomerang effect' and little or no learning will take place.

In this chapter I want to consider how best this problem can be dealt with within the school situation. Transfer from pre-school to primary education will inevitably present children with some form of discontinuity but there is no reason why this should not be seen as a positive piece of learning and not the traumatic experience encountered by some children.

There is a wide disparity in the age at which children commence their infant stage of schooling in this country. In some areas the new entrant is barely four years of age, while in others the child may have reached statutory school age, the term after the fifth birthday, the variance resulting from the individual policies of each local education authority. There will naturally be a big difference in the behaviour and abilities of the children who are barely four years of age and those who have turned five years, but both groups may experience problems if the transfer is not handled sensitively.

Certain discontinuities when children come from home or pre-school institutions to primary school are inevitable but in the next few pages an attempt will be made to identify some of these discontinuities which, although they may not always be removed, may at least be taken account of when dealing with the new entrant into statutory schooling. The chapter will end with a section containing guidelines which may be of help to pre-school and primary educators involved in the transfer process. Progress from pre-school to primary education should be seen as a continuous process in the child's total learning. The introduction of the *Desirable Outcomes for Children's Learning* (SCAA 1996b) can be seen as an attempt to ensure that there is continuity between the child's learning experiences in the two stages of schooling, as there are definite links between these outcomes and the National Curriculum.

WHAT ARE THE POTENTIAL DISCONTINUITIES?

In my view, there are four identifiable areas in which children may experience the type of lack of continuity which could lead to anxiety and distress and thus hinder later learning. The first and most obvious is the change in the physical environment and how it affects the child's movements; the second relates to the differences in classroom organisation in the two environments. The last two are concerned with discontinuities which could produce longer-term deleterious effects upon the child – that of curriculum content and the differing ideologies of the pre-school and infant educators.

Physical environment

The actual buildings in which schools are housed are varied and diverse: some will be lofty and Victorian with endless corridors, while others will be single-storey open-plan units. But whatever their architectural design there is a good chance that they will be strange to most children entering formal schooling for the first time. Even in those schools where the nursery class forms an integral part of the building, it is likely that there have been few opportunities to explore the remaining part of the school. Nursery classes are generally placed in a corner of the building with their own entrance, playground, and so on, and from the child's point of view can be as remote from the rest of the school as if she were in a nursery unit across a playground or on a different site.

The impact of the school architecture will naturally vary according to the children's previous experience. For some whose pre-school education has taken place in a large church hall or an expansive nursery where there has been plenty of room to run around, the new 'box-like classroom' may be inhibiting and restrictive of movement, while, for others, the lofty ceiling and long corridors may be totally intimidating. However, not all infant schools have 'box-like classrooms'; many are built on an open plan, providing large areas of space to allow for a flexible and stimulating environment. The children may have freedom to move around, but are they the best places to give the youngest children the sense of security which is one of their most important needs? In a Ministry of Education Building Bulletin (1955) it was written, 'sometimes we forget how near the ground children do in fact live' and how important it is for them to have their own self-contained area until they can gradually become accustomed to the school community.

The physical activity of some children may be curtailed as a result of entering the traditional classroom but research has suggested that small children may take longer to settle in open-plan schools. Among the earliest studies was an appraisal of the Eveline Lowe School in London, one of the newly designed schools of the 1960s which aimed at catering for children's needs in the light of the current knowledge of child development. This study showed that even when the children were well settled in an open-plan situation, they did not scatter around the school as their teachers had expected, but rather tended to stay with their own teacher, only moving away as far as the nearby teachers and their groups of children. The young children, four- and five-year-olds in particular, sought the security and comfort they needed in their own 'home corners' (DES 1972b). For them, a small part of the school had become familiar and they tended to stay in that area.

Neill and Denham (1982) looked at the effect of building design on the behaviour of staff and children and suggested that in the more closed unit situation staff and children are more likely to interact, whereas in large open-plan units it was the children who had to seek out the staff. Neill and Denham pointed out that in the open-plan situation staff tended to oversee rather than interact with the children. Whatever their previous experiences, whether they have come from playgroups, nursery schools, classes in units, day nurseries or directly from a home setting, all children need to feel secure in their physical environment. At four and five years of age the world can be a very frightening place if you are faced with too many strange and unfamiliar things and faces.

One of the features of the physical environment which causes many children distress and anxiety is the playground. The large expanse of asphalt or grass filled with many other children, the majority of whom are bigger and more self-confident than the new entrants, is a daunting place to spend long periods of time, particularly when there appears very little to do. The morning and afternoon breaks are difficult enough but the lunch hour is frequently associated with anxiety and stress for the youngest children, especially if they have had to eat their lunch in a noisy hall with tens of others. Any observer in a school playground can see many four- and five-year-olds standing in the corner, usually leaning against the school boundaries with their hands over their ears in order to shut out the noise.

Children who have been to nursery or playgroup will be accustomed to spending time running freely in and out of doors but always with an interested adult and a few other children, well known to each other. An essential feature of the preliminary school visits by parents and pre-school children should be to spend some time in the playground on each occasion so that the young child is at least aware of the new situation and is not suddenly thrown in at the deep end on the first day of schooling. Other aspects of the environment which will be different, not only from home but from pre-school provision in the voluntary sector, are the cloakroom and toilet facilities. Although in many schools the reception class has toilet facilities situated adjacent to or near the classroom, there are schools where the children have to walk along long corridors or even cross the playground.

Even if the facilities are close at hand, the actual toilets themselves are likely to be different from those encountered at home. Everything is child-sized and quite properly designed to make the child feel secure, but for many boys the use of a urinal rather then the more familiar toilet used in most households is a frightening experience. No wonder there are so many 'accidents' during the early days of schooling: wet pants are preferable to being terrified of either walking across the playground or seeing water gush out as it does in the urinals. Much distress could be alleviated if children were given sufficient experience to visit and use these facilities in the presence of a familiar, caring adult before being thrust into the situation with many other children.

Cleave, Jowett and Bate (1982) identified certain features of the environment as critical to the child, whatever their previous setting:

1 The scale and size of the building and its contents.
2 The range and extent of her territory and the siting of such facilities as play areas, toilets, and so on.
3 Organisational constraints in moving around the territory and within her base.

Children coming from the majority of pre-school settings have been allowed to move about the building with the minimum of constraints. For many, the tables and chairs of the infant classroom will seem strange and restrictive as they have been used to larger expanses with little or no furniture. Although those coming from the nursery sector will be accustomed to seeing small tables and chairs, there was always ample space for home corners, quiet areas, brick corners, and so on where the children can set out the equipment and play undisturbed for long periods of time.

However, in the primary classroom the increased numbers of tables and chairs and the need for more storage space for resources means the children find themselves with less room for physical activity. Furthermore, if children enter vertically grouped classes, they may find themselves in rooms where there is a greater range of equipment and apparatus to meet the needs of the older children and a resultant reduction in space and materials for the new entrant. For instance, in such classes it may be that either the 'home corner' totally disappears or else it is restricted to such a small area that it is almost impossible for high-level 'dramatic' play to take place. Many teachers try to utilise corridor space for brick building and other space-demanding activities, but children need to feel very secure before they will move from the close presence of their teacher to a strange environment in which teacher contact may only be on a very occasional basis.

The case studies offered by Cleave, Jowett and Bate (1982) showed that physical discontinuities are not detrimental to a child's progress provided that they are not too extreme and that adequate preparation has been made to ensure that the new entrants have visited the school on a number of previous occasions so that they do not feel total strangers in the environment. It is interesting to note that in almost all the studies carried out in this field, children with older brothers and sisters in the school have settled in better than those who are singletons or the first in their family to enter formal schooling.

The social environment

Reception-class teachers are well aware of the difficulties children face when they come from the cosy atmosphere of home, where it is likely that, at most, there will be two or three others needing mother's attention, to a social setting where, in all probability, there will be twenty or more children making demands upon a single adult. However, it is not only the child who has not had any previous experience outside the home who may have problems; the child who has attended nursery or playgroup will have to cope with a change in the social environment. Children from pre-school playgroups will have shared an adult with, at most, seven other children and the ratio of adults to children in a nursery school is one to thirteen or better. From whatever pre-school experience they have come, all children will have to become accustomed to less adult attention than they had previously been receiving.

This decreasing of the adult:child ratio inevitably affects the classroom organisation and the teacher's expectations of the children. Once in the infant classroom children will be expected to behave in a more independent manner, particularly in relation to dressing and undressing. Even though the majority of children who have had pre-school group experience are able to cope with their outdoor clothing, few will have had much practice in taking off dresses, shirts, shoes, and so on in preparation for PE and movement lessons. As a former reception-class teacher, I remember well the confusion and difficulties experienced by many children as they tried to dress themselves again after the PE lesson and how hard it was to cope alone with so many children.

However, although the children are expected to become more independent in this respect, there are situations in which there is a clash of attitudes and expectations between infant and pre-school educators and from the child's point of view it may seem that independence is being quashed rather than encouraged in the classroom.

In order to encourage decision making, nursery schools and classes allow children to select their own activities and to work independently with often minimal recourse to the teachers, the actual amount of time devoted each day to teacher-directed activities being quite small. However, as Cleave,

Jowett and Bate (1982) have pointed out, once in the infant classroom the situation changes and there is now a prevalence of no choice during the day: over two-thirds of the child's day is spent carrying out specific activities selected by the teacher. Furthermore, far from being involved for large parts of the day in various tasks, infants spend twice as much time as pre-schoolers in non-task activities such as lining up, queuing and waiting. Presumably these are organisational necessities in a situation where there is generally only one adult to as many as twenty to thirty children, but the situation is certainly alien to children who have spent up to two years in a nursery school or class, being encouraged to play constructively and follow their own pursuits. Similar situations were found by Cleave and Brown (1991) when they looked at four-year-olds in infant classes.

Management techniques vary from teacher to teacher but, where possible, a consistency of routine between pre-school and infant teacher would help to lessen anxiety and discontinuity for the new entrant into school. One routine which often differs between the two phases of schooling is that concerned with milk. In most pre-school settings children are free to take their milk from a table at any time during their half-day session, while in many infant classrooms children have to assemble on a mat at the teacher's command before the milk is distributed. Such organisational differences will undoubtedly confuse the youngest children during their early days of schooling.

Language and communication

The understanding of the language of instruction and communication in the classroom is another area in which children can experience considerable discontinuities. The child at home learns from an early age to interpret not only verbal communications but the non-verbal gestures and mannerisms which are characteristic of her own particular environment. The child may be in no doubt as to the meaning of a specific physical gesture from her parent or older relatives, but quite unaware that the eye contact or raised eyebrows of the teacher may be conveying a message upon which she is expected to act. As the child makes the transition from pre-school into formal schooling she may find that this new adult educator has different mannerisms which have to be interpreted and acted upon.

Even more confusing for the young child may be the language she encounters. As we are all aware, many children today enter school with poor linguistic experiences and this may not only present difficulties for them in articulating their needs and wishes, but may give rise to problems of interpreting the instructions and information given by the staff. Even the articulate child may not understand all the meanings of a word or sentence. The richness of the English language enables us to use a number of words which mean roughly the same thing; for example, such words as street, road and avenue are often regarded as interchangeable. Introduction to these different nouns at the appropriate time can only be beneficial to the child and help to widen her vocabulary. However, if the child is coping with early mathematical concepts and experiences difficulty in trying to come to grips with such ideas as 'big' and 'little', it may be very confusing if one teacher refers to something as 'big' and the other uses the term 'large' in a similar situation.

Children need to develop a wide and varied vocabulary, but if this learning is to progress smoothly, then it is vitally important that teachers from pre-school and primary education get together to ensure that their language approach is similar in the early stages so that there are as few misconceptions as possible. The able child will cope in spite of the different linguistic styles and indeed may benefit from the experience, but the low-ability or below-average child will be handicapped if instructions are given using different forms of vocabulary to express the same meaning. For these children, continuity of language experience is essential if they are to progress satisfactorily. Another group which has to be presented with very clear instructions, lacking in ambiguity, are those children for whom English is a second language. Many come into school with little or no grasp of our language and it is essential that they are helped to progress with as little discontinuity as possible, particularly as many of them no longer receive individual language support due to financial cutbacks.

DISCIPLINE

By the time children arrive at school they will have been exposed to a set of attitudes, value systems and expectations which are characteristic of their own family structures. One of the ways in which the family will have transmitted its ideas and values is by the use of discipline, reward and punishment. Hopefully, the young child will have experienced consistent discipline within the family setting, but as teachers are well aware, there is a good chance that for some children the values and discipline of the family may be at variance with those of the school. The child will then be experiencing a mismatch between what is acceptable behaviour in the home and what is acceptable in the school, a situation which can produce dissonance and conflict within the child.

Fortunately, children are very resilient and soon learn to appreciate that certain behaviours are acceptable at home and different ones expected within the classroom setting. This mismatch between what is acceptable at home and school will no doubt have been partially resolved by children attending nursery school or class, but unfortunately situations sometimes arise in which professionals are not in complete agreement over their expectations and attitudes towards children's behaviour.

Naturally, there are different levels of tolerance among everyone concerning what is acceptable and unacceptable in certain situations, but for the children's sake, there should be firm agreement between pre-school and primary institutions regarding classroom management and control. To experience conflict between home and school presents quite serious problems for young children, but to experience discontinuity between institutions, or worse, between professionals in the same institutions, is an inexcusable source of dissonance.

IDEOLOGICAL DIFFERENCES BETWEEN PRE-SCHOOL AND PRIMARY EDUCATION

Having looked at some of the current discontinuities children may encounter as they transfer from pre-school to primary education, let us now look at any differences that may occur in the underlying philosophies between the two groups of educators. In spite of the fact that training for teaching in the early years spans the age range three to nine years and teachers are prepared to work with children covering the whole age range, in practice there often develops a distinct difference in approach between the early years educators and primary teachers. Over the years, the early years workers have emphasised the importance of broad social and personal goals for children's development, an approach which has been characterised by an educational milieu in which the child has been encouraged to follow her own interests and inclinations and which has placed less stress on the development of obvious cognitive skills. Nursery educators have always stressed the value of traditional free play with greater emphasis on providing for individual children's social and emotional development and a conspicuous role for creative activities based on skills and competencies. Hopefully this approach will continue in spite of the introduction of the *Desirable Outcomes for Children's Learning* and baseline assessment. On the other hand, primary-school teachers have tended to place a strong emphasis on the teaching of the basic skills of reading, writing and mathematics, allowing free-choice activities only after the more formal work has been completed. Increasing pressure on teachers to be accountable for the children's progress, and the introduction of the National Curriculum with the associated SATs even in the first years of schooling, have resulted in more infant teachers becoming subject oriented. Both *Education 5 to 9* (DES 1982) and the report on *Primary Education in England* (DES 1978) stressed the competence and abilities of teachers in the basic skills, but criticised their lack of emphasis on the more creative aspects of the curriculum. However, in 1997 the Secretary of State for Education was urging a more rigorous approach to teaching numeracy and literacy.

The survey carried out by the British Association for Early Childhood Education (1984) into the needs of four-year-old children in school demonstrated clearly that there is a wide difference of opinion among the pre-school and primary educators. This clash of ideologies between professional groups is not just peculiar to the United Kingdom. An investigation by the Council of Europe (1975) into the procedures for transition carried out by the twenty-one member states showed that in about half of the countries there was official recognition of the existence of the 'link problem': most replies to the questionnaire gave as their explanation differences in ideology which governed the two sections. In discussing the problem with nursery teachers there seems to be a division of opinion between those who feel that nursery education is a stage in its own right and therefore should not be modified in any way to meet the needs of the primary school, and others who believe that in the last term of pre-school education certain constraints should be placed upon children so that they do not find the transition between the two phases of schooling too traumatic. These differences still exist between the two groups although in the last decade there has developed a greater understanding among nursery teachers of the need to ensure that they are articulate about the learning opportunities that they are providing. During the last few weeks of pre-school provision, many nurseries and playgroups modify their programmes slightly if they believe that the children will be entering a formal setting. If parents, too, are involved, then it should be possible for a smooth transition to occur.

CONTINUITY OF CURRICULUM CONTENT

Coming now to my final main area of discontinuity, let us consider continuity of curriculum content. It would seem that the introduction of a National Curriculum and the *Desirable Outcomes for Children's Learning* would ensure that this problem does not arise. Well-organised schools will be using a curriculum whose content has been geared to the developmental needs of the children and will see the content areas as progressing along a continuum, hopefully allowing sufficient flexibility to ensure that the individual interests of children in their community can be met. The implication for primary and pre-school education seems quite clear. There is no doubt in my mind that the learning experiences of the nursery school must anticipate what follows during the later school years. Likewise, education in the primary school must reinforce the learning which has occurred at the pre-school stage. What is important is that the situation does not arise where the young child is exposed to the National Curriculum at the expense of good nursery practice.

Walkerdine (1982) has looked at ways in which there can be discontinuities in children's early mathematical education: discontinuities between home and pre-school, as well as between nursery and infant classrooms. She cites as one of her examples the way children learn about money. At home and in many pre-school institutions young children regularly 'go shopping' for various items of food or other necessities and are involved in conversations concerning the high price of goods. They play at 'shopping', repeating and at the same time reinforcing these ideas of the high cost of various items, using token coins. However, two or three terms later, when they enter primary education, they do 'shopping sums' with very small numbers because we argue they cannot handle the large numbers involved. Now, I am not suggesting that young children should be asked to manipulate large numbers. What I am saying is that we may be producing nonsensical situations for children who are beginning to develop a notion of exchange value and who must surely experience some confusion when mother complains of the high cost of washing powder and the primary-school mathematics curriculum suggests that you can buy two packets for a very small amount of money. Perhaps the solution to this kind of problem is for us to ensure that when we are asking children to calculate the price of various items we should only choose goods which are of a low price and leave the other shopping experiences to the real-life or fantasy-play situation.

As one who has been involved for many years in training both nursery and primary-school teachers and therefore has spent many hours as a teaching-practice supervisor, let me give you a practical example of the way in which continuity/discontinuity of experience can occur in a specific area of the curriculum. Let us take sand and water play. Few educationalists would deny the value of such play or would disagree that it can provide a child with a wealth of learning experience. Yet time and time again I have been in nurseries where such experiences have been purposefully structured so that the child has gradually come to understand a number of basic mathematical and scientific concepts. That child is now ready to build on these experiences and to generalise them to other situations. However, the transition into primary school resulted in the sand and water tray being seen as 'somewhere to go when you have finished your work' and the child's understanding and progress in this area remains static. The child will simply repeat what has been learned earlier: the one thing that is not required – more of the same. No one doubts the value of reinforcement and practice, but constant repetition can only lead to boredom or frustration.

The school curriculum should offer new and challenging experiences to children, but these should evolve from previous knowledge and ideas. In this way children will cope with any discontinuity which results from the challenge since they will have internalised earlier experiences upon which to draw. This type of discontinuity is both valuable and necessary for development, but just as creative thinking normally has its basis in some rather mundane convergent approaches, so, in my view, the challenge of discontinuity must be grounded in sound early learning if it is to help the child move on to the next stage of development.

WHAT SHOULD WE BE DOING TO ACHIEVE CONTINUITY?

It has been suggested that one of the most effective ways of ensuring continuity of children's experiences is to use a curriculum model which takes as its starting point the child's life experiences as part of a family and community. We have, then, two ingredients which are likely to contribute to successful learning: previous experience and motivation. The child will be developing knowledge and skills based upon her earlier experiences and will be more likely to see the relevance of school-based activities if the ideas arise from her immediate environment. What is more, if parents are involved at these early stages in children's education, they will be more likely both to understand and support the school system.

Even if one does not accept this approach to the school curriculum there are a number of practical ways of ensuring that children experience continuity during the early years of schooling:

1 Parents should be involved as partners with mutual responsibility for their children's education. By encouraging parents to participate in their children's pre- and primary-school environment they can help to prepare them for the transition, e.g. changes in method, and in conditions of school life. Hopefully, many of the language and control problems about which we are often concerned might also disappear if parents become more actively engaged in school activities.

2 Pre- and primary-school educators should liaise regularly so that they can effectively prepare children for the transfer from pre-school to primary education. Children should be encouraged to visit and meet with their infant-school teachers so that the physical surroundings are less threatening and discontinuous and, where possible, children should be prepared for the transition for at least the last two terms of their final

year of pre-school education. This should be not only by means of visits, but maybe the daily organisation and routine should be modified so that the next stage is less traumatic.

3 Early years educators, working in the independent and voluntary sector know very little about what is going on in the infant classes, and even highly experienced nursery teachers do not feel that their expertise is valued by their colleagues teaching in the next phase of schooling. Equally, many Key Stage 1 teachers know little or nothing of their new entrants' pre-school experience and appear to discount it when assessing each child's needs. One way to overcome this lack of knowledge would be to encourage pre-school and primary-school educators to liaise and visit regularly so that they can effectively prepare children for the transfer from pre-school to primary education. In this way each would become aware of the organisational and curricular differences that exist between the two sectors of education. Naturally, there are problems in arranging exchange visits, particularly for nursery school staff who may send children to several infant schools, but with the increasing numbers of nursery classes being established it should be possible for more effective liaison to occur between pre-school and infant educators. If, during these visits, the staff of the two institutions could discuss their philosophy and approaches to early childhood education then I believe they would discover that ideological clashes would be avoided with only minimal changes being made by either side. But, above all, these meetings should lead to greater tolerance and understanding of each other's ideas so that the child's needs can be met more effectively.

4 Record keeping has an important part to play in maintaining the continuity of children's educational experience. Good records which are passed on and accepted by the receiving teacher should state clearly not only what the child can or cannot do, but give some guidelines to the next teacher as to the types of activity in which the children have been engaged over the previous one or two years.

Recent research and media coverage have highlighted for both parents and professionals the fact that young children may experience trauma and anxiety as they transfer from either home or pre-school to primary education. A number of writers have suggested ways in which these discontinuities can be minimised. Cleave, Jowett and Bate (1982) stressed that if discontinuity is to be reduced to as low a level as possible the following must occur:

1 Changes and the introduction of new experiences must be gradual rather than sudden.

2 People, places and things must be familiar to some extent rather than totally strange.

3 The children must have a sense of security rather than instability.

SOME GENERAL GUIDELINES

On a more practical level, I would suggest that all concerned with the education of the new entrants into school, parents, pre-school educators and receiving teachers, ensure that they are all well informed about:

1 The child's past experiences both at home and pre-school.
2 The provision and approach in the infant classroom and the possible effects of the changes on the child.
3 The individual needs of the child.

For children to develop fully they must be in a secure, stable environment and this can only be achieved if there is full understanding and cooperation by all concerned with the education of young children. Parents, primary and pre-school educators need to work together if they are to meet the best interests of the children in their care. If the liaison between parents and professionals advocated in the SCAA document (1996b) is effected then maybe children will experience fewer difficulties as a result of the discontinuities they experience when transferring from non-statutory to statutory schooling.

12 In conclusion

Nursery education in the United Kingdom is currently in a state of transition. Even though the nursery voucher system was short lived, the repercussions will continue as more and more primary schools introduce a once-yearly admissions policy, with the result that four-year-old children will no longer be in the nursery, but in reception or Key Stage 1 classes. Not only will there be a large number of four-year-old children in inappropriate provision, with poor staff ratios, but nurseries and playgroups will be catering predominantly for three-year-olds. As a society we have always advocated that mixed-age groups were best for young children and yet through political circumstances the opposite is occurring, and we are creating nurseries with chronological age groups. The three-year-olds need four-year-olds and four-year-olds need three-year-olds!

A positive side to these changes has been the increase in curriculum planning and evaluation which has taken place in many nurseries and playgroups since the introduction of the *Desirable Outcomes for Children's Learning* on entering compulsory schooling. The OFSTED inspectors will be looking closely at the curriculum being offered and will be checking that educators are not placing too great an emphasis upon sedentary 'reading and writing' activities. There is some concern that external pressures, particularly from parents, could lead to children being 'hot-housed' with a programme of learning which attempts to push them to attain the Desirable Outcomes by the time they leave the nursery/playgroup (generally as a young four-year-old), when they are designed as outcomes to be achieved by the time the child has reached the age of statutory schooling (the term after her fifth birthday). It is the role of the educator to provide experiences for children which will stimulate and extend, but not pressurise.

I hope that readers will agree that although there is no specific reference to the subject areas of the National Curriculum or the *Desirable Outcomes for Children's Learning* in this book, there is a close link between them and my approach to the curriculum. Although I have identified skills and competencies in five main areas which I believe are basic to all learning, I have not organised them into a specific programme of learning, such as the High Scope Curriculum, as I believe that early childhood educators should be free to find their own ways of implementing the curriculum based on the individual needs of the child and the social context of the setting.

I have advocated a balance between adult-directed and child-initiated activities and pointed out the importance of adult intervention in children's play, particularly socio-dramatic play, at appropriate times. Most of the time children spend in the nursery will be devoted to various types of free play when the skills and competencies will be practised naturally; however, there will be occasions when educators need to teach specific skills. For example, the use of scissors is a skill which most children need to be shown and to practise many times before they become proficient.

The amount of freedom given to children to make their own decisions and to select their own activities will depend upon the educator, but motivation studies suggest that giving children choice is a very positive part of encouraging them to 'learn how to learn'. However, educators may need to limit the choice of some children who may 'flit' from task to task without ever attempting to finish anything. For others, too much choice may be overwhelming and a limited selection is the kindest approach. The response to such children will depend upon the professionals' knowledge of the particular child or children.

As so many of our four-year-olds are entering primary classes alongside older children, I have tried where possible to point out not only the level of skill attainment one can expect from three- and four-year-old children, but how their abilities are likely to change during the first year or two of compulsory schooling. Will a particular skill have fully matured by the age of five or six or will it need several more years before it can really be perfected? In many respects four- and five-year-olds have different needs and it may be helpful for educators working with this age range, perhaps for the first time, to have practical guidance.

Adopting a skills model for the curriculum will involve educators in planning a programme of developmentally appropriate activities which will enable the children to practise their skills and competencies in a play environment. The learning outcomes which have been advocated by SCAA incorporate many of the skills that have been discussed and readers should be reminded that these are expected outcomes for the time the children reach statutory schooling, not when entering school at four years.

There are many ways in which the children will acquire these skills which lay down the foundation for later learning; sometimes it will be through play and on other occasions the children will have learned through observation or direct instruction. Hopefully, readers will have no doubt that the skills and competencies that I have written about are closely linked to both the *Desirable Outcomes for Children's Learning* and the National Curriculum.

For example, let us consider first the programmes of learning for the English curriculum at Key Stage 1. Turn to any book on the teaching of this area of the curriculum and you will find that the authors have placed emphasis upon on the importance of communication through language and the arts, the value of perceptual–motor and creative abilities and the place of movement in helping children to read and write.

If we look closely at the skills which children are expected to acquire in order to reach National Curriculum Key Stage 1 in Mathematics and Science it can be seen that analytical and problem-solving skills have a high profile. Other aspects of the primary curriculum such as creative activities and the Humanities can all be found to have their roots in the experiences which early years educators give their children in order to foster overall development. The skills and attitudes learned by three- and four-year-old children are parts of a continuous process of learning and offer a sound foundation for the subject-based curriculum in the primary school.

Hopefully, educators using the approach advocated here will find that children will be stretched and challenged, encouraged to solve their own problems and do things for themselves. Life in either the nursery or primary classroom should be fun for young children and I hope that children will be offered opportunities to develop fully in a well-planned learning environment where the educators have a sound understanding of children's development, and can offer them appropriate and fruitful learning experiences.

Part II

13 Some suggested activities for developing competencies

This second section of the book contains a selection of activities which early years workers may find useful to help promote children's skills and competencies in the various areas. They can all be carried out with children between the ages of two-and-a-half and five years of age. Naturally, not all will appeal to every child or every adult but it is hoped that the range is sufficiently wide to allow an appropriate selection to be made to meet the needs of individual groups. There is considerable overlap in some areas, and activities suggested to help foster one area of competence may prove useful in promoting other aspects of development. For example, in helping to enhance the child's awareness of herself and her bodily changes, the concept of growth will be discussed; this could well be linked to chickens being hatched or studying the growth of seeds into plants. All these activities could just as easily be identified as ways of developing scientific awareness in young children. The main purpose of providing educators with suggestions and ways of developing competencies and skills is to give busy people some concrete examples for the individual programmes they have planned. In no way should the activities be seen as independent items but should be regarded as a means of reinforcing the principles behind the skills and competency model I have suggested.

PERSONAL AND SOCIAL DEVELOPMENT

Activities to encourage self-awareness

Growing up

MATERIALS: Mother/father and a baby, visitors to the nursery. (Asking a father to join in could be helpful in attempting to dispel any sex-role stereotyping that may occur.) Equipment for baby corner: talcum powder, towel, bath, cotton wool, nappies, etc.

ACTIVITY:

1 Introduce mother/father and baby. Ask parent to talk about the baby to the children and encourage them to ask questions.
2 Ask the parent to bath the baby, if appropriate, and to change the nappy.
3 Discuss with children the differences between themselves as they are now and the baby. What can they do that the baby cannot? For example, speak, walk, etc.
4 Compare the needs of the baby with their needs.

What size am I?

MATERIALS: Large sheets of paper with crayons and felt pens, or a concrete paved area with coloured chalks.

ACTIVITY: Draw outlines around the educator and the children on to the paper or paved area. Then, after the children have decorated them, they can identify and discuss the parts of the body and compare the sizes of the body outlines. Varying the positions of the children while drawing outlines (e.g. stretched out, curled into a ball, etc.) can increase their interest and can also help them to relate physical size to body position.

What I like about me

MATERIALS: None

ACTIVITY: The adult talks about a particular part of the body and why it is appreciated so much. Then the children should be prompted into describing a favourite part of their body, what they like about it, its function and how it is used. The purpose is primarily to get the children to see their bodies as a physical entity, and to accept the differences between their own bodies and those of others.

Relaxer

MATERIALS: None

ACTIVITY: The adult identifies parts of the body in turn and shakes each vigorously. Lead the children through this activity and eventually into shaking the whole body. Then get them to sit down and quietly 'experience' the feeling as their bodies relax. After a pause discuss this experience and how it is actually resting and not being lifeless. Try to encourage the children to think up other occasions when they would relax.

Smelling jars

MATERIALS: Handkerchiefs (to cover the eyes), several jars of groups of scents, e.g. floral (pot pourri), fruity (lemons, apples), spicy (nutmeg, cinnamon), woody (lavender, pine).

ACTIVITY: Ideally, the children should be blindfolded for this activity. Let the children smell all the jars, after which they can group them into like smells and describe the sensation of 'smelling'. Some children may be able to identify certain scents and this can lead to a discussion on favourite smells. This activity could be preceded by an 'introduction' to their noses.

Simon says

MATERIALS: None

ACTIVITY: This well-known game can help children to identify various parts of their body. By having the educator prompt the children with 'Simon says touch your . . .', she can demonstrate which part is being identified. Depending on the level of the group some children could take over the role of the leader. This activity can also help children improve listening skills.

Reflections

MATERIALS: Mirror, dark container filled with water, polished spoon, silver foil.

ACTIVITY: Explain to the children that they are going to look at themselves in a variety of ways. The adult should demonstrate how each object reflects differently, and then let the children play with them. Encourage the children to experiment by pulling faces and by moving and/or distorting the reflective surfaces, i.e. dropping something into the bowl of water to create ripples. The educator should encourage the children to talk about the different reflections they see, which they prefer and why. Educators should also be aware that some children may be frightened by the reflections.

Follow the leader

MATERIALS: None

ACTIVITY: Children in turn assume the role of the leader, during which time any action they make or position they take must be mimicked by the rest of the group. It is intended that this will combine visual awareness with body awareness.

Activities for developing social competence

Name dropping

MATERIALS: None

ACTIVITY: The adult starts the activity by sitting in the middle of the group of children and suggesting that they guess the identity of a child she is thinking of after having given clues such as 'someone who likes to play with puppets'. The children should take turns in being in the central role. This should also help to encourage communication skills.

Let's all pull together

MATERIALS: A strong rope about forty feet long.

ACTIVITY: Tell the children that you all have to move a very big thing (preferably something large enough that only the group as a whole can move it). Tie the rope around the object and shout encouragement to the children as they move it (ideally, the adult should join in as long as it does not make the task too easy). When they have completed the move to a predetermined place, thank them and discuss with them the idea that no individual could move it alone and that it needed cooperation.

Three-legged tour

MATERIALS: Scarves or something suitable to tie legs together.

ACTIVITY: After a brief introduction on the value of cooperation the children should be put into pairs and their two adjacent legs tied together as they stand next to each other. Then, with the emphasis on cooperation within the pairs and not competition between them, the two children can try to walk around the classroom or outside area. Children who become proficient at this can be given a more complicated route to follow.

Pass the parcel

MATERIALS: One large parcel which is easy to handle and unwrap.

ACTIVITY: Despite the apparent simplicity of this game, children are, in fact, learning a number of social and motor skills during play. They must learn to listen carefully, unwrap presents, not snatch the parcel from another child, learn to accept that some people will have more than one chance to unwrap, and that only one person can be the winner.

Cooperative musical chairs

MATERIALS: Piano, record player and records or tape-recorder and tapes.

ACTIVITY: This is musical chairs with a difference. The game is played like musical chairs but the rules are quite different. When the music stops everyone must be seated on a chair or on someone's lap. The idea is to develop the cooperational element rather than that of competition.

Care and kindness

MATERIALS: A small tame pet (rabbit, hamster, etc.).

ACTIVITY: Discuss with children the meaning of such words as kindness, gentleness, warmth and affection. Tell the children how important it is to be gentle with things that are smaller than themselves. Let the children handle the pet, giving assistance when necessary. Praise any particularly gentle behaviour and suggest alternative strategies to those who are too rough.

Policeman's gaze

MATERIALS: Policeman's helmet, dark trousers, old blazer, blue shirt.

ACTIVITY: One child is chosen to be the policeman and to wear the helmet. While she is out of earshot, the rest of the group decide which child is going to be 'lost'. A boy and a girl are each chosen to be the parents who describe their 'lost' child – hair colour, clothes, etc. The policeman may also ask questions until she has spotted which child in the group is being described. Alternatively, the adult could play the part of the policeman who finds a 'lost' child who has to give her full name and address – children can take it in turns to be 'lost'.

Imaginative play

One of the most effective ways of encouraging cooperation and empathic skills is by giving children dressing-up props which will foster language and imaginative play. Through socio-dramatic situations children learn to cooperate and come to understand one another's point of view.

Activities promoting cultural awareness

The format in this section is different from that of the others in that the suggestions are of a more generalised nature.

Life in the community

Children should be given every opportunity to make close contact with the community at large. Where possible the children should visit institutions such as the fire station, post office, health centre, police station and local dairy. If this cannot be arranged, representatives from the local services should be invited into the nursery to talk about their work. It will probably be found that there are parents who would be willing to come into the nursery to talk about their work. As a follow up to the visit, children should be encouraged by means of appropriate props and materials to express their experiences in creative play.

Clothing

One of the most obvious signs of different cultural groups is clothing. All national costumes are intended to give an independent identity to each country. If the actual garments are not available, children can be shown pictures of men and women in a range of clothing, for example, kilts, kaftans, saris, kimonos, loin-cloths, anoraks, parkas, duffle-coats, turbans and fezzes. Adults should discuss these with children, pointing out, where appropriate, the relevance of each costume to the climate in which it is worn. If the nursery has parents who own any of these items of clothing, they should be encouraged to show it to the children and talk about how it differs from the customary dress of this country.

Housing

Show children pictures of different dwellings, for example, blocks of flats, terraced houses, semi-detached and detached properties, tents, mud huts, houseboats, log cabins and houses on stilts. Discussion can cover similarities and dissimilarities between where they live and the dwellings that they have seen in the pictures. Point out the reasons for the different kinds of material being used for housing in the other countries. The children can make models of the houses they find particularly interesting. It may also be possible to encourage enterprising parents to construct houses such as a log cabin or a house on stilts in the outdoor area.

Music

One way in which children can become more culturally aware is through listening to different types of music played on various musical instruments. Children should be given the opportunity to hear instruments such as bagpipes, harps, mandolins, balalaikas, didgeridoos and the various reed instruments used in Eastern music. There are many records and tapes available of music from all parts of the world, such as Irish jigs, kabuki music, Indian and South American dancing, aboriginal songs and so forth. These are generally available at large record stores but if any reader has difficulty in obtaining them, I suggest contact is made with the HMV shop, Oxford Street, London.

Cooking

Each culture has its own culinary specialities and although few of these can be cooked in the nursery it may be possible to encourage parents to bring in some prepared traditional dishes from their own culture to share with the children. If possible, they should bring in some of the ingredients so that children can see and smell them in their raw state.

Introduce various fruits and vegetables of the season, including potatoes, leeks, yams, sweetcorn, apples, ugli fruit, oranges, kiwi fruit, mangoes, papaws, okra, kelp. Discuss with the children the different tastes and textures and ask them which they prefer and why. Bring in a selection of spices and herbs such as nutmeg, cardamom, mint, thyme, cinnamon, saffron, turmeric, parsley. Let the children smell and taste them.

SOME SUGGESTED RECIPES FOR USE IN THE CLASSROOM

IRISH POTATO SCONES:

450 g potatoes, peeled; 2 level tsp. salt; 50 g butter; 100 g flour.
Cook potatoes in salted water until soft. Drain and mash well. Add salt, butter and flour to make a stiff mixture. Turn onto floured board, knead lightly, then roll out to 5 mm thickness. Cut into circles with cutter. Cook in greased frying pan until golden brown.

SCOTTISH SHORTBREAD:

100 g softened butter (or margarine); 50 g castor sugar; 125 g plain flour; 25 g semolina.

Cream butter and sugar until light and fluffy. Gradually stir in flour and semolina, mixing together with fingertips. Press into lightly greased sandwich tins. Prick well all over. Pinch up edges with finger and thumb. Bake in centre of moderate oven (160°C) for about forty minutes. Leave in tin for about five minutes. Cut into pieces and dredge with extra castor sugar. Remove from tin when cold.

GREEK SALAD:

Spinach leaves; small tomatoes; black olives; fetta cheese; olive oil; white wine vinegar.

Cut or rip the spinach leaves into manageable pieces. Quarter the tomatoes and slice the olives. Crumble fetta cheese on to the salad. Mix two-thirds oil to one-third vinegar in a bottle and shake vigorously until creamy. Separate into portions, pour on dressing and serve.

WELSH BAKED SCONES:

450 g self-raising flour; 150 g margarine; 100 g sultanas; 75 g sugar; 1 egg; milk to mix.

Mix ingredients together. Add sufficient milk to make into a stiff dough. Turn on to a floured board and knead lightly. Roll out to 5 mm thickness and cut into circles. Cook in a greased frying pan until golden brown.

INDIAN GAJAR KHEER:

225 g carrots; 4 cups milk; saffron strands; 4 tbsp. sugar; 2 tbsp. ground almonds; pinch of ground cardamom.

Grate carrots finely and add them to warmed milk. Add saffron for a few minutes and then remove. Stir in the remainder of the ingredients and simmer until carrots are easily pulped. Mash carrots into the liquid to make a mulch and serve.

Festivals

One of the important ways in which children come to understand cultural differences in our society is through the celebration of festivals. Christmas, Easter and Bonfire Night have been part of English tradition for many years but there are now many more dates in the calendar with which we should all be familiar. However, if we are to celebrate them in our classrooms, teachers need to be fully aware of their significance and not see them as yet another project. How many and which festivals should be celebrated will depend upon the cultural backgrounds of the children, but I have listed below a small selection which I hope will be of use to early years workers.

ADVENT   The start of the Christian year, beginning with a period of preparation for Christmas. It is also the time when Christians look forward to the second coming of Christ.

ALL SAINTS' DAY (All Hallows)   Originally it was probably the date for the beginning of the ancient Celtic year whose traditions linger in the Hallowe'en customs of the preceding day. It is now a Christian festival of thanksgiving for the witness of all holy men and women.

ALL SOULS' DAY (Chinese Buddhist faith)   The festival to help spirits who are homeless or who lack descendants. Each temple makes a large paper 'boat of the law' which is ceremonially burned in the evening to help wandering spirits reach Nirvana.

CHINESE NEW YEAR   Celebrated by the exchange of gifts and in London by a traditional carnival procession.

CHRISTMAS   Celebration of the birth of Christ.

DASARA   Hindu ten-day festival in honour of Kali. There are processions, dances and presents given.

THE DAY OF HIJRA   Islamic new year which starts on the day which celebrates Muhammad's departure from Mecca to Medina in AD 622.

DHU AL-HIJRA (The month of pilgrimage)   Pilgrimage to Mecca to be made during this month.

DIWALI   Hindu new year. A festival of lights when presents are given. Lakshi, the goddess of good fortune, visits every house which is lit by a lamp.

EASTER   The most important Christian festival, celebrating the resurrection of Christ.

FEAST OF THE TABERNACLES   Jewish harvest festival.

GOOD FRIDAY   Memorial of the death of Christ on the cross.

HANNUKKAH (Festival of the Lights)   An eight-day Jewish festival marked by the lighting of ritual candles.

HOLI   Hindu spring festival dedicated to Krishna. Originally a fertility ceremony celebrated with street dancing, processions and bonfires.

ID AL-ADHA (The Festival of Sacrifice)   Four-day festival marking the end of the pilgrimage to Mecca. Animal sacrifices are made and meat is given to the poor.

PASSOVER   Seven-day Jewish spring festival marking the deliverance of the Jews from slavery in Egypt.

RAMADAN   Muslims abstain from food and drink during the hours of daylight for the thirty days of this festival.

ROSH HASHANAH   Jewish new year.

WHITSUN/PENTECOST   Celebration of the day when God sent his Holy Spirit to the Apostles ten days after Christ's Ascension.

YOM KIPPUR   Jewish Day of Atonement. This is the holiest day of the Jewish year.

SAINT ANDREW'S DAY (30 November)   Patron Saint of Scotland.

SAINT DAVID'S DAY (1 March)   Patron Saint of Wales.

SAINT GEORGE'S DAY (23 April)   Patron Saint of England.

SAINT PATRICK'S DAY (17 March)   Patron Saint of Ireland.

DEVELOPMENT OF COMMUNICATION SKILLS

Activities to encourage communication skills

Growing water

MATERIALS: None

ACTIVITY: Ask children to sit on the floor in their own space. Have them drink an imaginary potion of 'growing water' that will make them very tall for a very short while. Talk them through the growing process until the room is filled with giants. Let them move around the room as giants until the potion wears off. As the potion becomes less effective tell children to shrink down to the floor back to their original size. Repeat process, using a potion that will shrink them down into the tiniest people in the world. This activity will enable an adult to discuss differences between sizes – large, small, tiny, big. It will also stimulate the imagination and encourage activity.

Mobile words

MATERIALS: None

ACTIVITY: Ask children to move around the room slowly, making their bodies move to the words. It is not essential for them to know the exact meaning of the words but merely to express how they understand and feel about them. Suggested words are: stretch, bend, turn, walk, bounce, roll, leap, skip, wiggle, squirm, fall, swim, crawl, curl and uncurl, etc.

This activity will help increase children's vocabulary and encourage them to distinguish between different types of movement. Various music effects can also be used to encourage different movement responses.

Talking about a picture

MATERIALS: Pictures of everyday scenes, including people.

ACTIVITY: Ask children what is happening in the picture. If appropriate, discuss with them what is likely to happen next and what the people in the picture will be thinking and why. Discussion of this kind will help children to recall, predict and elaborate on alternative possible outcomes. Children will also learn how to abstract the central meaning from a picture and report in detail what they can see.

Name the object

MATERIALS: Tape recorder and prepared tape containing the sounds of everyday objects such as vacuum cleaner, musical instruments (e.g. piano, drum, bells), door banging, telephone ringing, washing machine, tap dripping, etc. A space should be left on the tape between each sound recording.

ACTIVITY: Ask children to identify the sound by name. If a correct response is given, ask the children an appropriate question to discuss what they know about the object.

Are you listening?

MATERIALS: Any favourite story.

ACTIVITY: Prepare for story time in the normal way but this time 'pepper' the story at frequent intervals with comments to individual children. Do not change the tone of your voice while 'reading' these comments; children have to listen closely so that they do not miss any of the instructions. For example, once upon a time (close your eyes Mary) there was a big mouse (stand up Sharon) that lived in a hole (touch your nose Raiid) with his friends . . .'.

Poetry and stories

Poetry and stories are essential features of all early childhood education and there are many well-illustrated books and anthologies of poetry on the market today. The contents of these stories and poems are obviously important in developing children's awareness of the 'world of literature' but the actual artwork is just as important in many books for young children. The picture book is an art form in its own right, as children receive aesthetic stimuli through high-quality illustrations. It is valuable for children to encounter different illustrative interpretations of familiar tales, even though this may mean having two copies of the same book in the nursery. For example, the troll in Paul Galdone's version of the 'Three Billy Goats Gruff' is very different from that of William Stobbs.

DEVELOPMENT OF PROBLEM-SOLVING AND ANALYTICAL SKILLS

Activities for developing problem-solving and analytical skills

How fast do they go?

MATERIALS: One-litre plastic fizzy drink bottles (some full, some empty), ping-pong balls, billiard balls, cogs (Meccano or Lego have ready-made sets), heavy chipboard discs, paper plates, large spoons in pots of water, paint, glue, porridge and liquids of different viscosity.

ACTIVITY: Make display of interlocking cogs of different sizes such that if one cog is moved, all the others move but at different speeds. Get children to roll the plastic bottles down a slightly inclined ramp or across the floor. Discuss whether full bottles will roll faster than empty bottles of the same size. Do the same with ping-pong balls. Tell children to blow ping-pong balls along and then to do the same with billiard balls. Nail chipboard discs and paper plates through their centres to a board so that they can spin. Show children how to spin them and discuss why the heavy discs spin for longer and are more difficult to stop spinning with their hands. Also pour the liquids from the spoons back into their pots so that you demonstrate the different viscosities. Point out that thick things pour more slowly. These types of activities encourage observation skills and help children experience different forms of speed and momentum.

Puddle play

MATERIALS: Cooking oil, food colourings.

ACTIVITY: After it has stopped raining take the children outside to conduct some simple experiments by dropping cooking oil and food colouring into the water. Before adding anything to the water ask children to predict what they think will happen. Afterwards, discuss with them what they have discovered. This will not only encourage observation skills, but stimulate language.

Shapes

MATERIALS: None

ACTIVITY: Ask the children to look around the room and to name the many different shapes that they see. Discuss which shapes they know and the quality of each shape – is it round, curved, straight, bent? When children have made a number of suggestions ask them if they can make their own bodies into these shapes: can they make a tall and thin shape; a fat and round shape; a very big or very small shape; a bent or twisted shape? This should help children become aware of the differences in shapes and be able to describe them. This is not only a problem-solving task but will encourage understanding of opposites such as tall and short, round, big and small, high and low.

How do we get across?

MATERIALS: Pieces of wood, play equipment, rope suitable for making a bridge or boat.

ACTIVITY: Mark out an imaginary 'river'. Encourage the children to think of ways of getting across the water without getting wet. Place a selection of materials near by so that the children can solve the problem by making either a bridge or a boat.

Shadows and reflections

MATERIALS: None

ACTIVITY: On a sunny day take the children outside to look at the shadows and reflections made by the sun. Which is the longest and which is the shortest shadow? Show the children how to change the shape of their shadow by spreading out their arms, moving their heads or legs (warn children never to look directly at the sun). The concept of reflection can also be discussed when there are puddles. Encourage the children to look into the puddles when the water is absolutely still and then note what happens when the surface is disturbed.

Same and different

MATERIALS: Selection of items which are similar but vary along one dimension, e.g. blocks that are the same colour, shape and size but have different weights, spoons that are identical except for patterns on handles, forks that are identical except for their sizes, buttons which are the same shape, size and colour but have different numbers of holes.

ACTIVITY: Place objects in a pile on the table and ask children to sort them into sets, e.g. all spoons together. Then ask the children to look again at each group to see whether they are identical. Encourage the children to handle the materials and discuss the similarities and dissimilarities.

Walk in the neighbourhood

A walk along the roads around the school will provide many opportunities for developing problem-solving skills. Children can sort out the cars and lorries that pass them; which doors have knockers, which bells, and which both; different kinds of gate; different insects, those that crawl and those that fly. Discussions and observations will vary according to the environment in which the school is situated.

Time pictures

MATERIALS: A series of picture cards showing sequential events, e.g. getting dressed in the morning, going to a birthday party.

ACTIVITY: Mix up the cards and ask the children to put them in order. As children become more sophisticated at this activity, mix several sets together.

If . . . then

MATERIALS: None

ACTIVITY: Although the relationship between cause and effect is generally learned incidentally throughout the daily routine, adults may like to discuss some of these problems with children during quiet sessions. Some questions might be:

1 What must you do before going outside to play when it is cold?
2 If it were raining what would you do?
3 What happens if we hurt another child?
4 If paint is too runny what do we do?
5 What might happen if we run across the road?

Cooking

Cooking is an activity which is not only thoroughly enjoyed by children but offers them opportunities to develop many skills. Most recipes involve children measuring, counting and ordering, and those which require cooking enable the children to see how heat can transform the basic ingredients into different shapes and textures. A skilled adult will be able to use this activity to develop many aspects of scientific and mathematical awareness.

There are very simple recipes available, some of which have been included in the section on cultural awareness. Since it is an activity which is usually carried out on a small-group basis it also provides opportunities for language and social interaction.

Science experiments

Simple experiments using batteries, circuits and plugs, magnets, etc., to help children understand about energy and force. It should be possible to help children gain some understanding of light, sound and electricity through the suggested activities in this section.

PHYSICAL DEVELOPMENT

Activities to encourage perceptual and motor skills

Bouncing bodies

MATERIALS: Some large plastic footballs.

ACTIVITY: The adult can demonstrate two-handed ball bouncing and invite the children to try it out for themselves. Children are then told that they are going to bounce each other. The children are asked to take it in turns to put their hands on their partner's shoulders from behind and 'bounce' them around the room. This can encourage cooperation and get the bounced child into hopping.

Over and under

MATERIALS: One or more strong coffee tables or low tables.

ACTIVITY: This is effectively a follow-the-leader exercise although it could be made into a large circle. The children are introduced to a 'course' and shown that there are spaces under tables as well as on top. Then they are encouraged to make a line (or circle) and negotiate the circuit by crawling around the course, alternately wriggling under and climbing over the tables. This will also give a good example to them of the difference between 'over' and 'under', concepts that are not always immediately grasped.

Stepping stones

MATERIALS: Large concrete outside area and chalked out 'islands', or else distinctly different patches on an internal linoleum floor.

ACTIVITY: By using a simple story as a basis, an activity can be started consisting of moving from one 'island' to another. The sizes of the spaces between the 'islands' should be varied to encourage differing methods of crossing ranging from small steps to long jumps. The children can be invited to help each other move from 'island' to 'island', thus emphasising cooperation. This may be more suitable for older children in the group.

Shake and freeze

MATERIALS: None

ACTIVITY: Discuss the word 'freeze' with the children and what it means when water stops running and turns to ice. Have each child find a separate space and impress upon them the importance of not talking during this game. Tell everyone to wiggle one finger on one hand and then the same finger on the other hand (for older children in the group the terms 'left' and 'right' can be used). Add other parts of the body until they are shaking all over. Then say 'Freeze!' Practice of the control word will eventually bring them to an instant halt. Bring children out of the freeze slowly. After several practices children can be told that you want them to freeze into an animal or plant. When they do so adults should walk around and try to guess what each is, in the frozen state. This activity, besides developing motor control and directionality, will assist children in developing self-control.

The mystery guest

MATERIALS: A scarf.

ACTIVITY: Bring in a scarf and talk about how it feels if someone puts a scarf over your eyes. Discuss how you would learn about the world if you could not see it. Tell the children that they are going to play a game in which one child is going to be blindfolded and will have to guess which person is standing in front of her by touching with hands. Tell the volunteer to have a good look at everyone in the group before being blindfolded. Pick a 'mystery guest' and have that child stand very quietly in front of the blindfolded person. Ask the blindfolded child if they can tell the identity of the 'mystery guest'. (This activity could be repeated by asking the 'mystery guest' to speak and the blindfolded person would be expected to guess the 'mystery guest's' identity by the sound of her voice.)

This activity will help to heighten children's awareness of the sense of touch and develop an appreciation of how much they can learn by just touching an object. It will also help encourage problem-solving skills and foster empathy towards people with visual problems.

Mirror

MATERIALS: A large mirror.

ACTIVITY: Bring in a mirror and discuss what we see when we look into a mirror. Choose a child to be your partner to help you demonstrate the activity. Make sure there is space between you and your partner. The child who is the 'reflection' should copy your every gesture, but there should be no physical contact or communication between you. Once your 'reflection' understands what is happening you should change roles so that you become the 'reflection'. After a few moments, pick someone else to work with your partner. Divide the rest of the group into pairs. Tell one child in each pair to be the 'reflection'. Suggest that they change roles after a little while.

This activity should encourage muscle control as well as making children more observant of themselves and each other. Concentration should also be enhanced.

Feely bag

MATERIALS: A sock and a number of household and classroom objects.

ACTIVITY: One of the objects is placed in the sock. Children are then asked to feel the sock while the adult gives verbal clues about the object. Children take turns to hide objects and give clues. This should encourage tactile discrimination and language skills.

What is missing?

MATERIALS: Selection of everyday objects on a tray.

ACTIVITY: Children are allowed to look at and touch the objects on the tray for a short while. Then an article is removed from the selection which the children have studied and they must now identify which item is missing.
   This activity will help develop observation skills and visual memory.

Traffic lights

MATERIALS: Three coloured circles: red, green and yellow.

ACTIVITY: The adult holds up coloured circles and the children perform the appropriate action – stop for red, move forward for green and step backward for yellow. This encourages visual discrimination and concentration.

CREATIVE DEVELOPMENT

Activities to encourage creative awareness

See-through painting

MATERIALS: Paints, paper, roll of cling-film, brushes, rolling pin.

ACTIVITY: This is an alternative to fold-over painting on paper. Let children put blobs of paint on to the paper, and then cover it with a piece of cling-film. A rolling pin can then be used to spread the paint so that the children can see the colours mixing through the cling-film.

Salt carving

MATERIALS: Block salt (cut into small blocks), 'tools' such as wooden skewers, small spoons, wooden spatulas, small jars, tray.

ACTIVITY: Children should be given the salt 'blocks' on a small tray or dish and then be encouraged to bore, scrape, scoop and cut different shapes with their blocks. At first they will probably scrape the salt down to make 'snow' which they can then spoon into the jars. With experience they will be able to make unusual shapes in salt. Salt that has been turned into 'snow' can be used later with flour and water to make dough for modelling.

Imprinting

MATERIALS: Damp sand, assortment of objects.

ACTIVITY: Encourage children to make imprints of different objects in the sand and discuss how one can identify them by the marks they make. Initially this will probably be with toy cars, trucks, cups or their hands, but after the children have grasped the idea of 'imprinting' they can go outside and examine tyre-tracks, human and animal footprints.

A variation on this theme can be made after it has stopped raining. Powder paint can be added to a puddle in the garden and the children can make Wellington-boot footprints by stepping out of the puddle on to a sheet of paper. Prints can also be made with dough, clay or paints.

Spontaneous dancing

MATERIALS: Variety of tapes or records.

ACTIVITY: Children should be encouraged to move spontaneously to music and respond to the sounds in whatever way they wish. This activity should not only encourage concentration and listening skills but make children aware that we can communicate our feelings and ideas in ways other than language.

Some suggestions of music to create specific moods

MYSTERIOUS AND EERIE MUSIC
Saint-Saens: *Danse Macabre*
Mussorgsky: *Pictures at an Exhibition* (*The Old Castle* and *The Catacombs*), *Night on the Bare Mountain*
Berlioz: *Symphonie Fantastique*
Grofe: *Grand Canyon Suite*
Holst: *The Planets* (*Saturn, Uranus* and *Neptune*)

SEA AND WATER MUSIC
Mendelssohn: *Fingal's Cave*
Debussy: *La Mer*
Smetana: *Vltava* (from *Ma Vlast*)
Sibelius: *Swan of Tuonela*
Respighi: *Fountains of Rome*

QUIET AND PEACEFUL MUSIC
Beethoven: *Symphony No. 6 Pastoral* (2nd and 5th movements)
Debussy: *Prélude à l'après-midi d'un faune*
Rodrigo: *Concierto de Aranjuez for Guitar and Orchestra* (2nd movement)
Delius: *On Hearing the First Cuckoo in Spring*

STORM, BATTLE AND WIND MUSIC
Tchaikovsky: *1812 Overture*
Berlioz: *Symphonie Fantastique* (*March to the Scaffold* and *Witches' Sabbath*)
Holst: *The Planets* (*Mars*)

LOUD, EXCITING MUSIC
Mussorgsky: *Night on the Bare Mountain*
Prokofiev: *Symphony No. 5* (2nd movement)
Wagner: *Ride of the Valkyries*
Honegger: *Pacific 231*

LIGHT, HAPPY DANCING MUSIC
Prokofiev: *Love of Three Oranges* (March)
Tchaikovsky: *Nutcracker Suite* (*Dance of the Sugar Plum Fairy*)

Other music could include the types mentioned in the main text as well as Saint-Saens' *Carnival of the Animals*, Brahms' 'Lullaby', Prokofiev's *Peter and the Wolf*, and the *Sorcerer's Apprentice* by Dukas.

Texture rubbings

MATERIALS: Uncrumpled cooking foil, various textured everyday objects – tree bark, hessian, sandpaper, pebbles, coarse file, coins, manhole covers, etc.

ACTIVITY: Tell children to place foil over the various objects and press the foil on to them with their fingers and thumbs. Discuss with the children the differences between the imprints. Introduce appropriate vocabulary, e.g. rough, smooth, raised, flat, sharp, curved, hollow. Ask them which they prefer and why.

Pleasing pictures

MATERIALS: Collection of pictures of different types of painting, including abstract designs.

ACTIVITY: Discuss with children their feelings when they look at the pictures. Do they feel happy, sad, excited, surprised, angry, frightened? Ask them what they like best and what they like least about the paintings. Other vocabulary should be introduced when appropriate.

Colour matching

MATERIALS: Collection of different-coloured materials.

ACTIVITY: Ask children first to pick colours that go together and then those which are in contrast. Discuss why they think certain colours look better together than others. This activity will not only encourage aesthetic awareness but will help towards reasoning and logical thinking.

Experimenting with sound

MATERIALS: Elastic band, rulers, milk bottles filled with different levels of water, plastic bottles of different shapes and sizes filled with dried peas, rice, pasta. Tops should be firmly sealed to prevent contents being eaten or strewn over classroom floor.

ACTIVITY: After experimenting with the sounds made by the various objects, children should be encouraged to discuss the differences between these noises and that of a musical instrument. Which do they prefer and why?

What is a shape?

MATERIALS: Assorted collection of objects such as pebbles, driftwood, geometrical shapes, curved pieces and any unusual shape available. Clay, plasticine and junk materials including some rigid ones.

ACTIVITY: Encourage children to feel the shapes all over and draw their attention to various features of each object. Which shapes do they prefer, the regular or irregular? Supply appropriate vocabulary. After talking about the different types of shape children should be encouraged to make their own unusual 'shapes' using a variety of materials.

This type of activity should lead children to appreciate the different properties of malleable materials such as clay and plasticine as opposed to wood and metal and can lead on to discussions concerning shape and design of everyday objects.

Environmental awareness

Although some natural environments are very dreary and dull, many schools have a garden where children can see beauty in the form of flowers, trees and shrubs even when the surrounding area is depressing. For children living in grey environments it is essential that the indoor and outdoor areas of the school are made as aesthetically attractive as possible so that they can develop a sense of appreciation of beauty. Adults can draw the attention of children to the shapes, forms and colours of the various plants and trees around them and encourage children to listen to the sounds of the birds.

Children can be urged to listen to the various sounds in both the indoor and outdoor environments and comment upon which they like and which they dislike.

Bibliography

AAHPERD (1991). 'Physical education and health education in early childhood'. In: Elkind, D. (ed.) *Perspectives on Early Childhood Education*. Washington DC: National Education Association.

Adams, M.J. (1990). *Beginning to Read: Thinking and Learning about Print.* Cambridge, Mass: MIT Press.

Aldis, O. (1975). *Play Fighting.* New York: Academic Press.

Alland, A. (1983). *Playing with Form.* New York: Columbia Press.

Allen, Lady M., of Hurtwood (1968). *Planning for Play.* London: Thames and Hudson.

Andersson, B.E. (1992). 'Effects of day care on cognitive and socioemotional competence of thirteen year old Swedish school children', *Child Development*, **63**, 20–36.

Athey, C. (1990). *Extending Thought in Young Children.* London: Paul Chapman Publishing.

Ayres, J. (1978). *Southern California Sensory-Motor-Integration Test Manual.* Los Angeles, CA: Western Psychological Services.

Ball, C. (1994). *Start Right: The Importance of Early Learning.* London: RSA.

Ballard, P. (1937). *Things I Cannot Forget.* London: University of London Press.

Bate, M., Smith, M., Sumner, R. and Sexton, B. (1978). *Manual for Assessment in Nursery Education.* Windsor: NFER-NELSON.

Belka, D. and Williams, H. (1979). 'Prediction of later cognitive from early school perceptual-motor, perceptual and cognitive performances', *Perceptual and Motor Skills*, **49**, 131–41.

Bernstein, B. (1971). *Class, Codes and Control.* London: Routledge.

Blank, M. (1974). 'Pre-school and/or education'. In: Tizard, B. (ed.) *Early Childhood Education.* Slough: NFER.

Borke, H. (1971). 'Interpersonal perception of young children: egocentrism or empathy?', *Developmental Psychology*, **5**, 2, 263–9.

Bower, T.G.R. (1977). *The Perceptual World of the Child.* Cambridge, Mass.: Harvard University Press.

Bredekamp, S. (ed.) (1987). *Developmentally Appropriate Practice in Early Childhood Programs Serving Children from Birth through age 8.* Washington DC: National Association for the Education of Young Children.

Brownell, C. (1990). 'Peer social skills in toddlers: competencies and constraints illustrated by same age and mixed age interaction', *Child Development*, **61**, 838–48.

Bruner, J.S. (1956). *Studies in Cognitive Growth*. New York: John Wiley and Co.

Bruner, J.S. (1960). *The Process of Education*. Cambridge, Mass.: Harvard University Press.

Bruner, J.S. (1966). *Toward a Theory of Instruction*. Cambridge, Mass.: Harvard University Press.

Bruner, J.S. (1973). *Beyond the Information Given*. London: George Allen and Unwin.

Bruner, J.S. (1980). *Under Five in Britain*. London: Grant McIntyre.

Bryant, P.E. (1974). *Perception and Understanding in Young Children*. London: Methuen.

Bryant, P. and Bradley, L. (1985). *Children's Reading Problems*. Oxford: Blackwell.

Central Advisory Council for Education (Plowden Report) (1967). *Children and Their Primary Schools*. London: HMSO.

Chandler, M. and Boyes, M. (1982). 'Social-cognitive development'. In: Wolman, B.B. and Stricker, G. (eds) *Handbook of Developmental Psychology*. Englewood Cliffs, NJ: Prentice-Hall.

Chomsky, C. (1969). *The Acquisition of Syntax in Children from 5 to 10*. Cambridge, Mass.: MIT Press.

Clark, M. (1983). 'Early education issues and evidence', *Educational Review*, **35**, 2, 113–20.

Claxton, G. (1984). *Live and Learn: An Introduction to the Psychology of Growth and Change in Everyday Life*. London: Harper and Row.

Clay, M. (1975). *What Did I Write?* London: Heinemann Education.

Cleave, S. and Brown, S. (1991). *Early to School*. Windsor: NFER-Nelson.

Cleave, S., Jowett, S. and Bate, M. (1982). *And so to School*. Windsor: NFER-Nelson.

Clift, P., Weiner, J. and Wilson, E. (1981). *Record Keeping in the Primary School*. Windsor: NFER-Nelson.

Consultative Committee (Hadow) (1931). *Report on the Primary School*. London: HMSO.

Consultative Committee (Hadow) (1933). *Report on Infant and Nursery Schools*. London: HMSO.

Copple, C., Sigel, I. and Saunders, R. (1979). *Education of the Young Thinker: Classroom Strategies for Cognitive Growth*. New York: Van Nostrand.

Council of Europe (1975). DCCSCGT (75) 29. *The Link between Preschool and Primary Education*. Report of symposium at Versailles (France), 24–29 November 1975.

Council of Europe (1984). *Learning for Life*. Strasbourg.

Cox, M. (1997). *Drawings of People by the Under 5s*. London: Falmer Press.

Cratty, B.J. (1979). *Perceptual and Motor Development in Infants and Young Children*. 2nd edn. Englewood Cliffs, NJ: Prentice-Hall.

Cratty, B.J. and MARTIN, N. (1969). *Perceptual-Motor Efficiency in Children*. Philadelphia: Lear and Febiger.

Curtis, A. and Blatchford, P. (1980). *Meeting the Needs of Socially Handicapped Children*. Windsor: NFER-Nelson.

Curtis, A. and Hill, S. (1978). *My World: A Handbook of Ideas*. Windsor: NFER-Nelson.

Curtis, A. and Wignall, M. (1980). *Early Learning*. London: Macmillan Education.

Damon, W. (1977). *The Social World of the Child*. San Francisco: Jossey-Bass.

Dearden, R. (1968). *The Philosophy of Primary Education*. London: Routledge and Kegan Paul.

Dearden, R. (1969). 'The aims of primary education'. In: Peters, R.S. (ed.) *Perspectives on Plowden*. London: Routledge and Kegan Paul.

Dearden, R. (1976). *Problems in Primary Education*. London: Routledge and Kegan Paul.

De Bono, E. (1972). *Children Solve Problems*. Harmondsworth: Penguin.

Demon-Sparks, L. (1989). *Anti-Bias Curriculum*. Washington DC: National Association for the Education of Young Children.

De Oreo, K.L. (1974). 'The performance and development of fundamental motor skills in preschool children'. In: Wade, M. and Martens, R. (eds) *Psychology of Motor Behavior and Sport*. Champaign, Illinois: Human Kinetics.

Department of Education and Science (1972a). *Education: A Framework for Expansion*. London: HMSO.

Department of Education and Science (1972b). *Eveline Lowe Appraisal*. London: HMSO.

Department of Education and Science (1973). Circular 2/73. London: HMSO.

Department of Education and Science (Bullock Report) (1975). *A Language for Life*. London: HMSO.

Department of Education and Science (1978). *Primary Education in England*. London: HMSO.

Department of Education and Science (1980). *Education Act*. London: HMSO.

Department of Education and Science (1981). *Education Act*. London: HMSO.

Department of Education and Science (1982). *Education 5 to 9: An Illustrative Study of 80 Schools in England*. London: HMSO.

Department of Education and Science (1986). *Education Act*. London: HMSO.

Department of Education and Science (1988). *Education Act*. London: HMSO.

Department of Education and Science (Rumbold Report) (1990). *Starting with Quality*. London: HMSO.

Dewey, J. (1938). *Experience and Education*. New York: Collins.

De Witt, S. (1977). *Links between Preschool and Primary Education. Part II: The Establishment of Continuity*. Report on symposium at Bournemouth, 20–26 March, UK, CCC/EGT(77) 17.

Dion, K. and Berschied, E. (1974). 'Physical attractiveness and peer perception', *Sociometry*, **37**, 1–12.

Docking, J.W. (1990). *Primary Schools and Parents*. London: Hodder and Stoughton.

Donaldson, M. (1978). *Children's Minds*. Glasgow: Fontana.

Drummond, M.J. (1993). *Assessing Children's Learning*. London: David Fontana.

Drummond, M.J., Lally, M. and Pugh, G. (eds) (1989). *Working with Children: Developing a Curriculum for the Early Years*. London: National Children's Bureau.

Early Childhood Education Forum (1997). *Quality in Diversity in Early Learning*. (Draft).

Ebbeck, F.N. and Ebbeck, M.A. (1974). *Now We Are Four. An Introduction to Early Childhood Education*. Columbus, Ohio: C.E. Merrill.

Ehri, L.C. (1983). 'A critique of five studies related to letter-name knowledge and learning to read'. In Gentile, L.M., Kamil, M.L and Blanchard, J.S. (eds) *Reading Research Revisited*. Columbus, Ohio: Charles Merrill.

Eisner, E.W. (1972). *Educating Artistic Vision*. New York: Macmillan.

192   Bibliography

Espenschade, A.S. and Eckhert, H.M. (1980). *Motor Development.* Columbus, Ohio: Charles Merrill.

Ferreiro, E. (1984). 'The underlying logic of literacy development'. In Goleman, H., Oberg, A. and Smith, F. (eds) *Awakening to Literacy.* London: Heinemann Educational.

Fisher, J. (1997). *Starting from the Child.* Buckingham: Open University Press.

Forrari, K. (1988). *Music in the Pre-school.* Budapest: Corvina.

Froebel, F. (1896). *The Education of Man.* New York: Appleton.

Frostig, M., Lefever, W. and Whittlesey, J. (1966). *Administrative and Scoring Manual, Marianne Frostig Developmental Test of Visual Perception.* Palo Alto, CA: Consulting Psychologists Press.

Galdone, P. (1974). *Three Billy Goats Gruff.* London: Worlds Work.

Gallahue, D.L. (1982). *Understanding Motor Development in Children.* New York: John Wiley and Sons.

Gardner, D.E. (1956). *The Education of Young Children.* London: Methuen.

Gardner, H. (1983). *Frames of Mind: The Theory of Multiple Intelligences.* London: Paladin.

Gibson, J.J. and Yonas, P. (1968). 'A new theory of scribbling and drawing in children'. In: *The Analysis of Reading Skills: A Program of Basic and Applied Research.* New York: Cornell University Press.

Gipps, C. (1982). 'Nursery nurses and nursery teachers I & II', *Journal of Child Psychology and Psychiatry,* **23**, 3, 237–66.

Goffman, E. (1971). *Relations in Public.* New York: Harper and Row.

Goffman, E. (1972). *Interaction Ritual.* Harmondsworth: Penguin.

Goodman, M.E. (1952). *Race Awareness in Young Children.* Cambridge, Mass.: Addison-Wesley.

Godman, Y. (1984). 'The development of initial literacy'. In: Goleman, H., Oberg, A. and Smith, F. (eds) *Awakening to Literacy.* London: Heinemann Educational.

Goodnow, J. (1977). *Children's Drawings.* London: Fontana/Open Books.

Goswami, U. (1994) 'Phonological skills analysis and reading development', *Reading,* **28**, 2, 32–7.

Goswami, U. and Bryant, P. (1990) *Phonological Skills and Learning to Read.* Hove: Lawrence Erlbaum Associates.

Graziene, E. (1995). Personal communication.

Great Britain Committee of Enquiry into Discipline in Schools (Elton Report) (1989). *Discipline in Schools.* London: HMSO.

Green, J.A. (1913). *Life and Work of Pestalozzi.* London: U. Tutorial Press.

Gura, P. and Bruce, T. (1992). *Exploring Learning.* London: Paul Chapman Publishing.

Halsey, A.H. (ed.) (1972). *Educational Priority,* vol. 1. London: HMSO.

Halverson, F. (1958). 'A comparison of the performance of kindergarten children in the take-off phase of the standing broad jump'. Unpublished doctoral thesis, University of Wisconsin.

Hannon, P., Weinberger, J. and Nutbrown, C. (1991). 'A study of work with parents to promote early literacy development', *Research Papers in Education* **6**, 2, 77–97.

Harris, P. (1989). *Children and Emotion.* Oxford: Blackwell.

Harste, J.C., Woodward, V.A. and Burke, C.I. (1984). *Language Stories and Literacy Lessons.* Portsmouth, NH: Heinemann Educational.

Hartley, R.E. (1971). 'Play, the essential ingredient', *Childhood Education,* November.

Hartup, W. (1976). 'Peer interaction and the behavioral development of the child'. In: Schopler, E. and Reichler, R. (eds) *Child Development, Deviations and Treatment.* New York: Plenum.

Hartup, W. (1979). 'The social worlds of childhood', *American Psychologist,* **34,** 944–50.

Hendrick, J. (1980). *The Whole Child. New Trends in Early Education.* St Louis, Miss.: C.V. Mosby.

Her Majesty's Inspectorate (1985). *Discussion Document Curriculum 5–16.* London: HMSO.

Her Majesty's Inspectorate (1989). *The Education of Children under Five.* London: HMSO.

Hirst, P.H. (1969). 'The logic of curriculum', *Journal of Curriculum Studies,* **1,** 2, 142–58.

Hughes, M., Wilkeley, F. and Nash, T. (1994). *Parents and Their Children's Schools.* Oxford: Blackwell.

Hughes, M. and Westgate, D. (1997). 'Teachers and other adults as talk-partners for pupils in nursery and reception classes', *Education 3–13,* **25,** 1, 3–7.

Hughes, M. and Westgate, D. (forthcoming). 'Assistants as talk-partners in early-years classrooms: some issues of support and development', *Education 3–13.*

Hutt, C. (1970). 'Specific and diverse exploration'. In: Reese, H.W. and Lipsitt, L.P. (eds) *Advances in Child Development and Behaviour 5.* New York: Academic Press.

Inhelder, B. (1962). 'Some aspects of Piaget's genetic approach', *Monographs of the Society for Research in Child Development,* **27,** 2, 19–34.

Isaacs, S. (1930). *Intellectual Growth in Young Children.* London: Routledge.

Isaacs, S. (1933). *Social Development in Young Children.* London: Routledge.

Isaacs, S. (1954). *The Educational Value of the Nursery School.* London: BAECE.

Jenks, C. (1972). *Inequality.* New York: Basic Books.

Jowett, S. and Sylva, K. (1986). 'Does kind of pre-school matter?', *Educational Research,* **28,** 1, 21–31.

Katz, P.A. (1976). *Towards the Elimination of Racism.* New York: Pergamon.

Katz, P.A. (1982). 'Development of children's racial awareness and intergroup attitudes'. In: Katz, L.G. (ed.) *Current Topics in Early Childhood Education,* vol. 4. Norwood, NJ: Ablex.

Kellogg, R. (1969). *Analysing Children's Art.* Palo Alto, CA: Mayfield.

Kelly, A.V. (1994). 'Beyond the rhetoric and the discourse'. In: Blenkin, G. and Kelly, A.V. (eds) *The National Curriculum and Early Learning.* London: Paul Chapman.

Kensington and Chelsea LEA (1992). *Early Years Profile.* K and C Education Department.

Klaus, R. and Gray, S. (1965). 'An experimental preschool program for culturally deprived children', *Child Development,* **36,** 887–98.

Kuhn, D., Nash., C. and Brucken, L. (1978). 'Sex-role concepts of two and three year olds', *Child Development,* **49,** 445–51.

Laishley, J. (1971). 'Skin colour awareness and preference in London nursery-school children', *RACE,* **13,** 1, 47–64.

Light, P. (1979). *The Development of Social Sensitivity.* Cambridge: Cambridge University Press.

Lilley, I. (1967). *Friedrich Froebel, A Selection from his Writings.* Cambridge: Cambridge University Press.

Lloyd, I. (1983). 'The aims of early childhood education', *Educational Review,* **35,** 121–6.

Lowenfeld, V. and Brittain, W. (1975). *Creative and Mental Growth.* 6th edn. New York: Macmillan.

Lowndes, G.A. (1960). *Margaret McMillan, the Children's Champion.* London: Museum Press.

Maccoby, E.E. and Jacklin, C.N. (1974). *The Psychology of Sex Differences.* Stanford: Standford University Press.

McMillan, M. (1904). *Education through Imagination.* London: Dent.

McMillan, M. (1919). *The Nursery School.* London: Dent.

McVickers-Hunt, J. (1961). *Intelligence and Experience.* New York: Ronald Press.

Mallory, B.L. and New, R.S. (eds) (1994). *Diversity and Developmentally Appropriate Practice.* New York: Teachers College Press.

Matthews, J. (1984). 'The young child's early representation and drawing'. In: Blenkin, G. and Kelly, V. (eds) *Early Childhood Education: A Developmental Curriculum* London: Paul Chapman.

Maw, W. and Maw, E. (1970). 'Self-concept of high and low curiosity boys', *Child Development,* **41,** 123–9.

Maxime, J. (1991). 'Towards a transcultural approach to working with under sevens'. In: *Report of Two Conferences Combating Racism among Students, Staff and Children, Nursery Nurse Trainers.* Early Years Anti-racist Network and National Children's Bureau.

Menig-Peterson, C. (1983). 'The modification of communicative behaviour in preschool aged children as a function of the listener's perspective'. In: Donaldson, M., Grieve, R. and Pratt, C. (eds) *Early Childhood Development and Education.* Oxford: Basil Blackwell.

Michel, W. (1973). 'The optimum development of musical abilities in the first years of life', *The Psychology of Music,* **1,** 14–20.

Miller, L.B. and Dyer, J.L. (1975). Four pre-school programmes: their dimension and effects. *Monograph of the Society for Research in Child Development,* **40,** 936–50.

Milner, D. (1983). *Children and Race: Ten Years on.* London: Ward Lock Educational.

Ministry of Education Building Bulletin (1955). NNI955 No.1. London: HMSO.

Montessori, M. (1964). *The Absorbent Mind.* Wheaton, Illinois: Theosophical Press.

Moon, C. and Wells, G. (1979). 'The influence of home on learning to read', *Journal of Research in Reading,* **2,** 1, 53–62.

Moore, E. (1985). 'Microcomputers in the nursery', *Update Current Issues in Early Childhood,* **8,** 1.

Nash, B.C. (1979). 'Kindergarten programmes and the young child's task orientation and understanding about time scheduling', *British Journal of Educational Psychology,* **49,** 27–38.

Nash, B.C. (1981). 'The effects of classroom spatial organisation on 4–5 year old children's learning', *British Journal of Educational Psychology,* **51,** 144–55.

Neill, S.R. St. J. and Denham, E.J.N. (1982). 'The effects of preschool building design', *Educational Research,* **24,** 2, 107–11.

Newson, J., Newson, E. and Barnes, P. (1977). *Perspectives on School at Seven Years Old.* London: George Allen and Unwin.

Nutbrown, C. (1994). *Threads of Thinking.* London: Paul Chapman Publishing.

Parry, M. and Archer, H. (1974). *Preschool Education. Schools Council Research Studies.* Basingstoke: Macmillan Education.

Pestalozzi, J. (1898). 'Leonard and Gertrude', abridged by E. Chaning. Boston: D.H. Heath.

Peters, R.S. (1966). *Ethics and Education.* London: Allen and Unwin.

Peters, R.S. (1969). 'A recognisable philosophy of education'. In: Peters, R.S. (ed.) *Perspectives on Plowden.* London: Routledge and Kegan Paul.

Piaget, J. (1930). *The Child's Conception of Physical Causality.* London: Routledge and Kegan Paul.

Piaget, J. (1965). *The Child's Conception of Number.* New York: Norton.

Piaget, J. and Inhelder, B. (1969). *The Psychology of the Child.* New York: Basic Books.

Piaget, J. and Weil, A. (1951). 'The development in children of the idea of the homeland and of relations with other countries', *International Social Science Bulletin,* **3**, 561–78.

Plowden Report (1967). See under Central Advisory Council for Education.

Pushkin, K. (1967). 'A study of ethnic choice in the play of young children in three London districts'. Unpublished PhD thesis, University of London.

Reed, H. (1956). *Education through Art.* New York: Pantheon.

Robinson, J. (1982). *The Gulbenkian Report, The Arts in Schools.* London: HMSO.

Rousseau, J.-J. (1911). *Emile.* London: Dent.

Rowen, B., Byrne, J. and Winter, L. (1980). *The Learning Match.* Englewood Cliffs, NJ: Prentice-Hall.

Rubin, K. (1977). 'Play behaviours of young children', *Young Children,* **September**, 16–23.

SCAA (1996a) *Baseline Assessment.* London: School Curriculum and Assessment Authority.

SCAA (1996b) *Nursery Education: Desirable Outcomes for Children's Learning on Entering Compulsory Education.* London: School Curriculum and Assessment Authority.

Schools Council (1972). *A Study of Nursery Education,* Working Paper 41. London: Methuen.

Schutz, W. (1979). *Profound Simplicity.* New York: Bantam Books.

Schweinhart, L.J. and Weikart, D. (1993). *A Summary of Significant Benefits: The High Scope Perry Pre-school Study through Age 27.* Ypsilanti High Scope UK.

Sebastian, P. (1986). *Handle with Care: A Guide to Early Childhood Education Administration.* Melbourne: AE Press.

Shefantya, L. and Smilansky, S. (1990). *Facilitating Play: A Medium for Promoting Cognitive, Socio-emotional and Academic Development in Young Children.* Gaithersberg, MD: Psychosocial and Educational Publications.

Shields, M. (1985). 'The development of the young child's representation of emotion'. Unpublished paper.

Shields, M. and Duveen, G. (1986). 'The young child's image of persons and the social world'. In: Corsaro, W. (ed.) *Children's Worlds and Children's Language.* The Hague: Mouton.

Shields, M. and Steiner, L. (1973). 'The language of 3–5 year olds in preschool education', *Educational Research,* **15**, 2, 97–105.

Shorrocks, D., Daniels, S., Frobisher, L., Nelson, N., Waterson, A., and Bell, J. (1992). *ENCA 1 Project: The Evaluation of National Curriculum Assessment at Key Stage 1.* School of Education, University of Leeds.

Siraj-Blatchford, I. (1994). *The Early Years. Laying the Foundations for Racial Equality.* Stoke on Trent: Trentham Books.

Sleap, M. and Warburton, P. (1994). 'Physical activities levels in pre-adolescent children in England. *British Journal of Research Education,* Research Supplement, **14**, 2–6.

Smilanksy, S. (1968). *The Effects of Socio-dramatic Play on Disadvantaged Pre-School Children.* New York: Wiley.

Smith, D.K. and Syddal, S. (1978). 'Play and non-play tutoring in preschool children', *British Journal of Educational Psychology,* **48**, 315–25.

Smith, P. and Connolly, K. (1980). *The Ecology of Pre-school Behaviour.* Cambridge: Cambridge University Press.

Smith, R. (1989). *The Sense of Art: A Study in Aesthetic Education.* New York: Routledge.

Smith, R.H. (1981). 'Early childhood science education: a Piagetian perspective', *Young Children,* **January**, 3–9.

Snow, C. (1991). *Unfulfilled Expectations: Home and School Influence on Literacy.* Cambridge, Mass.: Harvard University Press.

Statham, J. (1986). *Daughters and Sons: Experiences of Non-sexist Childraising.* Oxford: Blackwell.

Steirer, B. (1991). 'Assessing children at the start of school – issues, dilemmas and current developments', *The Curriculum Journal,* **1**, 2, 155–69.

Stobbs, W. (1967). *The Three Billy Goats Gruff.* London: Bodley Head.

Stonehouse, A. (ed.) (1988). *Trusting Toddlers.* Canberra: Australian Early Childhood Association.

Sulzby, E. (1990). 'Assessment of writing and children's language while writing'. In: Mandel-Morrow, L. and Smith, J.K. (eds) *Assessment for Instruction in Early Literacy.* Englewood Cliffs, NJ: Prentice Hall.

Sylva, K. (1994). 'A curriculum for early learning'. In: Ball, C. (ed.) *Start Right: The Importance of Early Learning.* London: RSA.

Sylva, K. and Moore, E. (1984). 'A survey of under-fives record-keeping in Great Britain', *Educational Research,* **26**, 2, 115–20.

Sylva, K., Roy, C. and Painter, M. (1980). *Child Watching at Playgroup and Nursery School.* London: Grant McIntyre.

Taunton, M. (1984). '4-year-old children's recognition of expressive qualities in reproductions', *Journal of Research and Development in Education.*

Taylor, P.H., Exon, G. and Holley, B. (1972). *A Study of Nursery Education,* Schools Council Working Paper 41. London: Methuen Evans.

Teale, W.H. and Sulzby, E. (1986). 'Emergent literacy as a perspective for examining how young children become writers and readers'. In: Teale, W.H. and Sulzby, E. (eds) *Emergent Literacy: Writing and Reading.* New Jersey: Ablex Publishing Corporation.

Tizard, B. and Hughes, M. (1984). *Young Children Learning.* London: Fontana Open Books.

Tizard, B., Blatchford, P., Burke, J., Farquhar, C. and Plewis, I. (1988). *Young Children at School in the Inner City.* Hove and London: Lawrence Erlbaum Associates.

Tough, J. (1977). *Talking and Learning,* Schools Council Communication Skills in Early Childhood Project. London: Ward Lock Educational.

Tyler, S. (ed.) (1976). *Keele Pre-School Assessment Guide.* Windsor: NFER-Nelson.

Van der Eyken, W. (1977). *The Pre-school Years.* Harmondsworth: Penguin.

Vernon, M. (1969). *Human Motivation.* Cambridge: Cambridge University Press.

Vidler, P. (1977). 'Curiosity'. In: Ball, S. (ed.) *Motivation in Education.* New York: Academic Press.

Vygotsky, L.S. (1962). *Thought and Language.* Cambridge, Mass.: MIT Press.

Vygotsky, L.S. (1978). *Mind in Society.* Cambridge, Mass.: Harvard University Press.

Walker, A.S. (1955). *Pupils' School Records.* Windsor: NFER.

Walkerdine, V. (1982). Personal communication.

Waller, H. and Brito, J. (1992). *Early Milestones.* Walsall: Letterland.

Walsall LEA (1990). *Early Years Profile.* West Walsall: Learning Support Service.

Wandsworth LEA (1993). *Baseline.* Wandsworth Education Department.

Webb, L. (1974). *Purpose and Practice in Nursery Education.* Oxford: Basil Blackwell.

Weinberger, J. (1996). *Literacy Goes to School.* London: Paul Chapman Publishing.

Wellman, W. (1937). 'Motor achievement of preschool children', *Childhood Education,* **13**, 311–16.

Wells, C.G. (ed.) (1981). *Learning through Interaction.* Cambridge: Cambridge University Press.

Wells, C.G. (1984). *Language Development in the Pre-school Years.* Cambridge: Cambridge University Press.

Wells, C.G. (1987). *The Meaning Makers: Children Learning Language and Using Language to Learn.* London: Heinemann Educational.

White, B.L. (1959). 'Motivation reconsidered: the concept of competence', *Psychological Review,* **66**, 297–333.

Whiting, B. and Pope-Edwards, C. (1988). *Children of Different Worlds: The Formation of Social Behaviour.* Cambridge, Mass.: Harvard University Press.

Wilson, J., Williams, N. and Sugarman, B. (1967). *Introduction to Moral Education.* Harmondsworth: Penguin.

Wolfendale, S. (1983). *Parental Participation in Children's Development and Education.* London: Gordon and Breach.

Wolfendale, S. (1990). *All about Me.* Nottingham: NES Arnold.

Woodhead, M. (1996). *In Search of the Rainbow.* Netherlands: Van Leer Foundation.

Wragg, C. (1991). 'Primary profiles', *Special Children,* **March**, 8–12.

Wright, C. (1992). 'Early education: multicultural primary classrooms'. In: Gill, D. *et al.* (eds) *Racism and Education.* London: Sage.

Zimmerman, B.J. and Rosenthal, T.L. (1974). 'Observational learning of rule-governed behaviour by children', *Psychological Bulletin,* **81**, 29–42.

Zimmerman, M. (1975). 'Research in music education with very young children'. In: *Music Education for the Very Young Child,* Report of the 4th International Seminar on Research in Music Education, 1974. Wellington: New Zealand Council for Educational Research.

Index